SIGNS OF AGNI YOGA

# FIERY WORLD

I

# FIERY
# WORLD

# I

## 1933

Agni Yoga Society
319 West 107th Street
New York NY 10025
www.agniyoga.org

*Ur* is the root of the Light of Fire. From time immemorial this Radiant Principle has attracted the hearts of many peoples. Thus, from the Teachings of the past let us transport ourselves into future attainments.

# FIERY WORLD

## Part I

1. The element of Fire, the most all-pervading, the most creative, the most life-bearing, is least observed and esteemed. The human consciousness concerns itself with a multitude of empty and insignificant considerations, but the most wonderful of all escapes it. People quarrel over a pice in the bazaar, but they have no desire to stretch forth their hands to the treasure. Much that has been told about the heart must also be applied to the Fiery World, but with particular acuteness. The impetus of Fire is as strong as the structure of a crystal. Not by accident have globes and crystal spheres been employed by clairvoyants. Live embers are needed for the purification of the consciousness; the rainbow flame affirms the striving of the spirit. A multitude of applications of the work of Fire reveal themselves as the most striking conditions of existence. Beginning with the ordinary light formations visible to the open eye, up to the complex fires of the heart, we are led into the realm of the Fiery World.

2. While observing the fiery signs one may note certain subdivisions of people. Some strive eternally and cannot exist without this uplifting movement—be assured that these belong to the element of fire. Even though they err, they cannot remain inactive. Observe them, and you will invariably discover the flaming force. But do not seek the creative Fire in the inertia of earth, the rolling undulations of water, the gusts of air. We do not wish to extol the fiery people unduly, but in truth it must be said that they move the world.

One should not forget that these people do not find it easy to be in the midst of all other combinations. What is said about the Fiery Angel with scorched wings is correct. When he rushes to save the world, his phosphorescent wings brush against the rocks of Earth and are scorched, and the Angel is weakened thereby. Thus is disclosed the marked difference between the earthly world and the Fiery.

The earthly eye, though it be highly sensitive, does not usually assimilate even the subtle manifestations. But, in turn, the Subtle World does not discern the fiery dwellers to whom the flaming heart can lead one. Thus one can understand the veneration for Fire. Human strivings are needed for a natural affinity with the World of Fire. From early years they bear in themselves, as it were, a reflection of the Higher Fire. It is as if these sparks compel them to withdraw from contact with other elements; and those elements do not like these fiery orbs. Yet one cannot traverse the earthly path without contact with Fire, hence it is better to know its essential nature.

**3.** It should be pointed out that the tension of Fire reflects upon all functions of the body. One must not forget that, while the Fire of Space may heal wounds, on the other hand it can strain the tissues. Thus, let us be cautious.

**4.** It would seem that the Fiery Baptism already has been clearly expounded. Tongues of fire have been manifested above the heads of people, but they do not wish to accept the existing reality. They pretend to reverence the Scriptures but fail to accept them in life. Not all could accept and observe calmly the non-scorching flame as you saw it, yet it was quite real, with all the properties of fire except that of scorching. But one has to have an open heart to face the flame. People have grasped a crude manifestation in the form of electricity, but without applying the fiery properties of the human organism they cannot advance toward a refinement of the manifestation. A new dawn for mankind will come when the understanding of Fire enters life.

5. When we speak of the non-scorching fire, we must also not forget the consuming Fire. When the nun moans, "I burn, I burn!" no physician knows how to alleviate it. The physician may even apply cold water, forgetting that oil cannot be submerged in water. Fire can be allayed only by fire—in other words, by the energy of the heart, which flows during so-called magnetism. We treat inflammation with a current; such inflammations may flare up in various centers. But, actually, the chief danger lies close to the heart, the solar plexus and the larynx. These centers, being the most synthetic, may be exposed to the most unexpected attacks. Whoever has even once experienced the inner fire understands the danger of the conflagration of the centers. He knows what agony is experienced when the fire breaks through. In most cases man is not responsible for this, except perhaps because of irritation. Often the fire bursts out due to extraneous influences, and, in the case of a refined state of the organism, from cosmic causes. Fatigue of the heart actually opens the gates to the enemy. Thus the creative Fire can be transformed into a destructive flame. This should be remembered, for the outbursts develop from small beginnings. It should also be remembered that the use of fiery energy requires care. Great is the evil of needlessly spending the fiery energy of another. An Arhat can never be a vampire—this is a fundamental law of life. Therefore, wise is the law of eternal giving. It may seem that there is nothing in common

between sacrifice and Fire; however, flaming sacrifice is mentioned in all Teachings.

**6.** One must manifest special caution. You can see how even the morals of a nation change. Hence, ignorance reacts to the pressure of the atmosphere. One must observe that ignorance clearly affirms the foundations of darkness. One can imagine how easily an undeveloped brain deteriorates when the heart is silent. The morals of the peoples droop like a withered apple tree. Thus the danger of fiery epidemics is now great.

The Chaldeans classified all sicknesses according to the elements; and they were not far from the truth, for the elements and luminaries chiefly condition the organism—the cosmic as well as the human.

**7.** Just think! Each of us carries within himself the One Fire, immutable throughout the entire Universe. No one cares to imagine that the universal treasure is within him. The elements are not identical in the entire Cosmos; the change in their qualities does not permit us to ascribe to them identicalness. But the fire of the heart alone unites through its magnet all world structures. One must think about this pre-eminence. It is necessary to utilize this treasure in the entire structure of life. There is but one Light of Fire in all the world. We can understand that Fire manifests at the most remote distances. There is nothing supernatural or mysterious about it. Even a lesser disciple has heard about the all-pervading Fire, but he has failed to realize its application.

**8.** The manifestation of varied fires does not contradict the oneness of the essence of Fire. The rhythm of tension alone will change the color of the visible flame from silver through reddish-gold to an intense ruby-red. The ruby-red of tension is rare, for not every heart can endure it.

**9**. In order to accept and admit Fire as the path to Hierarchy, as the path of love and compassion, it is necessary to be affirmed irrevocably with one's entire heart. Only thus will the small stars become flaming giants.

**10**. Let the straitened times also be blessed. Precisely at such times do we learn to distinguish the significant from the mediocre. In the days of contentment our vigilance becomes obscured, yet this quality is especially needed when approaching the fiery spheres. Hence oppression and tension are so precious. They not only increase vigilance and impetuosity, they also force new fires from our innermost depths. Let the fire of the Tara be especially close. Thus, let us grow to love the unexpected as the source of new joy. Verily, the best fire is kindled through joy. Hence, straitened times are a horror only for the ignorant; for those who know, they are simply a source of events. The fires bring close even remote actions. To some, what has been said will appear to be a cold abstraction, but this will signify a heart that is cold and its fire extinguished. You already know the heat of the heart, and you appreciate the unexpected Messenger. Therefore it is so important to follow the Lords; one must leave behind dark determinations. Only the Fire of the Lords will kindle daring. Therefore, every word about the Lords must be valued. Though it be uttered unknowingly, yet there is in it the prana of daring. Let words about the Lords resound in all corners of the world. These are candles lit before holy shrines. They are lamps of Living Fire—a protection against all diseases. Solemnity is like a key to the lock.

**11**. During intense fiery manifestations, one can

observe one characteristic of the basic property of Fire. The surrounding objects appear to be translucent. You can bear witness to this. Fire seemingly transforms all fiery substances and reveals the luminous matter lying in the foundation of everything that exists. The same can be said about the magnet of a fiery heart; in its own way it discloses the fiery nature of everything that draws near it. Thus, through the fiery heart one can observe fiery qualities. It is only necessary to discover such a heart and with great caution utilize it in this experiment. In such experiments one must remember that the uncovering of luminous matter can be extremely dangerous under crude surrounding conditions. The danger of complete Samadhi is also dependent upon the same quality of Fire. Nevertheless, do not resist the fiery manifestations if they do not overburden the heart. In the years of Armageddon the manifestations become, of course, entangled, because the rhythms of the Fire of Space and of the subterranean fire are broken. Usually, such ruptures of rhythm are not taken into consideration, and hence they increase the cosmic perturbation still further.

12. The approaching fiery waves are extremely terrifying if one does not know about them and does not assimilate them with the fires of one's own heart.

13. You have heard of certain children who can see through solid bodies. Seek the solution in the karmic fiery nature. Actually, this is an entirely specific physical phenomenon, usually not conducive to the higher fiery attainments. Hatha Yoga intensifies separate centers and it can only be regretted that these partial endeavors do not lead to Raja Yoga and Agni Yoga. Thus, physical and fiery exercises are harmful, disturbing the surrounding equilibrium. Fire is the highest element, and the approach to it must be by way of the

higher consciousness. One can understand and learn to love Fire only through this higher consciousness.

**14**. Blood, blood,—is the cry of the peoples of the West and East. Unprecedented times! The salutary Fire is transformed through ignorance into a devourer!

**15**. "Surround yourself with Fire and become immune," is a most ancient advice. But, having grown more callous, people began to forget what Fire was indicated by the Wise. The fire became a physical one and magic circles of fire made their appearance. Thus, people always belittle their essential nature. Actually, any living fire is a healing one, but no resin can compare with the fire of the heart. Let them remember at least about the quality of earthly fire, yet in truth the time has again come to return to the primary source; otherwise it is not possible to cross the boundary near which humanity already stands. The earthly forces have been depleted and strained by humanity, and the Highest Powers are alarmed. Only the fiery, illumined consciousness can restore the broken bridge of ascent.

**16**. Is it possible for one belonging to the fiery element to be transformed into a creature of other energies? Impossible. But one belonging to another element can be transformed into a fiery being, because Fire is omnipresent. Of course, these leaps are not easy. Great exertion of spirit is needed to transmute the heart for unification with the higher energy. But the Fiery Gates are not closed—"Knock, and it shall be opened unto you." Thus, all Teachings summon to the Fiery Baptism.

**17**. The substance of fiery immunity was described by Zoroaster. He pointed out that from each pore of the skin people could call forth fiery rays to smite all evil. A man clad in a protective armor cannot succumb to any contagion. One can increase this resistance through unity with Hierarchy. Thus, the heart becomes like a sun reducing all microbes to ashes.

**18.** Indeed, the bacilli of cancer exist. They can be detected and killed primarily by the fire of the heart. If the absence of psychic energy contributes to their growth, then the fire of the heart, being the highest expression of consciousness, destroys them. In fact, everything that is readily consumed by the higher energy can be mitigated also, to a certain extent, by physical fire. The roots of many plants contain in themselves potent fires of the vegetable kingdom and can be useful where the fires of the heart are as yet inactive.

**19.** You already know about the significance of the thirtieth year for fiery manifestations, but one should especially guard the organism up to the seventh year. In children, even in the most highly developed, one should never force nature—Fire will not tolerate compulsion. One should know how to open the door, but each coercion may cause irreparable harm. On the other hand, one should not inordinately facilitate the child's striving, since excessive help creates weaklings. Therefore, the Golden Path is ordained. Thus, Fire demands cautious handling in all its manifestations. Clairvoyance and clairaudience are essentially fire-voyance and fire-audience. Fire is needed as the intermediary for all exalted actions. Six hundred times did We speak of the heart; so are We ready to speak six hundred and sixty-six times of the significance of Fire, if only to affirm the definition of Fire as a triumphal ladder. People cannot exist without turning to Fire; in the earthly world or in the Subtle World, they turn to the higher mediation. But We do not speak of fire worship, for there will be ignoramuses and fanatics who will try to raise this absurd accusation. I speak of the highest attainment, which will bring our subtle body to the Fiery World.

**20.** Every pilot will tell you not to turn the rudder too sharply. But one should speak even more emphatically about human consciousness; this crystal is formed slowly, yet each moment of cumulation is a spatial joy. Each one has a heartbeat, but one rarely observes the fiery substance. Therefore We do not always speak about Fire everywhere, except where Fire has already been accumulated.

**21.** The human eye does not see the most powerful electric vibrations. The same is true with regard to fiery gradations. Incidentally, this circumstance always hinders the Teaching of Fire. The smaller manifestations of fiery energies will be sensed, and thus admitted, but higher and more refined manifestations will become imperceptible to the modern apparatus, and to the consciousness which has not karmically approached the element of fire. But contemporaries do not readily admit the imperfection of the apparatus and especially their own inexperience. The lack of such acknowledgement becomes a great obstacle, and instead of moving forward valuable time must be spent in instilling an understanding of the nature of Fire. However, during these reiterations about the concept of Fire, a useful accumulation takes place, which will be indelibly inscribed upon the brain. Whatever is done, at least let those who cannot assimilate through the heart perceive through the brain. Our duty is to proffer the shortest paths, but patience will be found to follow the longest roads also. The chief requisite is steadfastness, when in your heart you yourself know that there is no other way; therefore the Subtle World is achieved only by means of Fire. Thus, knowledge of our essential nature is not only in knowing but also in sensing.

**22**. Non-perception of the highest currents of Fire is, to a certain extent, analogous to a priest who through daily contact becomes accustomed to the current of the sanctuary. It is known that saints, or exalted Spirits, surrounded by streams of Fire, did not perceive this highest manifestation. Indeed, those who live in the Subtle World do not notice its peculiarity, just as those who commune with Fire fail to regard this condition as extraordinary. A virtuoso does not consider it unusual that he plays beautifully, this is already customary for him. Thus, too, the Fiery World descends to earthly conditions, and those who are in contact with it lose the sense of strangeness.

**23**. Approaching manifestations of Fire, we must bear in mind various gradations. The so-called passages through fire differ greatly. The lowest type of fakirs rub their bodies with ashes mixed with a mineral dust, and thus gain a certain resistance to fire. Of course, this external, purely physical effect cannot be of interest. Yogis pass through fire by inducing the heart's energy as a counter-action. In this process the inner fire breaks through the pores of the skin and, being more powerful than the earthly fire, forms a strong protective armor. Such Yogis can also lead through fire without harm those who wish to follow them. To effect this the Yogi extends his energy to those who follow him, provided they can completely transport their consciousness into the heart of the Yogi. This condition of a complete transference of one's consciousness to the heart of the Guide is characteristic of fiery actions in general.

**24**. They will say that fire as an element is too elusive for observation. You may answer that fire makes itself even more apparent than other elements. In observing man's organism, are earth or water more evident? Fire is more easily evidenced in the temperature, the pulse, and especially in that tremor which accompanies all fiery manifestations. This is not a tremor of fear, but unification with the pulse of the element. Does intercourse with earth or water evoke such a tremor? But Fire, even in a small measure, produces a special sensation. Thus, let them not speak of the unattainability of the Fire of Space.

**25.** It is especially valuable to cognize in one's own heart communion with the fiery essence. In the Middle Ages, of course, they would have added to this the fire of the stake. But even in those times, valorous men were found who did not fear to speak about that which they perceived and sensed within themselves.

**26.** The Fiery Serpent rising above the Chalice in the form of the serpent of Moses, like the Arabic figure eight, indicates the tension of the Chalice, because the Chalice is filled with Fire. The accumulations and precipitations in the Chalice constitute the fiery substance. Thus, primarily we are fiery beings. Only with such conviction do we begin to grow the so-called fiery wings.

Are these tappings not fiery drops seeking admission? Are these not fiery waves, which intensify the rhythm? Let each reminder about Fire serve as a saturation with solemnity.

**27.** Observation of people who love the structure of flame constantly yields new deductions. Approaching Fire, we begin to discern the rhythm of energy, which produces all combinations. One should love this element with full understanding, in other words, with thoughts in harmony with space. If we are prepared to remain earthly gnomes let it be remembered that the best gnomes serve Fire. Thus one should understand that even the lowest consciousnesses are being drawn upward. Even fairy tales speak of gnomes who cannot exist without devotion to the Fiery Beings. Thus the ancients tried to inculcate fiery conceptions in the children's consciousnesses. Nowadays science, through the caloric theory and astrochemistry, gives the identical fairy tale about the Great Fire. But the exceptional character of the fiery manifestations still does not permit the average man to introduce the concept of Fire into his daily life, so that Fire remains within the confines of an undesirable abstraction. One must overcome this limitation; I speak as a physician.

I affirm that, serving Fire, we can cross all dark abysses! If even flying machines need a special gas, how much more is the subtlest energy needed for uplifting the spirit!

**28.** All achievements and heroic deeds are essentially fiery actions. The higher energy transports people across the precipice. It may be asked, "Does not the fiery energy participate in the rise of crime?" Certainly, this same energy can raise a bloody knife; therefore We advise not to turn the Fire of Benefaction into the flame of destruction. Besides personal harm, the flame of destruction contaminates the surrounding space. Moreover, a flame of evil is aroused by the decomposing vortices of the lower strata. It has long been said that sinners themselves feed the fires of hell. People are themselves responsible for the extent of evil. As it is, a vast amount of evil is not realized, and people refuse to recognize whence come these hideous burns. In various countries you saw different concepts of hell. If such forms are embodied on Earth, likewise they exist in the Subtle World. How carefully must one avoid all ugliness on Earth! The Fire of Benefaction creates the most beautiful transmutations. Let us then be toiling and blessed smiths. Beneficent Fires are borne high up by the vortexes of the far-off worlds.

Once there existed a trial by fire. He who was tried approached the fire, and the fire, at contact with truth, rose upward, but a lie deflected the flame. With all its imperfections, this trial brings to mind the possibilities of the reaction of Fire.

**29.** You have seen Our apparatuses for measuring the compression of fire. The erupting flame records a terrific pressure. The fiery essence is under the pressure of many atmospheres; in order to burst into flame, the mass of compression must be overcome. If the flame has formed and burst forth, it indicates that the pressure and the power of the flame are extraordinary.

**30.** On finding himself beyond the boundaries of the three dimensions even the most cold-blooded person will be terrified if his heart is unprepared for the next realization. One cannot leap from one state to another without a fiery tempering. Thus, it is impossible to assimilate the beauty and solemnity of the Subtle World without a timely refinement of the heart. One can stand insensate in the dark before the most wondrous works of art, but the darkness is within ourselves! And one can kindle the Spatial Fire only by the fire of the heart. It has been said many times that the Great Fire is manifested through our hearts. Therefore, let him who remains in darkness blame only himself. But it is terrifying to remain in the darkness of the fourth dimension, and all the succeeding dimensions become hideous nightmares when not illumined by the fire of the heart.

**31.** Of course the flow of saliva or various pains of the nerve centers correspond to different degrees of cosmic perturbations. But the question arises as to whether these signs are a refraction of cosmic events or cooperation with world energies. One must accept the latter. The refined microcosm will be a true collaborator of the Macrocosm. It is said that Abraham walked before the Lord. Let us understand this as full cooperation. From this completeness is also born the fulfillment of the law of Existence.

**32.** It is difficult for a refined heart to exist in the lower strata. To a certain extent the heights are helpful, but still the intervening breaks between the heart and its fiery birthplace are too great. But these polluted strata should not have existed—people created them; hence they must strive to purify them. Artificial ozone helps but little. Prana is purified by the highest Fire, and only this quality makes it creative. Yet even in the plains, even in the city squares, before expressing a decision, try to inhale as deeply as possible. In this inhalation perhaps a particle of the prana of Benefaction will reach you through all barriers. Thus, let us nowhere despair, and let us everywhere make a final effort. One can observe how a sincere heart-felt sigh becomes like a long-drawn-out trumpet-call. Thus, let us not forget that all the best manifestations of the human organism not only are powerful in their chemical reactions but penetrate many strata by their psychic force. Let us not in any way depreciate the sacred microcosm created by the will of the pure heart.

**33.** Let those who can hasten in thoughts act without delay. One must become accustomed to the fact that each thought is a communion with Fire. Hence, it is shameful to have an ignorant or insignificant thought.

**34.** Let us be like those who await the Great Advent; let us harken to the Steps and know that our hearts are proffered in help to the world. Let us not permit confusion and denial, for these qualities turn the tongues of flame against us.

35. Upon the great Path it is better to be slandered than to hinder a decision of the Lords. Let us learn to enjoy being slandered, for we cannot name any fiery path without its carpet of calumny.

36. Let no one be disconcerted by My demand for battle. Those who stand on one spot are a thousand times more exposed to danger than those who strive. However, the striving must be in the heart and thoughts, and not only in the feet.

37. The so-called herb of truth actually exists. A combination of seven plants unlocks the controlling centers and a man freely utters his thoughts. This is not hashish but an evidence of the most ancient curative factors. It was primarily used for the diagnosis of disease, for no one knows better than the man himself the causes of that which occurs in his organism. But the inner consciousness cannot reveal these secret causes without a special influence. Later, however, rulers and courts of law utilized this as a means of securing evidence, and thereby they introduced the element of compulsion. But everything coercive and artificial is contrary to the fundamentals of Existence.

38. People often complain of the isolation of the Subtle World, which is already inaccessible to Earth. Yet the Ayur-Vedic traditions foresaw this earthly alienation. There exists a plant extract which, when rubbed into the skin, permits an approach to the Subtle World, facilitating its visibility and tangibility. But for this a complete detachment of the consciousness from Earth is required. Moreover, such coercion is impermissible in the reconstruction of the world. Let us not disparage the significance of the heart and

Fire in any way. Are small roots of any use during the flights of the spirit?

**39.** If we gather all the details of our life, we shall find innumerable evidences of the Subtle World. We will also find that in the majority of cases the voices of the Subtle World do not reach Earth, just as our voices do not reach deaf ears. Indeed, this comparison becomes precise when we realize that the cries of the Subtle World do not reach Earth. Nothing can equal the despair of the Subtle World when its warnings do not reach their destination. In its own way, the Subtle World greatly desires to help our world. But true cooperation can only be attained by cultivation of the heart and by understanding the quality of the nature of Fire.

**40.** In the ancient pharmacopeias and in various ancestral medical records you are struck by the number of allusions to mixtures for bringing the organism into a transcendental state. You feel that this is not a form of necromancy or witchcraft, but a special way of seeking one's future. Hence, it is clear that our remote ancestors were far more solicitous and thoughtful of the future than our contemporary scholars. For us, the future is relegated either to the confines of hellfire or to the province of an electrical manifestation. The powerful life-creating potency of Fire is unrealized; the effulgent, radiant manifestations are not comprehended, and the very Hierarchy of Light itself is regarded as either a phantom or a bugbear. There are many who wish to evade the future, preferring to call themselves dust. Yet even the learned shudder at the question as to whether they wish to pass through Fire.

Nevertheless, how often have we been drawn out of the three-dimensional state! When we are immersed in thought, do we notice time or temperature? We are entirely unaware of the numerous minutes that run together in the twinkling of an eye or become an eternity. Such experiences occur daily, and each one can be a witness to wonderful phenomena.

**41.** The concept of Shambhala is actually linked inseparably with fiery manifestations. Without the application of purified Fire it is impossible to approach the higher concepts. Throughout the entire world people are divided into those who are conscious of Shambhala as the Highest Measure and those who deny the future. Let the word *Shambhala* be known to but a few; each has a different tongue, but the heart is one. One must manifest solicitous attention to each one who is ready to proceed toward Light. The heart must embrace each manifestation that reverberates to the Good. But only under the Flaming Dome are all equal.

**42.** Upon the sky you inscribe words in smoke. Perhaps you do not know that the Chaldeans up on their ziggurats wrote in space when the dates approached. Thus, cooperation was established with the luminaries, and chemical rays speedily fortified the earthly solutions. In their turn, scientists affixed in space their findings.

**43.** To a certain degree, the difficulty of understanding is due to the limitations of the earthly language. All the symbols and higher concepts are conventionalized to an absurd degree. When man observed something beyond the limits of daily life, he began to speak of it in vague and unusual terms, which meant something entirely different to his neighbor. To this were added the anomalies of sight, taste, and hearing, resulting in a complete babel. When man attempted to express the supreme Hierarchic Concept, he tried to string together the best syllables and only achieved extreme confusion. Notice that everyone who speaks about a transcendental concept meets with the most surprising explanations. People frequently speak about the same thing, but in such different terms that there is no possibility of reconciling these concepts with words. Then, do not tire yourself with argument, but remain silent in cordial solicitude. Let the fiery energy work, it will know how to find at least a narrow entrance. Thus, in all circumstances, remember that you possess a store of the all-pervading energy.

**44.** Also remember that the fiery energy grows and works incessantly if the heart is aflame. Thus, it is easier to understand the already mentioned divisibility of the spirit. Flame is divisible without harm and does not require either space or time. Thus, when you are seen simultaneously in different countries, you need not be surprised, for this is only one of the qualities of the fiery tension. Of course, this fiery tension produces a pressure on the solar plexus. One must realize how the unification of the fire of the heart with the Fire of Space tenses all centers.

**45.** Work like sculptors. Their hands know how to approach the stone in order not to distort the form. But, then, the one who eats knows how much food he requires. Naturally, overfilling the stomach will not be the right measure. On the contrary, the requirement is not determined by earthly measurements. The fire of the heart gives the sign to the consciousness. Thus, it is cause for rejoicing that the true measures are found in the fiery knowledge.

I have in mind a well for the safekeeping of treasures; for since time immemorial a treasure was always hidden in the depths. We also see that achievements are preserved in the depths of the heart, and are verily surrounded by Fire.

**46.** The sculptor's touch cannot be described in words. He himself will not be able to say precisely why he used a stroke of just such a depth. Similarly, you should correlate straight-knowledge with reality. The Teaching makes it possible to consider as reality that which yesterday was still unrealized.

**47.** The approach of the Subtle World to the earthly one is one of the great fiery tasks. Imperceptibly, much is being done toward this end. But, in addition, it is necessary to strengthen a consciousness of this in the minds of people. One should affirm its reality and remove it from the category of a fairy tale. It is not sufficient that somewhere results have already been achieved, for the slightest improvement demands a conscious acceptance. If this is apparent even with everyday discoveries, then how much more is it felt when it concerns man himself! It is difficult for man to yield even in the smallest! Rare are the heroes who shed their blood for the good of their fellow man, yet this inner impulse fills the organism with new forces. One should understand the transmutation of the physical body also as a form of heroism. It must serve as an encouragement to realize that the experience of such an approach has already produced excellent and tangible results. People must become accustomed to the fact that the perfecting of conditions of existence must be accelerated, but this must not resemble convulsions. On the contrary, people should not be satisfied with outworn customs; they should learn to rejoice at the new. Joy about the new is already wings to the future.

**48.** To co-measure one's actions with the actions of co-workers is also a fiery quality. When lighting a lamp, no one intends to set fire to the house. On the contrary, everyone seeks a safe place for a lamp. Fieriness is not madness. It is awful to listen frequently to ignorant conversations about the chaotic state of Fire. It must be understood that this element demands the highest co-measurement, profound circumspection, and caution. Each Agni Yogi is primarily wise in the apportionment of this substance. He will be thrifty rather than extravagant. As a faithful guardian he knows that the highest substance is purified through lofty labor and suffering. He knows that each energy of Fire is like a rare blessing. The Fire of Space demands manifestation; and he understands the value of this finding. Only then can he be entrusted with the ocean of Fire.

Therefore I ask all co-workers to be sternly circumspect. Thus will they preserve the treasure that grows in the heart. It is best not to scatter it into the abyss of darkness, where each torch will be used for a ruinous conflagration. The pillar of co-measurement, even in Fire must be a safeguard.

**49.** No one should approach Fire with fear. No one should approach it with hatred, because Fire is love!

**50.** Each endeavor may be fulfilled in three ways—through external muscular exertion, outwardly through a nerve center, or through the heart's fiery energy. If the first effort is animal, the second is human, and the third is of the Subtle World. The third effort could be utilized much more frequently if people could consciously apply the concept of the heart and Fire. But unfortunately this tension arises only in exceptional cases. Naturally, when a mother saves her child, she acts beyond earthly conditions. When a hero dedicates himself to the salvation of mankind, he multiplies his strength tenfold. But this unconscious enflaming rarely occurs. We watch over the constant increase of forces through the realization of the predestined powers. It is not so difficult to transform and kindle the consciousness when constant attention is applied to it. Constancy is also a quality of Fire.

Everywhere, under all circumstances, the essence of Fire is the same. Fire cannot be formed out of any elements, any compounds; one can only manifest Fire. Likewise it is possible to draw near to the Fiery World. The most astounding regenerations occur through fiery manifestations. The earthly world is regenerated only through Fire. People believe in the Light of Fire. People become blind because of Earth, and are regenerated through Fire. One can cite many examples of how Fire brings about world upheavals. Without the manifestations of Fire you cannot even enter upon a path of regeneration. Many will scoff at the mere word regeneration, yet even a snake renews its skin. Thus it is better consciously to approach the Fiery World.

**51.** It is not terrifying that the oceans change their beds. Should not people be primarily mobile in thought? The ability to transpose one's being into thought will provide a channel to the Fiery World.

**52.** One should become accustomed to the fact that drowsiness has many possible causes. It is wise to understand that the activity of certain centers is especially transcendental and is apt to cause physical drowsiness. But We know how significant the state of semisleep can be. Do not reject drowsiness.

**53.** A thoughtful physician may ask concerning the fiery illnesses, "Are they named as quite specific sicknesses, or are they spread through the majority of diseases?" The second is closer to the truth. Fire can aggravate all illnesses, therefore great attention should be paid to the state of fiery striving. Besides, it must be remembered that any fiery manifestation cannot be abated merely by water or cold, but rather through psychic energy, which resists Fire everywhere. This energy, as a sort of condensation of Fire, can absorb the fiery surplus. Thus, attention should again be directed to psychic energy when We speak about the heart, about the Fiery World, and about Our affirmation of the existence of the Subtle World. When you read about being consumed by the inner fire, bear in mind the reaction of psychic energy. It can be manifested in three ways: through autosuggestion, through physical action, or through the highest action at a distance. However, physicians often forget that it is not the medicine but some external condition that helps. We recall one remarkable case when a physician possessed powerful psychic energy, yet stubbornly attributed its effects to his medicine. One can easily realize the extent to which such benefits would increase if the physician understood wherein his power lies. Only, do not confuse the heart's energy with external magnetism and so-called hypnotism. Both of these manifestations are artificial and hence, temporary. The heart's energy is not applied forcibly, but is to be transmitted by contact with the current. If, prior to all physical means, the physician and the patient would simultaneously think about the energy of the heart, in many cases the reaction would be instantaneously useful and healing.

54. I ask not to forget that the Fiery World does not tolerate procrastination. Affirming it in the consciousness is already a step of approach.

55. In world events, is it not possible to perceive the manifestation of Fire? Observe the relationships of nations, the magnet of ideas, the dissemination of thoughts, and all the signs of public opinion. These flashes of flame are not caused by any means of communication, but by something else, which stands beyond.

56. Joy and courage are indispensable, but without Fire these qualities are not created. Reason can deprive one of all joy and thus close the gates to the future.

Yet a fiery world outlook does not fall from heaven, it must be discovered. This method of discovery must begin in childhood. We see how children already accept inwardly the most difficult tasks of the spirit. Even all impediments placed by their elders serve only to crystallize their straight-knowledge. But crystallization is a fiery action. The best beds of crystals are molded by fire. Thus, the invincible heart is also formed by fiery impact. This is not a symbol, but a purely laboratory deduction. Yet how far from fiery considerations are people!

57. Not only about Fire must we ponder. Events are driving onward like an ocean wave. You understand correctly that the dark force surrounds each benevolent inception. We observe how every ordinary action is instantly turned into evil. Thus, one should get rid of all yesterday's gnats, and replace everything usual with the most unusual. Even an award, as it were, should be granted for unusualness. One should not expect unusualness from the old world. Over and above the usual conditions, one should touch the most unexpected angles. Therefore I rejoice when new elements are dealt with.

58. Pulmonary plague, in certain forms, is a striking evidence of a fiery epidemic. From time to time it has visited Earth, preparing the consciousness for the possibility of calamity. Also, the type of strange coughing about which you have heard is symptomatic of this ailment.

It is manifested generally in both children and adults, and even in animals. But people prefer not to recognize this preliminary form of dreadful calamity. They will superficially attribute it to the most varied diseases; anything to keep from thinking about the unusual. All such patients should be isolated, and the dead cremated at once. People who have lost their psychic energy may easily succumb to this contagion. It can be intensified by various additional forms, both internal and external. The darkening or inflammation of the skin will suggest smallpox or scarlet fever; the majority of fiery manifestations are reflected upon the skin. Learn to pay attention to these unusual manifestations. Musk, and hot milk with soda will be good preventives. Cold milk is not assimilated by the tissues, whereas hot milk with soda penetrates into the centers. Having tried to reduce temperature with cold applications, people often find that a mustard plaster or hot compress results in unexpected improvement. We definitely oppose cupping glasses and leeches, because they affect the heart and may be dangerous.

We often send people on most dangerous missions, but at the same time We take care of their health. It is unwise to destroy a useful substance.

**59.** Fire bears within itself an understanding of beauty; it envelops creativeness and transmits imperishable records into the treasury of the Chalice. Hence, We value these incorruptible achievements more than all those that may be destructible. Therefore, help human thought to strive toward the Imperishable.

**60.** He who does not help the regeneration of thought is no friend of the New World. Many times you have noticed that improvements and refinement occur imperceptibly when calculated in human measurements. It is difficult to perceive each bit of the growth of a plant stem; yet the beautiful flower differs so strikingly from the seed. Equally astounding are human transformations; it is precisely these fiery blossoms, rarest of all, which sustain the balance of the world.

**61.** One cannot help but observe how unexpectedly

the scroll of events rolls up. Merely observing them molds the entire Epoch of Fire.

**62**. Fire must be alive. Inactivity is unnatural for Fire. Energy generates energies. It is especially harmful to tear man away from his customary labor. Even through the lowest forms of labor man creates a manifestation of fiery energy. Deprive him of labor and he will inevitably fall prey to marasmus; in other words, he will lose the Fire of Life. One should not propagate the concept of people's retirement from work. They do not age because of advanced years, but from the extinction of Fire. One should not think that the extinguishing of Fire exerts no harm on the surroundings. Harm occurs precisely when a space occupied by Fire suddenly becomes accessible to corruption. This decay of life is opposed to the law of Existence. On the contrary, human society should sustain Fire in all its surroundings. The fire of the Druids was a reminder of the maintenance of the Fire of Life. It is inadmissible to quench Fire in anything, not even in the smallest. Therefore, do not interfere with the festival of the spirit, even though its language be incomprehensible to you. That which is unintelligible to you today will become clear tomorrow. But Fire once extinguished cannot again find the same application.

**63**. The festival of the spirit is of pan-human value; it is a treasure which has been built up. Let no one infringe upon this worthy structure. Among the impermissible invasions of karma, interference with the festival of the spirit is regarded as very grave. On the other hand, to send a smile to the festival of the spirit is the most flaming flower of the heart's offering.

**64**. It is necessary to realize the difficulty of discerning the different currents. Many would not be able to distinguish the intricate variations of currents and rhythms. I highly commend Urusvati for attention to the currents—only thus can one accumulate observations. In two years' time it will be possible to inform about one of the most complex currents, which cannot be withstood without previous accumulations.

**65.** Last night's current is one of the highly tensed Fiery impacts—the so-called dual arrows. The past heavy current of Mahavan also has a significance for this new tension. It is given as a special defense against grave impacts. Thus, one can arm oneself fierily, provided the spirit itself accepts such an armor. This acceptance is essential for the cognizance of the Fiery World, because the gates may not be opened where there is opposition.

**66.** Not few are the fires in the fields and forests—but people regard them as supernatural. This can be explained only by lack of imagination.

**67.** Besides Our affirmation, even people themselves observe the subsiding of certain continents. Yet no importance is given to this. This is also due to ignorance.

**68.** Stand firm, stand more firmly than a rock. The miraculous fire is intensified by steadfastness of spirit.

**69.** The quality of observation is one of the principal fiery qualities, but it is not attained easily. It is acquired as slowly as is consciousness. You noted correctly that consciousness is strengthened by life itself; observation is strengthened likewise. There can be no abstract consciousness, nor can there be theoretical observation. But human absent-mindedness is monstrous, it creates a seemingly unreal world. In their egoism people see only their own delusions. In such wanderings there can be no discourse about the New World. Hence, by all means, training in observation should be introduced in schools, even for small children. An hour devoted to observation is a true lesson in life, and for the teacher this hour will be a lesson in resourcefulness. Begin the refinement of observation upon everyday objects. It would be a mistake to direct the pupils too rapidly to higher concepts. If, for a beginning, the pupil is capable of observing the habitual contents of a room, this will already be an achievement. This is not so easy as it seems to an unobservant eye. Later, by a series of experiments we can accelerate the ability to form impressions. We can propose that the pupil pass through an unfamiliar room at a run and yet with concentrated observation. Thus, it is possible to reveal blindness and assert true keenness of vision. It is necessary to outline a program of tests for all the senses. Thus is fiery action expressed in a simple exercise. Children are very fond of such tasks. Such exercises of consciousness carry one into the higher spheres. The most ordinary routines can become the gateway to the most complex. Imagine the exultation of a child when he exclaims, "I've seen more!" In this "more" can be comprised an entire step. The same joyous exclamation will greet the first fiery starlet that is observed. Thus, true observation begins.

**70.** Flights into the Subtle World may be difficult; even an experienced consciousness may meet obstacles. Today Urusvati experienced such a difficulty. An effort was needed in order to pierce chemical strata which are formed by astrochemical fusions. The days around full moon are not favorable for flights. The so-called lunar glass can impede, and very strong perseverance is required.

**71.** Each blow of the hammer produces a fiery manifestation, but each sword stroke also yields a fiery display. Let us approve the work of the hammer, and warn against raising the sword. Let us discern each touch of Fire. Let us accept with utmost responsibility each evidence of the great element. The manifested Fire does not return to its primeval state; it will remain in a special state among fiery manifestations. It will be either life-creating or destructive, according to the intention of him who sends it. For this reason I stress the significance of Fire, this inseparable fellow traveler. By the most varied means one should impress people with the significance of the elements. They have forgotten how filled their life is with the most responsible actions. Words and thoughts beget fiery consequences; yet the tongue continues to prattle and thought continues to wound space. Ponder this fiery production! Do not pride yourselves on some dead knowledge as long as you continue to spew slander against the Highest. Remember that this slander will lodge with you forever. The world has been set aquiver by the flames of malice. Its progenitors hope for the ruin of others, but they themselves will perish from leprosy.

72. Before you is another manifestation of a high degree—the Kundalini bestirs itself, from its base to the very highest joint. The pharyngeal glands are highly inflamed, but this physical aspect is indispensable for the fiery reaction. In this condition the Kundalini acts at the furthest distances. You realize how necessary just now is this reaction of Urusvati. Without this fiery action, there could have been no victory. But the battle is difficult indeed, and the waves of attacks are increasing. Therefore, let us be very cautious. Let us be attentive, benevolent, and very careful.

73. Sound and color are among the principal fiery manifestations. Thus the music of the spheres and the radiance of the fires of space are the highest manifestations of Fire. Hence, it is impossible constantly to hear the sounds of the spheres or to see the scintillating fires. Such frequency of emotions would separate the

earthly body from the fiery one to too great an extent. Thus the equilibrium so needed for Eternity would not be created. It is true that in consciousness we should separate our four bodies in order that their functions may be divided. The disturbance of equilibrium leads to premature destruction of the lower body.

74. There is no reason to think that black magic is now especially increasing in Tibet. Of course it has increased there greatly, but this is only one phase of its world-wide development. One cannot imagine to what an extent this black network is being spread. It is impossible to conceive the entire diversity of its participants. It is impossible to reveal all the unsuspected combinations which sustain each other. Can one be reconciled to the fact that heads of states, prelates, Freemasons, rebels, judges, criminals, physicians, the sick and the healthy, are all at work in the same black field? The difficulty of detecting them is that one cannot indicate any definite organization; all is based on separate individuals, who are deliberately placed in the most varied activities.

75. The associates of the black lodges themselves distinctly recognize each other. There actually exist obvious signs. Thus, if you notice an inhuman cruelty, be assured that this is a sign of the dark ones. Each Teaching of Light is primarily a development of humaneness. Remember this definitely, for the world has never before been in such a need of this quality. Humaneness is the gateway to all other worlds. Humaneness is the basis of straight-knowledge. Humaneness is the wings of beauty. The essence of humaneness is the substance of the Chalice. Therefore, above all, on Earth let us be clothed in humaneness and recognize it as an armor against the dark forces. A fiery manifestation will visit the heart through humaneness. Thus we shall realize

once again to what a degree the farthest is the nearest. We also recognize each other through humaneness. Thus, in this hour of danger, let us labor for the most imperative.

**76**. The inner Lotus can be observed open as well as closed. When the protective purple aura is needed, it can be seen how the petals of the Lotus contract and become covered by the precipitations of the blood vessels. During such a manifestation an experienced Yogi realizes that great danger is near. As in nature, long before the clouds appear the petals of flowers turn increasingly toward the sun or at twilight promptly fold up, so also the Fiery Lotus senses the approach of cosmic storms. And through the development of Yoga one can observe a similar tension also in the outer Lotus. Thus is called the circular rotation of the Kundalini, which touches the chief centers, and forms, as it were, the outer Lotus of defense. This particular tension is usually preceded by the manifestation of arrows, which has already been spoken about. The outer Lotus is also called an armor. We consider its formation not only a sign of danger but also of the attainment of a degree of Yoga.

**77**. The absentation that you observed of course has not a physical but a yogic significance. It is induced by an urgent need of appearing without delay in distant countries. One should get accustomed to such summons when there is so much tension everywhere. For only the blind can think that tomorrow will be as yesterday!

**78**. It can be noticed that before the evening certain flowers not only close but even droop to the ground. So also with the inner Lotus.

**79**. It may be asked in what relation Our Teaching stands to the one already given by Us through

36

Blavatsky. Answer that each century, after the manifestation of a detailed exposition, a conclusive culmination is given, which actually moves the world, along the line of humanness. Thus, Our Teaching includes the *Secret Doctrine* of Blavatsky. Similarly, Christianity was the culmination of the world wisdom of the classic epoch, and the Commandments of Moses were the culmination of the wisdom of ancient Egypt and Babylon. However, one must grasp the signification of fundamental Teachings. It is hoped that people not only read Our books but accept them without delay, for I speak only briefly of that which must be remembered. When I speak of the need of fulfilling My Indications, I ask you to fulfill them with complete precision. I can see more clearly, and you must learn to follow the Indication, which has in view your own good. A man fell under a train merely because he stepped upon the rails, but he had been forewarned and should not have done so.

**80**. People say that before a war or calamity forest fires and other conflagrations occur. Whether or not they always occur is of no importance; what is significant is that popular belief takes note of the fiery tension before world upheavals. Folk wisdom assigns to fire a remarkable place. The Lord visits people in Fire. The same fiery element was chosen as the Highest Judgment. The purging of evil is performed through Fire. Misfortunes are accompanied by burning. Thus, in the entire current of folk thought one can perceive these fiery paths. People like the shrine lamps and carried torches, displayed for the services. In the people's understanding the element of fire has a solemn meaning. Thus, let us draw not from superstition, but from the folk heart.

**81**. Sincere striving for self-perfection is not

egoism, but has universal significance. The thought about improvement does not concern oneself alone. Such thought carries within itself the flame needed for many kindlings of hearts. As fire, when brought into a place filled with inflammable substance, will unfailingly ignite it, so fiery thought pierces space and infallibly attracts seeking hearts to itself.

**82**. The responsibility of the kindled heart is great. It transmits rhythms and currents along the line of Hierarchy. Therefore, those around it should not overburden a heart so strained; this should be understood as a basis of Existence.

**83**. The dark forces have brought the planet into such a condition that no earthly solution can restore its conventional prosperity. None can regard the earthly standards of yesterday as suitable for tomorrow. Hence, humanity must understand anew the meaning of its transitory sojourn in an earthly state. Only through a fundamental defining of one's existence in the carnate form and through an understanding of the Subtle and Fiery Worlds can one strengthen one's own existence. One should not think that the delusion of trading can even temporarily insure a secure existence. Life has been turned into trade, but who of the Teachers of Life has ever been a shopkeeper? You know the great symbol of driving the moneychangers out of the Temple; but is not Earth itself a Temple? Is not Maha Meru the foot of the Summit of Spirit? Thus one can indicate the predestined Summits to the inhabitants of Earth.

**84**. Let us not forget that each instant must pertain to the New World. Observe that in enumerating the worlds We seem to omit the world of thought. This is not by accident. The Mental World constitutes a living link between the Subtle and Fiery Worlds. It enters in as the impellent nearest to the Fiery World. Thought does not exist without Fire, and Fire is transformed into creative thought. The manifestation of thought is already understood; let us also realize the Great Fire—Aum!

**85**. One can distinguish the labor of Fire in the most diverse manifestations. Nowadays a crystal globe is often used for concentration, in order to call forth subtle impressions, but this is a later form. In the ancient East a block of rock crystal was chosen and placed over a covered fire. Then the structure of fiery creativeness was brought to life, and it attracted the manifestations of Spatial Fire. Thus one can observe to what a degree the ancient power of fiery observation has degenerated.

**86**. It can also be noticed that around certain people things wear out, while others seem somehow to preserve them. At times people erroneously say, "Everything burns on him." In reality it is quite the opposite. Pay attention to the preservers. They will be close to Fire. Precisely the fiery principle preserves the durability of things. I have already spoken about the reaction of the psychic energy of workers upon the quality of their production. Here also we shall look for the participation of Fire. Psychic energy will give fiery evidence of the influx of the fires of space.

**87**. One can place the Teaching of Fire into the foundation of each day. So long as we wander among illusory allurements we will not be affirmed in the sole basis of life, and thus will not come close to ascent. I have in mind those wavering ones who not only lose their own path but who also impede the movements of their near ones. The waverer not only dissipates his own treasures but also plunders that of others. It is frightful to see how the manifestation of doubt contradicts all fiery foundations. In this, observe that the waverer usually does not doubt himself, but others only, and thus he gives admittance to decomposition.

**88**. It need not be thought that only karmic conditions create wavering. Often the cause must be sought in obsession. The waverer himself thinks that he must proceed warily—but as if this anxiety concerned only himself! The past of many waverers would be instructive for the schools.

**89**. In schools one should not read only about heroes. Examples of the fate of a few anonymous waverers would be worthwhile. The bright flame of achievement would shine still more by comparison with the fate of the extinguishers.

**90**. Rejected possibilities can be discussed not only morally but also chemically. In truth, what words are adequate to describe the destruction of an already formed reaction when precious fiery energy, gathered by great and lengthy labor, is ignorantly dissipated? But these fiery particles, invoked for a definite combination, remain discordant for a long time, and double effort is required to again utilize them for creation. I repeat, it is inadmissible to violate someone's spiritual festival. It is criminal to invade an already molded integral consciousness. Does not the evidence of karma issue from these same irrational intrusions? Coercion is especially inadmissible in the fiery domains.

**91**. Let us mentally collect all the fiery approaches, let us examine the signs of inspiration or illumination. We will find identical signs indicating the common foundation, which actually lies beyond. And so it must be, the fire of the heart comes into contact with the Fire of Space. Only thus can be effected the conception, or more correctly, the impregnation of thought-creativeness. Moreover, one must manifest the highest respect for the complexity of the apparatus that forms the contact with Fire. The most delicate golden networks of nerves are almost imperceptible to the eye. One must peer into them with the third eye in order to remember them forever and be imbued with respect for them.

**92.** The golden network, seen by Urusvati, forms the foundation of the Chalice; one can judge the delicacy of the inner apparatus. Thus, refinement can turn thought toward consideration among human beings. People should not offend one another. In the name of Fire no offense should be given. Not all adjustments are effected with a hammer; small implements and careful touches are also necessary. Again an old truth, but as yet scarcely applied.

**93.** In general, few can understand the glow of the flaming heart. Yet those who have beheld these fires of illumination know how vital is this manifestation. The Fire-bearer himself notices these instants of light, but for those present many conditions either permit or impede seeing the miraculous Fire. Without doubt the natures of those present have an influence upon the character of the manifestations themselves. One can easily imagine such a mass of extinguishers that even the star of Light will be only a glimmer. But at times a simple yet most beautiful heart sets ablaze a new force of the Fire-bearer. Besides human reactions and conditions of the Subtle World numerous manifestations of nature exert an influence. Thus, during a thunderstorm the luminosity can increase at the moment when the electrical mass also intensifies the inner fires. Water that contains certain mineral properties can also facilitate the manifestation of inner radiance. Naturally, the worst atmosphere is the stale, poisonous air of unventilated houses. Surely, if this air can be the breeding place of disease, how much more can it suppress the emanations of the heart! The manifestation of luminosity is more frequent than is thought, but prejudice and sophistry will always draw their own conclusions. The misfortune is that people cannot detect unfettered judgments. The heralded emancipation, about which people like so much to speak, will be primarily not slavery of opinion.

**94.** When I call, "Help through thought." I show a special trust. Not everyone can be asked to help in thought. One must be certain of the quality of thought and of the concentration of heart energy. Such choice thoughts are like a powerful radio. One should know how to muster complete devotion, and how not to encumber thoughts with irrelevant feelings. A hurricane is necessary to carry sendings—steadfastness also will be urgently needed. It is erroneous to think that thought is important only for the earthly plane; perhaps it is even more important for the Subtle World, to create a powerful collaboration. During the tension of the world, equilibrium can often be created precisely by thoughts.

**95.** The reactions from the currents noticed by you have a dual significance—they balance the cosmic shocks and multiply the force of the sendings. This is so-called psychophysical therapy. During the condensation of darkness such powerful currents are useful.

**96.** Achievement should be the subject of conversation on each significant day. One should regard achievement as something invoked and not become weary of speaking and thinking about it. Misfortune is begotten by disparaging achievement. It is as if a large temple image were being carried through a narrow door, and in the jostling the most precious ornaments were broken.

It is dangerous to bring one's complaints on a

significant day. How can one convey that such crude ways are like the fall of a hammer upon the strings of an attuned instrument? The man who spatters the most destructive words adds, like a child, "Well, the heavens haven't fallen!" He cannot perceive the rupture of the inner threads which nothing can in any way tie together; thus irreparable harm is often wrought. But each heart that has realized Fire affirms the concept of achievement, for without it life is straitened and unbearable. Thus, let us carry the achievement of all three worlds.

97. Shambhala is manifested under the most varying Aspects, in relation to the concepts of a century. It is correct to study all the cycles of the legends of Asia. Thus one can go back as far as the most ancient Teachings connected with Siberia, as the least known and most archaic part of the continent.

The relation of the hieroglyphics found in India to the inscriptions on Easter Island is unquestionable. Thus is disclosed the manifestation of a new relationship of peoples, which fully corresponds to the most ancient sources. Thus, once more you see how the chronicles have preserved the true historical data, but people accept them with difficulty. You observed justly that the facts about the Kalachakra are passed over in silence; this is due not only to ignorance but to an abhorrence of touching the fundamentals. Humanity passes over with equal shudders all the wells of knowledge—this applies to all worlds—and people will shudder just as much over the world of Fire.

98. Try to divide people according to the elements. Not only according to the type of blood but also according to the character of the nerve substance will it be possible to observe a direct reaction in accordance with the elements.

**99**.  During every illness one can apply thought as a means of healing or relief, but such thought should eject the sickness from the organism with full force, without hesitancy or delay. However, if such force be lacking it is generally better not to think about the sickness at all, but to leave to the lower Manas the carrying on of the inner battle. It is most harmful to waver in thought and to visualize a victory of the sickness. In such cases it is better to distract the attention of the patient from his condition. When people speak of the fatal outcome of a sickness, they themselves bring it closer. The least serious sickness can assume dangerous proportions if nourished by thought. Observations should be made in hospitals concerning the effect of thought upon the process of illness. Even the healing of wounds depends upon psychic energy. Thus we arrive again at the very same Fire generated by thought. All treatments by rays, thermal action, and applications of light comprise the same fiery influences, which are weak in comparison with the power of thought. Hence, the most vital advice is to develop fiery thought.

**100**.  Consideration of the significance of synthesis in earthly existence is correct. The entire force of consciousness should be preserved during the attainment of the higher spheres of the Subtle World. Yet only a synthesis of consciousness affords this possibility. One should also become accustomed to the most rapid orientation, and what could better contribute to this than synthesis? People speak of vigilance, but under this quality they think of vigilance in only one direction. But even trusted sentinels have perished from striving in only one direction. Can we value all nature's riches if our eye is unaccustomed to mobility?

**101**.  No justification is possible where there is hatred. I summon to magnanimity, not to weakness.

One may renounce everything for the Service of Light, but one must test good will in the Fire. This must be understood with the strings of the heart. But when you encounter a tiger, do not think of helping him; there is a limit to abomination.

**102.** In its timelessness and spacelessness thought belongs to the Subtle World, but still deeper possibilities must also be discerned in this construction. Fiery thought penetrates deeper than that of the Subtle World, therefore fiery thought more truly manifests the higher creativeness. With attention, everyone can distinguish these two strata of thought. During the usual trend of thought we are often conscious of a current, as it were, of a second thought, which clarifies and intensifies the first. This is not a division of the thought, on the contrary, it is a sign that deeper centers have begun an active participation. This flaming process is indicated by special terms in Hindu metaphysics, but we shall not dwell on them, for it will lead to dispute and Western arguments. Such controversies are of no use, all that is needed is a simple reminder of the fact that thought is linked with the Fiery World. Even children exclaim, "It came like a flash!" or, "It's dawned upon me!" Thus are called the moments of correct and instantaneous decisions. One may remember how Mme. Kovalevsky solved mathematical problems. Such a fiery condition linked with the Fiery World is characteristic. You know that above the subtle thoughts there are profound thoughts, which are sometimes difficult to separate from the thoughts of the Subtle World. This is not possible in the present state of our planet. The experience alone of this dual trend of thought should compel us to realize the division of the worlds.

**103.** Of course, at times we are dealing with remote

recollections, but there may also be cases of fiery illumination. It was thus in the case that you recalled. The Fiery World brings us flashes of illumination, similar to lightning flashes in the coarse manifestation of a thunderstorm. Just as storms always supply Earth with a purified store of prana, so does the Fiery World constantly pour out waves of influences. It is a pity that the receivers are few, but if one were to begin to exercise the consciousness for communion with the Fiery World, then such a receiver could become naturally affirmed. But the simplest for all worlds is to adhere firmly to Hierarchy.

**104.** Cruelty of the heart is death of the heart. Dead hearts fill the world with disintegration.

**105.** If one can distinguish between the strata of thought, one can also sense various kinds of activity. At first all activity seems to be taking place on the earthly plane. Later, in so-called dreams, straight-knowledge becomes separated, as if it were an independent activity which takes place not on the earthly plane alone. Thus comes the first realization of an entry of other worlds into our existence. Then, in a state of complete wakefulness, instantaneous absences may be observed which have no connection with any ailment. Thus the bond between the worlds and our participation in them can be traced still more profoundly. It is not easy for the consciousness to assimilate the concept of the invisible worlds; due to our dense shell we can realize only with difficulty all the possibilities outside our vision. One should become accustomed to thinking of entire worlds which actually exist. The Subtle World is not only our state of being, it is actually a complete world with its own potentialities and obstacles. Life in the Subtle World is not far removed from that on Earth, but it is on another plane. All the fruits of labor do not disappear, on the contrary, they multiply. However, if it is difficult here to preserve clarity of consciousness, there it is even more difficult because numerous manifestations are encountered of orders of evolution new to us. Thus, one should preserve especially the dictate about clarity of consciousness. This is expressed as true synthesis. And if consciousness is so greatly needed for the Subtle World, how imperatively is it needed for the Fiery World!

**106**. The master smelter counseled the new worker on how to approach the fiery furnace. But the worker's only concern was to learn the chemical composition of the flame. The master said to him, "You will be burned alive before you reach the flame. Knowing the chemical formula will not save you. Let me give you the proper clothes, change your footwear, shield your eyes, and indicate the proper breathing. First, keep in mind all the rapid transitions and fluctuations from heat to cold. I can make the most fiery work attractive to you. You will love the flashes and the glow of fires. In the tension of the flame you will find, not terror, but the tremor of ecstasy, and a proper conception of fire will fortify your being."

Thus may one advise each one who begins to think about the Fiery World. At the outset let us bring complete devotion and cultivate that step of love which acts as an inextinguishable Light. Since the earthly world is based upon manual creativeness, to approach thought-creativeness is more attractive.

**107**. One Chinese philosopher, knowing the frightful aspects of the lower strata of the Subtle World, determined to deaden their impression. For this purpose he filled his sleeping chamber with the most frightful images. In the presence of these revolting masks, he hoped that nothing worse could be expected. Such methods are abominable, although people love them whether in this or in another form. On the contrary, We teach the eye to become nonreceptive to the repugnant. Besides, it is impossible to imagine the complete gamut of horrors created by people's vices. Even here in the earthly world we often are horrified by inhuman visages, but imagine the aspects into which these are transformed when their essential nature is unmasked! And here also We often experience the attacks of these dark entities. They attempt to annihilate everything dangerous to them. During sleep they try to weaken one, in order to inflict injury more readily during the disturbance of the balance. One should not consider these dark engenderings as superstitious fancy. Every scientist must realize the depth of the perspective of Existence. The scientist has grasped the incalculability of infinitesimal organisms; he has seen the bones of giant animals, and he can see still more if he peers into the vastnesses of the Himalayan caves. Thus the scientist measures into infinity and calculates infinite magnitudes by simple mathematical solutions. This means that precisely the scientist must admit the infinitude of fiery formations. Thus, from the merest arithmetical zero one must send one's imagination into the Infinite, remembering that a vacuum does not exist.

**108**. Ask Urusvati to tell about the multiformity of the fires seen by her. Let all these rays, stars, fiery Lotuses, flowers, and all the other manifestations of the Fiery World live and be affirmed. It is impossible in earthly words to describe all the quality of these fiery visions. Beyond certain boundaries the Fiery Realm is disclosed like a vision. It cannot be defined by time, nor can the cause of its emergence be determined, for the Fiery Element is entirely beyond earthly dimensions. But if we can see it, both in its grosser manifestations and in its subtlest, it means that even our carnate being can anticipate the higher sphere. Fiery communion is unforgettable once it has been experienced. Thus let us gather courage for the ascent.

**109.** The three dimensions are demon's chains—as someone has said. Truly, he who chained the human consciousness with three dimensions was a veritable jailer. How could it have been possible to conceal that other beautiful, higher dimension! In their first questions children often strive beyond the boundaries of conventional limitations. At no time did the ancient wisdom insist upon three dimensions. Only with the gradual coarsening of humanity did this limitation take possession of the mind. It is remarkable that when the lamps of the heart become extinct, people begin to concern themselves with limitations. One can quote numerous historical examples of this self-abasement. But the human consciousness prefers to ignore the fundamentals of self-perfectment. Thus it attempts to conceal the most precious possibilities.

**110.** Cognizance of fiery reactions is divided in accordance with the senses. The first impression is that of vision, with all its fiery diversity. Then hearing is added, with the music of the spheres, bells, and the chords of nature. Then comes the refinement of touch, with the sensations of rhythm, of heat and cold. The most difficult of all are the sensations of smell and taste. Yet Urusvati knows the meaning of scenting a man at a remote distance. Now Urusvati also knows something else that is very difficult: to sense the taste of a metal in the Subtle World, which is already an extraordinary subtlety. But one should not only possess the power to discern such sensations, one should know how to observe them. Such discernment is very rare, but by passing beyond the three-dimensional boundary it becomes attainable.

**111.** On approaching the Fiery World one must firmly assimilate the quality of steadfastness. This is not a very easy quality to attain in connection with mobility. Neither quality implies that one should chew only one and the same crust, or scurry about in the same mouse-trap. It is not easy to affirm these qualities in the spirit as long as the three-dimensional boundaries are not discarded.

**112.** It has been correctly observed that in order for the organism to adapt itself to a vegetable diet after a meat diet three years are needed. But if, for purely physical conditions, such a period is necessary, no less a period is required for the transformation of consciousness, unless karmic conditions induce special possibilities. To transform the consciousness means to enter a special world; it means to acquire a special evaluation of all that occurs; it means going forward without glancing back; it means leaving behind all complaints and acquiring good will. Does it not seem strange that alongside a period for a diet one must put the ethical concept of benevolence? But, fortunately, every physician will support us in this, because benevolence is the best expedient for the digestion. People like to have the spiritual foundations supported by dietetic advice.

**113.** A principle permits us to form a concept of the successive steps of the very same orderly process. Everyone can learn to swim as soon as he conquers the element in his consciousness. Following this principle a man can lie upon the water, and through a certain exercise, can sit upon the water. Advancing further, the Yogi can stand upon the water. Of course, such standing, and also levitation, are already fiery actions. You have knowledge of levitation, and you recall what fiery tension is required beforehand. But levitation is not so difficult, for the element of fire is akin to air. At the slightest doubt, despite all physical accomplishment, the man will immediately drown or fall. The reflex of doubt is a most striking one.

**114.** One need not be surprised at the dark entities swarming about. If you should find a lion in your flower garden, no doubt there would be an uproar in the house. To the dark ones you are that very lion in their backyard. Not a few efforts did they expend in cultivating their thistles, and then, suddenly, an uninvited lion made his appearance! Truly, sometimes one must pity all these labors of human hatred. But, for all that, the absence of doubt is stronger than all the dark snares.

**115.** Before human eyes many spiritual actions having physiological consequences take place, yet people are unwilling to notice them. The same can also be observed in visiting the Subtle World, where these manifestations are far more distinct. The decomposition of the astral body depends upon fiery contact. When a fiery being approaches certain strata of the Subtle World, a striking manifestation can be witnessed. The fiery substance is a touchstone, as it were. At its touch some subtle bodies are intensified in their fiery capacity, whereas others immediately disintegrate. This process takes place with great rapidity, as if from fire. Thus, one can compare a series of remarkable ascents and deserved departures. Fiery qualities can be manifested not only in the Fiery Sphere but even in fiery earthly incarnations. One should gradually become accustomed to the thought that even here on Earth there can be manifestations of the highest fiery qualities. One should admit this not only because it is immutable but also because of the diversity of nature's manifestations. Some may not admit that the projected subtle body can perform as purely physical an action as writing, but you know that this is possible, and there is no need for Me to convince you of it. Of course, fiery energy is necessary for such action.

116. Effort is needed for the directing of fiery energy, which for abbreviation we shall call Agni. This exertion is actually not a physical one and not even one of a subtle order. In the East people understand this lightning-speed quality. In Western speech there does not exist at all a designation for this most subtle concept. That is why it is so difficult to speak about the Fiery World. In the Eastern tongues also this concept sometimes becomes obsolete because it is unfit for contemporary consciousness. This is why many of the signs of Tao have been reduced to an outward depiction.

117. How many lofty discourses are taking place! What a multitude of signs of higher knowledge are being poured into people's lives and scorned as husks! And yet, who thinks courageously about the morrow? On the contrary, tomorrow usually remains a hotbed of terrors into which the consciousness sinks. Attention needs to be directed to the wonders of each day. Let us pursue from the cradle the entire path of trust and self-perfectment.

118. The path of good will actually should be expanded. It has been affirmed as the essence of our being. Let us not forget this talisman even for an hour. It is like the wonderful stone of which you know. Let us not forget the quality of the stone, and let us affirm it by our banner.

119. All that has vital capacity should be welcomed.

Each spark should be welcomed; from it grows Fire. Thus, be benevolent.

**120.** The use of alcohol and opium are ugly attempts to approach the Fiery World. If Samadhi is a natural manifestation of Higher Fire, then the flame of alcohol is a destroyer of Fire. True, narcotics evoke illusions of a fiery approach, but actually they will remain for a long time as obstacles to the mastery of the true energy of Agni. Nothing brings such misery later, in the Subtle World, as do these unnatural attempts to evoke Fire without a fitting purification. One may imagine that in the Subtle World a drunkard not only is tormented by craving for alcohol but suffers still more from unnaturally manifested Fire, which, instead of strengthening him, consumes the tissues prematurely. The combustion of the subtle body is accomplished quite differently during its transition into the Fiery World; it bursts into flame like an outworn envelope, accompanied by a feeling of liberation. But, like everything in nature, this must be accomplished only in accordance with the basic law, and it does not tolerate violation.

**121.** Violence is the scourge of humanity. It springs from ignorance, for even a man who thinks but little feels terror in his heart when faced with the unnatural.

From every manifested terror let us turn to magnanimity. Although We shall not weary of reiterating about magnanimity, yet this is the last chance for many to realize it. Pay attention to the word L a s t.

**122.** Even in physical illness seek a psychic cause. Nations have composed many sayings about these influences; they say, "Because of the heart the eye has been darkened," or "He has lost his teeth from strain," or "His breast has been split from thinking,"—thus do people remember about the principal cause of illness. And a thoughtful physician discerns the difficulty of treating a spiritual condition. It can be affirmed that any illness passes away more quickly when it is not supported by a psychic cause. The same peoples have attributed various curative qualities to Fire. Even incisions have been made using red-hot metal. Thus, fiery neutralization was affirmed even in the primitive consciousness.

123. The state of illumination is called "fiery aid." This state of consciousness should be approached with all the senses refined. Indeed, it may be noticed that sometimes I speak about things that are almost the same, but in this "almost" is contained one complete turn of the spiral. If you compare all these "almosts," you can discern the stratifications of the consciousness. It is not very easy to assimilate the rhythm of these strata, which differ individually. Yet through many observations it is possible to understand what a most subtle substance our consciousness is. Precisely, I emphasize refinement of the stratifications of consciousness. People often imagine that Fire is something turbulent, unencompassable, almost terrifying, thus they themselves plant fiery thickets. "As you call, so shall the call be answered."

124. It is not easy to cure eyes that are darkened with the dust of discord. An eyewash of true magnanimity is the first expedient. Likewise, note that this is true of many other ailments.

125. The situation in the world is difficult; everywhere there is a kind of ossification. People think to entrench themselves in a bog, but whole mountains are splitting as a reminder of what is coming.

126. In place of the Diplodocus, kangaroos leap; in place of the Pterodactyl, bats fly; in place of the dragon, lizards. What is the meaning of this? Can it be degeneration? Actually, it is only adaptation. Similarly,

the club of Hercules would be only a museum rarity nowadays. Thus, also in life, evolution should be understood, not as the growth of the fist, but as condensation of the spirit. From the swinging of the club let us turn to a new understanding of everyday life. The element of fire is majestic, yet even this must be learned in daily routine. It is not right to clothe heroes in a toga alone, depriving them of other forms of garment. Evolution should be accepted from life, amidst life, and for life. The beauty of evolution is not an abstraction, for each abstraction is a misconception. One should well remember this concept of evolution as a vital capacity; thus we shall approach the most complex formulas, where the symbol Aum will not be an inscription but the expression of the highest ingredient. Let us exercise our consciousness toward this.

**127.** It should not be thought possible to have one universal remedy for illnesses which may have a thousand causes. Special sections of therapeutics can be instituted which will partly correspond to a considerable number of the causes of illness. Thus, it must be understood that a universal expedient is impossible, because the origins of illnesses are entirely different. Likewise, in the methods of Yoga it is impossible to apply the same means for all. And yet, quite often in lectures and discourses general methods are mentioned, and those present are deluded into thinking that the prescription is for one and all. Only a very attentive scrutiny of the spiritual condition of the individual in question will give the right guidance to the indications for him. It seems very primitive to consider the diversity of organisms, particularly the conditions of the spirit, but mankind so loves panaceas. Still, there is only one panacea—the uplifted consciousness!

**128.** Many animals live up to three hundred years.

But if there should be discovered a means for prolonging their life, even for five years, it would be of no benefit for evolution. The life of the spirit is the basis of evolution.

**129**. If we begin to speak about firespouts, many will altogether fail to grasp the meaning, and others will think we refer to coarse electrical manifestations. Yet, one should ponder deeply upon this subtle fiery action. You have just seen how a mere scratch has caused a fiery burning. Such a manifestation is not from a physical infection. A firespout touched the torn tissue. Similar manifestations can be observed which conform to external fiery tensions. The torn tissue, with all the nerve outlets, serves as a magnet, as it were, for the fiery waves. Indeed, those people who possess vigorous heart energy can more strongly attract the waves of tensed Fire. Therefore, in such cases I recommend water compresses, but no alcoholic preparations. During the tension of Fire alcohol must be avoided, for it concentrates the fiery waves. Many drunkards could give instructive testimony about the fiery waves that cause such sufferings! Of course, I am not speaking now about nerve conflagrations, which only a few have observed. Even so, the firespouts must not be forgotten in such a tense time.

**130**. These same spouts and spirals are created by the disordered strivings of surrounding people, though not with bad intentions. You also know the effects of the striving of carnate and subtle bodies. They do not realize that in their tension they almost become vampires. Besides, one should distinguish the sendings of the intellect from those of the heart. Mentioning a name a great number of times may prove to have almost no influence, but a heart-sending, by its anguish of striving, can act as a spiral of asphyxiation.

It may be truly said, "Do not strangle, even for your own good."

**131.** During the sendings of good thoughts one must acquire the lightning-speed quality of these arrows. For this one should not encumber the consciousness for protracted periods, for it is useful to launch this arrow. The fiery dynamo labors like a light through all space. One must become accustomed to this work when the contact with Hierarchy is constant.

Seeing a dark star indicates a very great danger. Thus, in everything, such signs can be given. A small consciousness does not realize all the disturbances, but a developed consciousness understands the significance of the agitation of waters by the swords of the Angels.

**132.** Western physicians talk without cause about the difficulty of working with Us. We have never been opposed to experimental methods. On the contrary, We welcome each unprejudiced action. We approve when a member of the British Medical Society speaks about accurate methods of research. We are prepared to assist the Russian scholar in his work on immunization and immortality. We rejoice when the Japanese surgeon makes use of astrological dates. We are giving assistance to the Latvian physician in discovering the ocular symptoms of obsession. We are ready to assist each one, and to rejoice with each one. Indeed, We unceasingly insist on observations, and We direct to attentiveness in every way. We speak about reality; We affirm the absurdity of abstractness. Thus, We wish that physicians and scholars of the West would consider justly Our collaboration. It must be understood that the time has come to clarify the facts by discarding the husks. It is time to acknowledge that many superstitions are still growing in the backyards of isolation.

Thus, to superstition will belong the condemnation of all that is "not mine." The liberation of thinking will indeed be the adornment of true knowledge.

**133.** Is it not necessary to remind about liberation of thinking each time that you gather to talk about Fire? Will you not insist on justice when you refer to cognition? Do you not evoke smiles of pity when you mention the invisible Fiery World?

**134.** In the carnate condition the Fiery World is invisible with rare exceptions, but in the Subtle World a fiery mist can be sensed. True, upon approaching it, lower beings feel a particular suffering, as if before the unattainable. For these lower beings the Sons of the Fiery Mist are seemingly armed with fiery rays, which are nothing but the radiations of their extremities. It is necessary that the conventional conception of the mist should be changed into that of a harmonious fiery universe, but for this the consciousness must be transmuted. How many shocks must be experienced in order that the visualization of Existence uplift the consciousness in all fearlessness! One must rid oneself of fear of the mist, and, by honest thinking and a developed imagination, one should advance beyond the monsters of superstition.

**135.** Thought-creativeness and suggestion are completely different, although they are both related to fiery manifestations. Suggestion is a coercion of Fire, whereas thought-creativeness is a manifestation of basic law. When We spoke to a certain sahib about permeating his dwelling with Our Aura, We naturally had in mind thought-creativeness, and not suggestion, which We willingly leave to petty hypnotists. Thought-creativeness is far more powerful than any suggestions. First of all, suggestion is transitory; it strikes the aura and creates karma, whereas thought-creativeness saturates the aura and does not interfere with independent action. In fact, space saturated with thought-creativeness concentrates the fiery power. The inviolability of karma remains one of the subtlest conditions of all. To give, to assist, and even to guide, without infringing upon the personality—this is a difficult task. Each one must confront this solution. Thought-creativeness, devoid of self, provides the way out of these labyrinths. Kindness, cordiality, and cooperation likewise help, but the fog of unsteadiness is a particularly poor guide.

**136.** Any ribaldry and quarreling are already a tribute to darkness. The most deadly dagger is not at the belt but at the tip of the tongue. Sometime it will have to be understood that the spoken and also that which is thought are indelible. Each one intending good can rejoice at this, and vice versa.

**137.** Add, when writing to the Latvian physician: During observations of the eyes of the obsessed he must not lose sight of the fact that an observed symptom may change. At the approach of fiery energy, the symptom may disappear, as it were. The obsessing agent may begin to rave, or it may withdraw, taking the symptom with it. Therefore, the observation should be carried on without sending the fiery energy beforehand, otherwise this action will turn into expulsion of the obsessor. Such an action is excellent in itself, but it is beyond the scope of the oculist. The same reaction is sometimes observed in skin diseases which, under the influence of fiery energy, alter their appearance and even disappear. Let us not forget that obsession is sometimes manifested cutaneously, or by twitchings of the face. Nevertheless, the Latvian physician deserves praise, for it is not easy to perceive the crystals of brown gas.

**138.** For the last time let us turn to friendliness as a basis of life. Friendliness is not the rouge and powder of malice. Friendliness is not a veil. Friendliness is not a mask of treachery. Friendliness is not an affable grimace. Friendliness must be understood as a feeling coming from the heart, devoid of hypocrisy. There are many errors concerning the concept of friendliness, for people have become accustomed to deceive even themselves. But since the quality of friendliness is indispensable for the Fiery World, it must possess genuine honesty. First of all, Fire does not tolerate fluctuations. Hence, one must understand the quality of friendliness in its entirety. Friendliness should not be considered as some sort of achievement. One should not give praise for the quality of friendliness, for it is inseparable from an expanded consciousness. How is it possible to imagine the transformation of the Fiery Mist into a whole beautiful world, without having the strength to purify one's own thoughts from small splinters? Let us realize how petty these splinters are! And it is not difficult to rid oneself of them; one has only to uncover them in the consciousness. Let us not be afraid that people in general cannot return to friendliness, there is enough of it in each of us, therefore, let us assume the same thing about others. But let us not make of this fiery quality, weak will, subserviency, and pitiful hypocrisy.

**139.** Again the low strata of the Subtle World have been revealed in order once more to convince people of how close they are to similar strata of the physical world. It is regrettable that people enter the Subtle World so unprepared for it; they bring their base habits along, and they squander the forces of thought on imperfect forms. In the Subtle World the creativeness of thought is developed in all domains. It is difficult even to imagine on what delusions the precious power is expended! People should be advised to get used to thinking, even a little, about the beautiful, in order to avoid manifestations of ugliness. Not few are the beautiful creations and remarkable manifestations of nature, but it is necessary to observe them. A dark state of mind is the source of all misfortune. Even the low strata of the Subtle World differ in the distinctness of the illusions. Where there is aspiration there are no confused dreams, and all details are clearly impressed. But what a danger there is if the striving is base or trivial!

**140.** Science has already established the existence of particular organisms that can hear distant radio stations without receiving instruments. Indeed, this manifestation of a fiery order discloses paths to realization of the possibility of receiving thought from a distance. If the law of sound waves be understood, it is possible to delve into the same principle. It is fortunate that even the timid contemporary science admits the obviousness of such natural possibilities. But it is deplorable that science does not take the trouble to investigate such individuals. One hears that "with the exception of this phenomenal ability the organism is perfectly normal." This is a most ignorant observation. It means that the physician examined such a phenomenal man as carelessly as he would a recruit before a march. We do not wish to offend the physician, because often there is no place for him to carry out the proper observation. Indeed, the conditions of life render difficult all work of a subtle nature. Try knocking at the door of experimental institutions, and you will be met with an absolutely hostile stream of requirements, which will be beyond the capacity of a seeker. It is necessary to change this situation, otherwise where will it be possible to investigate various evidences of a fiery basis? Try to find the means to investigate necessary manifestations, and you will see how hostile your listeners will be; they will remind you of the Inquisition. As if their task were not to assist that which is highly useful, but to destroy possibilities! Thus it has been, thus it is, and people desire that it should always be so. Otherwise, there would be no Armageddon. One should understand whole-heartedly how many of the subtlest conditions there are that can determine important changes in all of life. Yet how necessary it is to knock for admission, to persist, to submit to derision, in order to reveal that which, it would seem, is open to all. Golgotha is erected by lack of understanding and ignorance.

**141.** Even a savage can fly in an airplane, but let us not think that formerly it was any better. I have shown you the records of the Thirty Years' War in order that you may understand how, even in comparatively advanced countries, coarseness and ignorance have ruled. Records of refined Rome, Egypt, and Babylon could be cited, at which the heart would shudder. Hence, all who look to the future should continue to knock for admission.

Also, one must become accustomed not to overburden Hierarchy and not to hurt each other. I have called upon you to display understanding of this law, but often the ears are so deaf!

**142.** A demon decided to place a holy hermit in a helpless position. For this the demon stole some of the most sacred objects and offered them to the anchorite with the words, "Wilt thou accept these from me?" The demon hoped that the hermit would not accept the gifts, and thus would betray the holy objects; if, however, he did accept them, he would be entering into cooperation with the demon. When this horrible visitor had voiced his proposal, the hermit did neither one nor the other. He rose up in indignation and with all the force of his spirit commanded the demon to leave the objects on the ground, saying, "Dark spirit, thou wilt not retain these objects, thou wilt vanish, annihilated, for my command has been manifested from Above!" Thus must one rout the dark ones, and when one's confidence is fortified by Hierarchy, no dark force is able to keep back the flame of the spirit. Let us not consider these legends unnecessary. The demons are of many forms and each toiler of Light undergoes attacks.

**143.** A headache may have many causes, but it also may come from the non-acceptance somewhere of mental sendings; this can also be reflected as needle pricks in the heart. Hence, I am anxious that this harm should not take place. With some people a routine of negation is formed imperceptibly, and it becomes, as it were, a habit to feel offended. On the basis of these errors, people become impervious to the manifestations of mental sendings. In this state the most benign thought recoils from the obstruction of resentment. Moreover, the thought may return and only cause trouble to the sender. One should urge everyone not to do harm. Besides, a touch-me-not attitude is most petty and is nurtured by an undeveloped consciousness. Thus, in everyday life there exists a routine of resentment. It must be recognized and ejected as a most noxious insect. Petty earthly feelings are turned into a fiery Gehenna.

**144.** Much is going on roundabout and especially where there is a Magnet. The Teacher forewarns that nowadays the most unusual conflicts may be expected, so crowded have the lower strata of the Subtle World become. People have decided to fill the Subtle World with great numbers that are arriving before their normal time. No one has thought what the consequences will be for the people themselves. It is impossible to slaughter millions of people with impunity, without setting up a most grave Karma. Even if the karma is not a personal one, so much the worse, because it increases the Karma of nations and of the whole planet. What has been said about peacemakers is the more correct, since because of them there arises a proper attitude toward the future. The lower strata of the Subtle World must not be filled with the horrors of uncompleted karma. One should not think that this will have no reaction upon the condition of the planet. But the principal cause is that no one thinks about the Subtle World at all. The isolation is most frightful; precisely the dark force exults at each alienation.

**145**. Let us observe each movement. Our organism reveals many facts which concern the Subtle and physical worlds. It can be noticed how much one's consciousness is changed during a flight into the Subtle World. It is as if it were sifted, and even our favorite formulas remain with the earthly consciousness. This observation is very difficult to comprehend. I rejoice the more when one not only notes this but also recalls the sensation of the slipping away of even a familiar formula. This does not mean that an already developed consciousness is lost in the Subtle World; it is rendered even more acute, but it passes, as it were, through a fine sieve, which transforms the remaining subtle substance. But for this observation a well-developed keen-sightedness is needed. Also, you do well to remember moments of absentation. In time you will know where your presence was needed. Not only in the Subtle World but here on Earth the exchange and assistance of consciousness goes on. You may be assured that if absence has been repeated again and again, it means you will learn about great events, about collisions where consciousnesses are confused and require assistance. It is indeed necessary to know how to observe these moments of cooperation. To save their near ones people sometimes give their blood for transfusion; will they not, then, lend fiery consciousness when their near ones are troubled?

**146**. Also, one should learn not to expend labor unproductively. Mental confusion compels people to neglect primary considerations. See how lacking in the essential are the two letters received by you; I do not blame the writers so much as those who confused them. Such a disregard for the principal issue is an already irreparable harm. The person who disconcerts the consciousness of his fellow man is a corrupter. He brings no joy to himself; on the contrary, his life will be darkened, for his consciousness has digressed from the main issue. To discern the principal issue and to remain on the path to it means to proceed to victory. But to begin by plunging into an abyss of uncertainty, does it not mean being a stone on the neck of one's fellow?

**147**. Co-measuring the main issue and the dust of the threshold is that test which each one must have clearly before him. No one has a right to pierce a heart or cause a headache, while irreplaceable treasures go by! People do not consider irreplaceable that which they do not notice.

**148**. It is possible to read a closed, unfamiliar book. You have seen this. It is possible at will to learn the time, mentally evoking a view of the timepiece. Thus it is possible to impel the Fire of Space to remove all obstacles. People call this manifestation clairvoyance, but it is better to call it fiery transvision. Yet it may be noted that this fiery possibility is not always the same. Also, it can be shown that great shocks increase this faculty just as complete repose does. But there exists a certain intermediate condition of the spirit, which, like a cloud, enshrouds our consciousness—this is confusion of the spirit. It is that same wavering which breeds the cloud of doubts. The clarity of reception fades not only because of the receiver's own confusion but also from that of those about him and bound to him by karma.

**149.** When the photographing of auras shall be instituted, it will be possible to see a significant phenomenon. The aura in complete repose will be equal in intensity to the aura in great shock. But on the other hand the waves of the intermediate reactions recall the shaking of a dusty sack. That is why I so protect you from petty waverings and discords. One can picture the gray spots of dissension which, like a canopy, conceal the light of possibilities.

**150.** One must not look upon the labor of Fire as something psychic. Consider Fire as something physical. It will be easier for the average consciousness to think thus.

**151.** Sleep can have the most contrasting causes, just as contrasting auras can be alike. It may be a hazy state of repose, or it may be a tense labor of the subtle body. When, besides nightly sleep, absentation during the day is also required, it means the labor is great. Often this imperceptible labor has a world significance. Governments would like very much to have such co-workers, but due to human limitations they do not even know how to find them. When, however, such a possibility arises, they are filled with an animal terror, exclaiming, "Most dangerous people!" Thus, each concept reaching beyond the limits of the crudest material conventions will be accompanied by an animal fear. One must be consoled by the fact that it was ever thus.

**152.** Whoever is unable to comply with the conditions of the Teaching of Knowledge dwells in fear. One has to see the aura of fear in order to understand how absurd this feeling is. Such an aura is not only agitated but coagulates, as if frozen, and, deprived of vibrations, it hangs like the yoke of a criminal. One should pay attention to the photographing of radiations. Even phosphorescent fish are easily photographed.

**153.** We shall return later to the question of birth, so bound up with the Fiery World. But now I shall reply to the question about light in the Subtle World. Indeed, the transcendental nature of the condition communicates a corresponding aspect to the whole world-content. When you visited Dokyood, you saw sufficient light. But certain regions of the Subtle World are striking because of their twilight. The Light is within ourselves and we open up the way to it. So, too, the inhabitants of the Subtle World who desire light have no scarcity of it. The inhabitants to whom the need of Light is alien dwell in twilight. This refers to unlimited thought-creativeness. That sun which we on Earth perceive under one aspect, can be transformed into many conditions under the power of thought-creativeness. He who desires Light gives access to it, but he who sinks into a twilight of thought receives that to which he has limited himself. This is why we repeat so often about clarity of consciousness, about boundlessness of thought, and about containment. Such an adaptation of the organism to the future produces the most desirable results. How many inhabitants of the

Subtle World look about themselves in the Fiery Mist and dimly regret something that has been lost!

**154.** When I say that the enemies of Good will suffer defeat, I have in mind a reality. One can see how people who have lost the bond with Hierarchy lose their place and pass into oblivion. You have just seen how it is possible to slide downward, not from the Sword of the Angel, but by popular decision. Thus it happens when that which is already near, already given, is not accepted. One must not wait until the messenger hurts his hand from knocking, one must summon heart-understanding in time. One cannot sever the threads with Hierarchy with impunity. The clouds come because of our very selves! Thus, observe these fiery signs in life.

**155.** During great fiery tension lesions of the skin should be avoided. A fiery conjunction of unnatural order causes a particular burning. This phenomenon can be of interest to physicians. And even scratches should be viewed from a spiritual angle. Psychic energy is at work, but one must take into consideration the special fiery tension. Each eruption of a volcano likewise takes place because of particular pressures. The manifestation of fiery tensions occurs in many sides of life. Once again in the Pacific Ocean new islands have risen, like fiery abscesses.

**156.** We observe with regret to what an extent a cruel action destroys many already prepared manifestations. One can only be amazed at such profligacy!

**157.** Toward what shall we strive, to the finite or the infinite? The earthly sojourn is of short duration, the Subtle and Mental Worlds are of fixed date, but the Fiery World is beyond dates; this means that one should strive toward it. In the worlds of limited sojourn the fiery armor is acquired. The earthly world is like an impasse—either ascent or destruction. Even the Subtle World will not satisfy a striving spirit; all the other lives are only preparations for the all-encompassing Fiery World. A weak spirit is terrified by the distance to the Fiery World, but the spirits in which ascent is innate can only rejoice. The physical forms are beautiful, but the music of the spheres is incomparable. Yet beyond this subtle illumination is displayed the Fiery Grandeur. Ozone here on Earth appears as a messenger from Above, yet it is the grossest manifestation of the atmosphere. The earthly azure is lofty, but it is like wool compared to the fiery radiance. Those who have entered the Fiery World cannot breathe the air of Earth. Nirvana is actually fiery ascent. In every Teaching we find a symbol of this fiery ascent. St. Sergius received the fiery sacrament. Thus, graphically is the sign of the higher possibility given. The time is coming and is already near when people will not know how to accept the fiery possibilities. In their confusion they will forget that fiery communion has been ordained. They will excel in counteracting, instead of being filled with, the power of Fire. Therefore I reiterate and remind about the necessity of fiery union. Many dangerous chemical combinations will cause consternation. Precisely the encumbrances in the Subtle World can indicate how sick the planet is. Since this danger has become obvious, it is Our duty to forewarn.

**158.** Psychic energy, that is to say, fiery energy, or Agni, is manifest in every living being. Everyone can discern in himself dense, subtle, and fiery elements. Wherever we sense a manifestation of psychic energy, there already is the fiery domain. From these fragments an entire fiery conception of the world can be formed. Each one, through attentive observation of the reflexes of his being, can note a great number of characteristics of the fiery domain. This should be observed, because in such manner we cease to think of the Fiery World as something abstract. Such a conception of the Fiery World is especially harmful, nor do all abstract interpretations assist evolution.

**159**. We can distinguish among our qualities the traits of the Subtle World; they will not always relate to psychic energy. But many remembrances, many aversions and inclinations may be products of the Subtle World. So, also, recollections about certain persons and localities that one has never seen may prove to be not from the physical world.

**160**. Likewise it is possible to cognize the Subtle World in isolated facts as an entire world-concept, but for this attentiveness is needed, or rather, that refinement which is called culture.

**161**. You are right in observing that precisely a lack of inner well-being is especially ruinous. One may win all lawsuits, one may meet new friends, but inner dissolution can drive away the very best friend. When pepper dust is in the air, all begin to sneeze. Thus can imperil be spread. You have seen more than once how new circumstances have appeared, but they have to be met. Thus, it is necessary once and for all to understand about the infection of imperil! It is inadmissible to refer light-mindedly to decomposition! This process is transmitted like leprosy. There can be either an increase of strength or disintegration, there can be no third condition. One should not advise strengthening by force. It is impossible to save anyone from leprosy by coercion. It is impossible to keep anyone from imperil by violence. Friendliness is not violence. Growth of the heart comes not from a whip, and a beautiful garden can be grown only by beautiful actions. Offense to Hierarchy is irreparable.

**162**. A sadhu pointed to a mango, saying, "Here are three worlds: first the skin, which has no value; next the pulp, transitory yet nourishing; and finally the seed, which can be preserved unto eternity." Thin is the skin, more substantial is the pulp, and mighty is the seed. The egg, too, presents the same analogy: The shell, which is a transitory manifestation; the white, which is nourishing though not for long; and then, the fiery yolk. Man represents the synthesis of all the kingdoms, and yet the symbol of the three worlds is everywhere evident. Thus, the custom of exchanging colored eggs on a commemorative day is a most ancient symbol. People have wished to remind each other about the path of the three worlds, about the path of ascent and resurrection. Thus, let us not forget that the path has been marked out even on simple objects.

**163**. Perfectly comprehensible is the desire to know why in visiting the Subtle World we are not struck by the polychrome of the auras. In the first place, the consciousness transposes many impressions, but the main thing is that there exists a synthesized harmony. It is indeed possible to distinguish the degree of illumination, and the radiation itself, just as in the carnate world, can be evoked mentally. It would be unbearable if the whole Subtle World were atremble with many-colored rainbows. Even on Earth the rainbow can sometimes be irritating. But the Subtle World is actually aglow in perfect harmony. We are not speaking about the lower strata, where it is impossible to find harmony.

**164**. So, too, one should not think that in the Fiery World its beings are constantly surrounded by tongues of flame. Fire can be crystallized, but its habitual state may be characterized as light. These communications are simple, but it is better to mention them in order to avoid the usual misunderstandings.

**165**. The fiery aura may be regarded as an actual indicator of the Fiery World. We must become accustomed to the fact that in the midst of life we encounter signs of these tensions. Crude examples are the electric eel and other animals that discharge electricity. But actually there are some people who, even apart from containing electricity, carry such charges of this energy that at contact they give off shocks and sparks. This means nothing in particular, but it is instructive to observe how the basic energy is precipitated.

**166**. It should be remembered how accurate is each of Urusvati's indications, and also that each of her sensations has a basis. Not only fiery eruptions and earthquakes, but even distant hurricanes are registered in the sensations, and these perceptions are infallible, for the fiery consciousness contacts everything sensitively; also, there are no errors in judging people, for each one displays his essential nature to the fiery consciousness.

**167**. Where, then, is the mite that can turn the lever of events? Where is the mite that can decompose that which is already composed? It is not necessary to seek a mountain of Good, it may appear as a grain of sand. One should not seek shelter from a black cloud only. Calamity creeps in more easily than the smallest worm. In all circumstances it is necessary to apply small measurements also. The atom is small, but it contains many a destiny. Thus, as we approach Fire, small is the boundary line between burns and the pleasant warmth that comforts the freezing one. By all similes I am striving to bring you an understanding of the subtlety of the fiery element.

**168**. Fire has as its antipodes earth and water.

Unfortunately these two elements are too tangible, and thus they avert fiery perception. That is why it is so difficult for people to comprehend that Fire does not have a constant state; it is eternally in evolution or involution, and both movements are subject to the law of progression.

**169.** Once again we are faced with a series of threatening events. Again I remind you about the Lion Heart. I am not speaking about failures, because grave events are pregnant with many consequences. Be not amazed at the tension and at special alternating waves. One must know the manifestation of derangement of rhythm. Wherever all is well let us not have to reiterate that you hold fast to Me as the only support. Execute My Decree in the most precise manner; precision is essential, for small clefts are very dangerous. One must hold out with the Lion Heart. Let us not think that the enemies are weak, for they are strong; yet I am not speaking to distress you, but only in order to affirm the Lion Heart.

**170.** Once, after a state council, a certain ruler took an earthenware vase and smashed it before the eyes of everyone. When asked the meaning of his action, he said, "I am reminding you about irreparability." Even when we break the simplest object we understand irreparability, yet how irreparable are thought-actions! We have become accustomed to surround ourselves with crude concepts, and they have thrust out all the higher concepts. If rulers would remind more often about the irreparability of mental decisions, they would forestall a great number of misfortunes. A ruler who is ignorant of the spiritual principle of self-perfectment cannot lead the multitude of consciousnesses entrusted to him. A ruler is a living example. A ruler is the one who lays out the paths through all the worlds.

He lays the foundation for prosperity, but it will not be prosperity on the material plane alone. Thus, he will be no true ruler for whom Fire exists only at the end of a match. His scope will be equal to that of his concepts.

171. The need for fiery knowledge will, like the imagination, lie in the domain of accumulated life experiences. Indeed, remembrance of the Fiery World is incomparably rarer than subtle impressions. Often people have no words to express fiery impressions. People usually do not think with their minds, but limit their thinking by the conventional words of others, thus introducing dead words into the vast domain of thought.

172. The hurricane, whirlwinds, and like destructions call to mind irreparably broken vases. Therefore one must unite one's thinking with Hierarchy. Only thus will the earth not sink under foot. I assert that an earthly foundation is gradually losing its finite meaning. People will comprehend to what an extent the conditions of the world are impelling them to the next steps!

173. The heart, the Chalice, the solar plexus, are truly cosmic barometers. It must be understood what tension there is in the world, therefore I speak about the preservation of magnanimity as the basis of good health. It must be understood how urgently the heart requires magnanimity. There are a great number of small black stars, as if they were signs of the onset of darkness.

174. That transitional state which links us with Hierarchy is called the "spark of wisdom." This is not emptiness, nor apathy, nor coercion, but a completely conscious opening of the heart.

175. What is especially important is usually entirely neglected in thinking. The most real circumstances

become elusive. People are unwilling to notice how the capacity for observing sensations beyond the physical is leaving them. Whereas, even during an ordinary cough, yawn, or sneeze, one can notice an instant of a special condition which is not a physical one. We shall not even enumerate other, more complicated tensions, but whoever has felt the above-mentioned sensation of being outside of the physical state, can already begin to gather manifestations of the other planes.

**176**. Before you is the tension of the synthetic center of the throat; one must understand how many different tensions must be united in order to strike upon the center of synthesis. One must deal very attentively with this tension, for it reflects upon the heart. During such a condition one should protect the throat ligaments, at least externally, and not strain them by talking.

**177**. Does an Arhat rest? You already know that a change of labor is rest, but the true repose of an Arhat is his thought about the Beautiful. Amidst various labors, thought about the Beautiful is the bridge and power and stream of benevolence. Let us weigh a thought of evil and a thought of good, and we shall prove to ourselves that the beautiful thought is more powerful. Let us organically analyze different thoughts, and we shall see that a beautiful thought is a treasury of health. In beautiful thinking an Arhat beholds the ladder of ascent. In this active thinking is the Arhat's repose. In what else can we find another source of benevolence? Thus can we remember when we are especially oppressed. When the shutters of selfhood are being fastened everywhere, when fires are extinguished in the darkness, is it not the time to reflect about the Beautiful? We anticipate a miracle, we strive to break the lock, but the ladder of the Arhat is only in the Beautiful. Let us not sully, let us not belittle this path! Only thereby will we attract that which seems so miraculous. And the miracle, is it not the indissoluble bond with Hierarchy? In this bond lies all of physics, and mechanics, and chemistry, and the panacea for all things. It seems possible with a little striving to move all obstacles, but the fulfillment of this condition is immeasurably difficult for people! Why have they clipped the wings of beauty?

**178**. Only through conscious striving can human evolution be advanced. When you think about particular measures for evolution, it is necessary to invoke all cooperation. A teacher says to a pupil, "You will not solve the problem as long as you have no desire to solve it." Thus, too, in life one must voluntarily wish to move with evolution. Let each one understand this in his own way, but positive action contains at least a small possibility. Mobility of thought already belongs to the fiery domain.

**179**. Dreams have been examined from many angles, yet the most significant is usually overlooked. Knocks at night, poor digestion, irritation, and a great number of superficial influences are not overlooked, but all the reflexes of the Subtle World, all the influences of thought at a distance, and, finally, all Hierarchic warnings and fiery sensations are disregarded. One must possess a highly atrophied imagination and perception to neglect these fundamentals of dreams. Not only did the materialist turn his attention merely to the superficial data of dreams, but this observer was of a limited nature. Materialism can be accepted as a striving for reality, but not for belittlement and not for limitations. Dreaming has an immense significance during earthly life. Almost half of life is passed in contact with the Subtle, and even with the Fiery World.

One must have respect for a state in which one spends time equal to that spent in wakefulness. One cannot regard overeating as the primary consideration. One must conscientiously and undisparagingly remember all four fundamentals mentioned above. Thus it will be possible to discern much that is both instructive and beautiful.

**180.** Hierarchic dreams can remind about much that has already been formed in space. Thus, when it is necessary to remind about the urgency of collecting all data, the symbol of a searching man may be seen. Let us not forget that the indication is always a very careful one in order not to violate karma.

**181.** It is often necessary to remind about events that have already been molded. This is not an encouragement but a statement of fact. People are directed far more often than they think. But still more often they do not think at all, being carried away by a stream of prejudices. Yet We can but send a vision or a dream wherever something concerns the Common Good. At present the world is especially in need of such indications, otherwise the confusion of minds may close the principal path.

**182.** Confusion of minds does not permit humanity to think about the Fiery World. Perverted materialism has actually turned thought away from matter as a source of light. The spirit has been rejected and matter forgotten—the bazaar has remained! People think that what has been said is an exaggeration, but here is a simple example—dispatch one courier with a request for good and one with a request for evil, and compare the results. Counting up the replies, you will comprehend why it is necessary to make haste.

**183.** Soulless beings are known to all. This is not a figure of speech but a chemical reality. It may be asked,

Do these people incarnate in this deplorable state? The question indicates ignorance of the fundamentals. No one can be incarnated without a store of fiery energy. Without the torch of Agni, no one enters the physical world. The squandering of Agni takes place here, amidst all the wonders of nature. To dissipate Agni it is not at all necessary to commit any violent crimes. From various Teachings we know enough about even the reformation of robbers. Ordinarily the dissipation of Agni occurs in everyday life when the spirit slumbers. The accumulation of Agni is arrested by trivial actions. It must be understood that the benefaction of Agni grows naturally, but when darkness blankets the process of perfectment, then the Fire imperceptibly—though it can be chemically proven—departs from the worthless receptacle. Beautiful is the law of eternal motion, either evolution or involution. Beautiful is the law that permits each incarnate being to have within him eternal Agni, as a Light in the darkness. Beautiful is the law that, even in spite of karma, issues Light to each wayfarer. Beautiful is the law that does not prevent the growth of the fiery garden within one, even from the age of seven. Though these first blossoms be small, though they bloom in very small thoughts, they will be a true inception of the future trend of thought. What a multitude of beautiful thoughts are born in the heart of a seven-year-old when the dim images of the Subtle World have not as yet disappeared from the brain and the heart! Dissipation may also begin then if the soil of the plant proves to be rotten. In case of such depletion it is possible to help much, or, as it was said long ago, to "lend Fire." This lending takes place also in the very smallest actions. Thus, already thrice have I reminded about crumbs. From these sparks grow huge fires.

**184**. Do not think of soulless people as monsters. In various fields they even attain mechanical preeminence, but Fire has left them, and their works have become darkened.

**185**. Of course, every one is at liberty to determine his own destiny and even his final disintegration. But soulless beings are highly infectious and harmful. Obsession occurs easily during such a depleted condition. Do not regard it as an exaggeration that almost half of the planet's population is exposed to this danger. True, it varies in degree, yet once the decomposition sets in it progresses rapidly. One can notice the same thing amidst past cultures. The fires of the spirit died out like smoky bonfires, and all smoke is poisonous unless some useful substance is added to it.

**186**. The contact with the Fiery World bestows advantages not only for future lives but also for the present. Not in vain is it said that a fiery wish will be fulfilled. Let us not regard this as a hidden, illusory conjecture, let us accept it as a reality. Fiery thinking so crystallizes corresponding spheres that thought in itself will already be affirmation. Indeed, let us not calculate according to earthly dates, for the spatial fires are timeless. Let us not divide life, for life is eternal. But the fiery wish will be fulfilled. Thus, many images indicated in advance had already been formed in unalterable storehouses. Let us look upon these fiery desires in full consciousness, and let us not be superficial when we are concerned with the essence of Existence.

**187**. Many times have I spoken of the harm of divisions. If life is eternal, if we understand one another not by conventional sounds but by something beyond language, then we are obligated to utilize this force toward unity. He who divides is wrong. He who permits separation is wrong. It is correct that the best ones are the containing ones. This is no time, after the fashion of cave dwellers, to flaunt ourselves as chosen workers. All are workers, along the entire line of Hierarchy, but let none obstruct the fulfillment of the fiery wishes.

**188.** Even for a simple examination by means of rays, the physician prescribes a special diet. Yet how much more subtle is contact with the Fiery Domain. One must prepare oneself not only through diet, but also by other external and internal means. Food requirements are not complicated. The chief thing is to avoid blood, since it is an element which introduces emanations unfit for the refined organism. But even in case of extreme necessity, one can avoid blood by using either dried or smoked meat. Similarly, in planning cereal or vegetable diets, one should be guided by the condition of one's organism. Yet even without Yoga anyone can understand that any excess is harmful. And everyone knows about the vitamins in raw products. But all these conditions, like excessive pranayama, are nothing compared with the heart's comprehension. You yourselves know how the fires flash up and how the most beautiful thoughts guide one. You may have heard more than once about robber sadhus, and they are probably quite zealous about counting their pranayama. You have heard also of certain Rishis who, even under the most intolerable conditions, did not shrink from helping people. It is especially good on each memorial day to recall the heart's acquisition of Fire. All other conditions are applied in accordance with the intrinsic worth of the heart. The heart will not fill itself with alien or animal blood, for the quality of the heart will not accept it. The fiery heart will not choke with evil speech, for this is contrary to its nature. Thus, let us welcome and always assist the natural kindling of the fires.

**189.** Measure is cognized by the heart. Words are unfit for the expression of measure. Nevertheless, every developed heart knows the measure of each application.

**190.** The New Era can be built only by means of culture. Therefore, culture will be proclaimed as the one defense against disintegration. Nowadays one should strive only in this direction. Our Command is to miss no opportunity of reminding people about culture. Though We be regarded as fanatics on the subject, people will nevertheless harken and become accustomed to it. Thus We introduce brain patterns.

**191.** We have spoken about solemnity, friendliness, magnanimity—let us complete the square with gratitude. From the most minute through the entire line of Hierarchy, shine the sparks of gratitude. Precious are these fires!

**192.** Even if someone does good by accident, praise him. Commend each crumb of good. To him who cries out in the darkness it matters not who brings the Light. Widening the field of vision means the bringing of Light. This action is beneficial, both for the giving one and for him who receives the Light. Transmission of Light connotes the transmitter's expansion. There was one flame, now it has become two. It means good has been accomplished.

**193.** In human hands benevolence is like the evening lamp. Darkness falls, but the lamp is ready and an experienced hand is there to light it. But again I say—praise each good deed, it is a manifestation of generosity. Let each spark of good be blown into a flame. Though good be accidental to a great extent, it still is good. It would be too much to demand always a conscious good action; let the darkness be dispersed, even by dim lights. Even with one spark of light, absolute darkness will no longer be such. Behind the thought, word, or deed, Light is already standing. Thus, he who knows how to find a spark of Light is already an illumined co-worker.

**194**. Upon cognizing the Fiery World, one must forever forget the small, since it does not exist. As a physician does not regard anything as insignificant while mixing a curative compound, so, too, a grain of gun-powder in a powder magazine is not small in effect. We sensitize ourselves by examples of that which exists. What good is education if the brain remains crafty and the tongue false? People can be divided according to refinement of heart, but not according to falseness of consciousness. Do not think that falseness of consciousness has no significance for the Fiery World. Thus again from morals we come to chemistry.

**195**. Every physician will tell you that a mixture of the most useful ingredients often produces an even destructive compound. In all fields, a mixture is very dangerous. Ugly complications sometimes arise from mixture. How cautiously must one follow the path of consciousness, lest one find one's feet on different paths! The goal of life is to find oneself in the Fiery World with all the acquisitions of consciousness.

**196**. It should not be thought that, in his consciousness, an Arhat could lose sight of the Guiding Will even for an instant. He proves to be a simple mortal, if he does not always solemnly bear the chalice of achievement. The power of His heart becomes dormant as soon as He ceases to feel the Hierarchic thread in His hand. In this realization of constant vigilance lies the uniqueness of an Arhat. When I speak of vigilance, I am teaching you the fundamentals of cognition. But this solemnity is not easy in the confusion of the atmosphere. To be strivingly vigilant is not easy when the dust of decay is whirling about. One cannot exact the same demands when the earth is convulsed. Indeed, only an Arhat can save humanity in the confusion.

197. The new race may be born in different parts of Earth. Do not be amazed if separate manifestations appear in the most unexpected places; for magnets are also placed in ways most unsuspected by humanity. Yet in placing magnets numerous circumstances are taken into account. Thus, the network of the race that is being generated is spread to distant frontiers. But one part of the world determines the destiny of the century; I shall not name that part of the world, but the history of all movements has marked it sufficiently.

198. People frequently distinguish fragments of the music of the spheres, just as they do the vibratory differentiations of light, and only a false attitude toward everything prevents them from concentrating on this. Thus begins the charmed circle of insincerity. The manifestation of reality falls into the category of the inadmissible. It is sad to see how people are ashamed of their best manifestations. Thus they not only violate their own significance but also become creators of ugliness in the Subtle World. Those people who have rejected reality bear the lasting stigma of a lie.

199. One must bury one's head in illusionary conventionality in order to fear confessing even to oneself what one sees and hears. No sophistry is required to estimate with honesty and without egoism that which occurs.

200. One should not forget how many stones are cast upon the path of ascent. Only an experienced consciousness will not lose sight of the existence of

a by-path. Irrepressible striving must also embrace complete resourcefulness. Sometimes madmen set an example of resourcefulness in their striving. It would seem that the intellect ought not to delay a traveler!

**201**. Not only by song and the rhythm of music but by every machine a vibration is created which contacts fiery energies. So, also, each tension, or rather, shock, is a conductor of the very same manifestations of Agni. Hence, one must become accustomed to distinguish and recognize the spark in each tension. One need not emulate the morbid people who avoid tension. One should welcome each fiery vibration as a purifying principle. What ordinary people regard as a calm life is nothing but extinction of fire. They have even invented entire systems of extinguishing fire from early childhood.

**202**. Striving toward the rocky path is not acquired externally, it grows from within, solely through cumulative experience. One must know the complete immutability and eternity of life in order to proceed without fear. One must understand the indestructibility of our essential nature in order to place this value upon the scales. One can accept only an unchanging value; thus we shall learn to safeguard this value and affirm it. It need not be thought that many can corrupt the value of spirit—so be it. For we carry the ark of the monad, knowing that by uplifting it the world will be benefited.

**203**. The new cannot be new for the Arhat. So much has been impressed upon His eyes. It is instructive to observe how in various epochs the same knowledge and discoveries were not only termed differently but were brought into life in diametrically opposite ways. Thus, many verbal contradictions can be explained.

**204**. Deepened breathing is a sign of special tension. Therefore one must not regard a shock only as the result of misfortune and suffering. More than once you have heard about moments of ecstasy before an attack of epilepsy or certain other ailments. But this is only the transference of consciousness into a fiery manifestation. Hence, some monks and sadhus at times would not exchange this fiery feeling for any treasure.

**205.** The knowledge of vitamins is a sign of the coming age. But to the physical substance of vitamins one should add conscious psychic energy, and then numerous questions of physical and spiritual healing will be solved. Thus, one can begin to accompany the taking of vitamins with a corresponding thought. Even upon the simplest physical actions one can notice the influence of thought. For instance, one may throw a ball with an unvarying physical effort, but by accompanying it with different thoughts, the force imparted to the ball will of course vary. Thus one can observe how greatly we either hinder or augment even our ordinary actions. One must introduce similar experiments in schools in order to demonstrate the power of thought upon simple physical apparatus. Vitamins themselves pertain to the domain of psychic energy. In other words, they belong to the fiery sphere, meaning that their fusion with fiery thought produces a most powerful combination.

**206.** Among the useful discoveries one must distinguish those which pertain to the fiery domain. Their correlation can lead to most useful results. They will guide one toward new refinements, and will indicate how many useful substances are driven out of use because of ignorance.

**207.** The root of feeling is its boundlessness. Thus, one can understand why I speak about the approach and constant deepening of feeling. Consider that the fiery approach knows no boundaries—it is beyond our dimensions! Such a condition must be taken completely scientifically. Only recently it was asserted that the atom was indivisible, but, as was proved, this limitation is only relative. Thus, one can conjoin oneself with thought about Infinity. But, as we agreed, substance is feeling and vice versa. Thus, let us begin to comprehend feeling as Infinity. In other words, feeling will bring us to the Fiery Gates.

**208.** You are amazed that before the earthquake measures were taken for the elimination of the heart spasms. Does not feeling primarily guide such telegraphy? Precisely the vital substance of straight-knowledge does not require any conventional apparatus. But of course it is necessary to reciprocally nourish this substance. Urusvati's thoughts were actually the best nurture for this current.

**209.** Lacking straight-knowledge, who can imagine the reality of the Fiery World? But this quality must be cultivated with all devotion; and this devotion must be precisely in the heart, not on paper. Also, acceptance of the Fiery World proves courage, for any ignorant thought primarily rebels against the fires of the heart.

**210.** We are consoled by the fact that even a few understand the purpose of life and acknowledge the fiery worlds. Do not count upon multitudes anywhere, but at the same time have entire nations in mind. The manifestation of the nodes of Existence occurs in unusual ways.

**211.** I approve of your gathering the evidences of psychic energy and of the corresponding glands. For this it is necessary to observe the time sequence of the communications. In this sequence a deliberate rhythm can be perceived. It is not by accident that hints are given to various people in different countries. The alternation of the waves of East and West is also not accidental. The forgotten domain is gradually being conquered anew. Once again we approach the fundamentals of Existence. Precisely in this way shall we again understand life as a process of self-perfectment, and thus solve the ethical as well as the economic postulates. Hence it is so important to gather with great care all data about psychic energy, from various sources, not being constrained by their seeming contradictions. Nothing else has stirred up as much controversy as psychic energy. These flowers of Existence can be gathered only by a trained hand, otherwise the hand may be unsteady in the midst of the signs of all ages and peoples. There has never been a nation which did not dream about Agni, gathering for it the best consonances. A one-sided consciousness inevitably stumbles over dogmas and is frightened by sophistry. Yet Sophia is not sophistry, and experimentation is not prejudice—thus one may gather a useful collection.

**212.** I approve of the Kalachakra, now being compiled. This fiery Teaching is covered with dust, but it should be proclaimed. Not reason but wisdom gave this Teaching. It should not be left in the hands of ignorant exponents. Many domains of knowledge are united in the Kalachakra; only the unprejudiced mind can find its way among these stratifications of all worlds.

**213.** Swelling and sensitiveness of the glands is especially evident during school years. Physicians endeavor in every way to drive this manifestation inward, or they remove the glands. But hardly anyone has thought of the fact that the special sensitiveness of the glands is due to fiery manifestations awakened by new tension of the brain and heart. It is neither a cold, nor the stuffy atmosphere of quarters, but the new activity of the fiery centers which causes the tension of the glands. Also, a similar tension reacts upon the surface of the skin. Of course, treatment by means of pure air reduces the tension, for the fieriness of prana corrects the unbalanced condition of the glands, establishing a fiery harmony. But each removal by force of a fiery apparatus undoubtedly has a powerful effect in the future, lowering the sensitiveness of receptivity.

**214**. In antiquity it was considered useful to place on the glands the roots of *igniridaceae*, but this is a very primitive way of healing, because the fiery property of these plants can be utilized far more advantageously. They can yield an extract useful for increasing the fiery activity. Apparently the ancients intended to apply the cure of like by like. Wormwood is good, and so is rose oil, which acts as a sedative, although not so quickly. Indeed, the fiery property of plants has many uses, and can enter into the composition of tonic remedies.

**215**. The misfortune of people lies precisely in that they like to grasp at the second thing, neglecting the first. But the approach to the higher energies obliges them to understand that which is fundamental.

**216**. It is essential to remind about the action of the mind which desires to catch the distant, overlooking the close. During the confusion of minds this inexcusable neglect of that which is nearby is especially apparent.

**217**. During the fiery tension it is especially useful to gather together and to give the fire a new direction. But people may gather only if there is no irritation. So, too, the moments of silence are like a balsam of tranquility by which a near one's heart can be sustained.

**218**. Actually, the red light does not betoken calm. One must perceive how tense is space. If only the heads of governments would understand that cosmic conditions have a certain significance! But, unfortunately, even the few astrological efforts are surrounded by absurd explanations. One should, as in everything, return to the simplest and most precise. All Teachings are infiltrated with arbitrary commentaries. The past must be understood as interpreted by an honest historian.

**219**. Which of the conventional types of humanity expresses the fiery heart? The customary trend of thought may surmise the type to be of sanguinary nature, or, at least choleric, but this conclusion is an ignorant one. The fiery heart is a synthesized essence and cannot be fitted into purely conventional categories. It can only be asserted that the hypochondriac does not reflect the fiery essence. Thus, one must imagine the fiery heart as an all-containing receptacle. The fires of such a heart will also not be uniform. Who can limit Buddhi by blue color? It may be asked of which shade is this vibrating blue color? In any scale there will be a blue tone, depending on the outer and inner chemism. Also, let us not forget daltonism, which is widely developed. Thus, within a single law the fiery heart will find all the riches that befit the splendor of the Cosmos.

**220**. Let us learn to discriminate—thus we will become generous. No limited person can become spiritually rich, but one should have compassion for a neighbor's color blindness. For, up to the highest steps, each one is subject to such diversities. Let us not demand that all people think alike. It is good if they can discriminate between Light and darkness. But subtle vibrations are not easily perceived.

**221**. Especially during eating, the inner fire should not be tensed. It is not without reason that some people prefer to eat in silence. Indeed, through all daily life necessary information is scattered. Men rarely utilize wholesome truths. Thus, for example, people like not only to buy quantities of things but also to use them immediately, forgetting that each object carries many complex stratifications. The ancient custom of fumigating each new object had an obvious reason. However, this custom was a precaution not so much against physical stratification as against the subtle, with all its psychic effects.

**222**. So long as humanity continues to dwell in a corporeal consciousness, the methods of conventional experimental medicine can hardly be altered. Only by directing the consciousness toward psychic energy can the senselessness of vivisection be stopped. Working with living plants, on one hand, and applying psychic energy, on the other, will lead the trend of thought into a new channel; but, in any case, each protest against vivisection already has Our approval. Such protests indicate a knowledge of the manifestations of the Subtle World and an understanding that vivisections can become new sources of contamination. In the future, an adequate prophylaxis, together with application of psychic energy, will make diseases entirely non-existent. But meanwhile, it is necessary as far as possible to stop the cruelties of vivisection and to reiterate about psychic energy. Through such a constant reminder, the energy itself will become more manifest. For fiery thinking is also a kindling of the torches.

**223**. New thinking does not mean the overthrow of all that is old. Indeed, it will be the best friend of all that already has been discovered. Such thinking does not reject a formula that is not understood merely because it is not clear at the moment. Our friend will carefully lay aside an obscure formula. Often something obscure is not a concealed attainment, it is dependent upon a great number of transitory idioms. Every language is not preserved; even in the course of one century the meaning of expressions is changed, which leads to a growing complexity of ways of thinking. Let us not regret running waters, but let us not forget that we are looking upon old achievements with new eyes. Even a great number of isolated ancient terms may appear strange, because they have been inserted into alien dialects and often are distorted in pronunciation. In antiquity people sang these significant words to memorize them, but the rhythms have been abandoned as something unnecessary. Yet by losing rhythm people have forgotten the significance of vibrations. New thinking does not forget about the basic laws.

**224.** Benignity is one of the fiery qualities. But what have people made of this quality? Not flabbiness but full justice is included in benignity. The fiery heart distinctly understands the inadmissibility of malice. It knows about the creativeness which excludes malice as a worthless expedient. Benignity also senses goal-fitness, that is to say, the higher measure of justice. About the sense of justice We have spoken much, but it is so fundamental that one should affirm it in each statement. Otherwise what will balance personal feeling when one has to gaze at the Light from behind a screen of blood? Not without cause do people say of an unfair judge that he has blood in his eye. Thus, amidst discourses about fiery reactions we must continually regulate the fiery currents of our nerve centers. Each mention of Fire already evokes a certain tension of it. Therefore, whoever wishes to think fierily must also know about fiery responsibility. Such responsibility is most weighty, for it includes the most contrasting inceptions. Yet between the subterranean fires and the higher Light there is a broad domain!

**225.** Amidst the battle it is possible to have a moment of respite and reciprocity. You have sensed something like prickly currents. The currents themselves are not prickly, but seem so because of the resistance with which the earthly strata are filled. These arrows of the demons hide the sun. We must intensify all energies, and hence reciprocity is especially needed.

**226**. During the transmission of thoughts, the difficulty arises not so much from the sender, but in the reception. The sending takes place through tension of the heart and will, hence it depends entirely upon the sender himself. But the recipient is usually in other conditions. Not only may he be mentally overburdened but his thought and consciousness may be absent. Moreover, the most unexpected currents can intersect space and thus distort some portion of the sendings. In order to even partially avoid this impediment, We teach alertness and vigilance. When the consciousness becomes used to these conditions, the receiver remains tensed and open. This method of continuous vigil is not Ours alone, it was already employed in remote antiquity. Each initiation into the Mysteries contained the question, "Is thy ear open?" Such opening signified primarily the ability to maintain keen vigilance. The condition of intersecting currents was avoided by striving toward the Hierarch, with whom a contact was established. True, harmful attempts can be made with intent to break off or to fasten upon the currents. Besides the already indicated aerial conduits, it is possible to avoid eavesdropping by means of mutual striving—this is like galvanizing the conduit. Thus, it is possible by degrees to achieve many useful things. Moreover, let us not forget that these achievements are ineradicable.

**227**. People must not keep anything rotten in their houses. The presence of fermentation or of stagnant water attracts undesirable entities. When the photographing of entities of the Subtle World becomes more advanced, it will be possible to record on film the difference between the surroundings of a bit of cheese or meat and that of a fresh rose. Obviating logical arguments, one can actually see that the forms attracted by meat are repellent. These lovers of decomposition even accompany to the mouth itself the dish fancied by them. Also, before photographing auras one can gain experience by taking pictures of objects with their surroundings. As always, the experiment requires patience and perseverance. It should begin with indicative objects. Of the pure aromas, one must prefer the rose; it contains a very lasting oil. But it should not be forgotten that flowers should be gathered before decomposition has set in. I point out roses because they contain the greatest quantity of fiery energy. Thus, lovers of roses are near to fiery energy. The entities that feed on decomposition avoid the aromas of fiery energy. One must accept this indication in all simplicity, and just as information from a pharmacy.

**228**. During the investigation of loss of weight, the laying on of hands is used, just as during increase of weight; this means that the hands transmit certain fiery energy. But this will be only a certain fiery step, the next one will be transmission of the same energy by means of the glance, in which the question of distance will be secondary. Thus it is possible to increase or diminish the weight of an object at a distance. In truth, would it not be a pleasing occupation for a merchant! Therefore it is well that the manifestation of such energies is not common in the present state of humanity. It is possible to point out many experiments that can alleviate everyday earthly life; but, actually, people would make use of them for increasing the number of killings. Meanwhile the fiery energies are knocking at their prison doors.

The date is coming when they will either be applied intelligently or they will pour forth as fiery sicknesses or cosmic cataclysms. Three alternatives lie before humanity. It remains for it to choose one according to the state of its consciousness. Freedom of choice is always given. No one can deny that before the disaster of a world war a great number of warnings were given. Even not very far-sighted people observed them, but madness blinded the majority. This manifestation was before the eyes of the living generations, yet their circumspection was not increased. Ten million victims crowded the strata of the Subtle World. People prayed for killing but did not think about atonement for the violation of the law of Existence! Instead of intelligent understanding, people are ready for new killings; they do not reflect that fiery energies will flood the planet as a natural effect of the law of nature. Thus, in the "Fiery Book" it is necessary to write for those few who are willing to think about the future.

**229**. When it is asked, Are the worlds habitable? reply affirmatively. True, from the earthly point of view, there is not residence everywhere, but in the sense of existence the worlds are habitable. Actually, all these different evolutions are not always accessible to each other. Yet it will not be a great mistake to say that all manifested space is habitable. The microscope indicates life throughout the entire planet; the same law applies also to space. Let us turn again to the harm of killing. Each explosion violates the equilibrium of many beings invisible to us. Not millions but incalculable billions are injured by war. One must not forget all the atmospheric turbulence from gases and explosions. This is not occultism, but scientifically sound common sense. Thus, let humanity not forget about the counterblow.

**230**. Thought about the counterblow, or karma, should not weaken one; on the contrary, it should prompt one to beautiful actions.

**231**. Actually, Fire is a unifier. When the fire departs, decomposition immediately sets in. True, in fermentation decomposition accumulates new fire, but this is already a particular conjunction of particles. One should think similarly about each action. It will not be incorrect to say that the expulsion of Fire from thought generates decomposition. When I speak about unifying, I am also presupposing fiery welding. As the caster knows the proper quantity of metal for a group of figures, so does Fire act on the unifying of peoples. This unification can be represented as the creation of one gigantic figure, with all the power of a giant. And we must strive for the formation of these collectives of the spirit. Let us not regard them as artificial Golems. The monster, Golem, remained without the fire of the spirit and therefore destroyed itself. The spirit is a fire-bearing magnet, and it is possible to join to it a portion of the higher energies.

**232**. They will come—the extinguishers; they will come—the corrupters; they will come—the slanderers; they will come—the forces of darkness. It is impossible to avoid decomposition once begun. But he who is wise does not look back, for he knows that Fire is inexhaustible when invoked. Not without reason do I charge you to reiterate about the Decrees. Repetition even in itself already strengthens the foundation.

**233**. It is not fitting to dawdle when the clouds are gathering. I remind you that the chief basis is the one anchor. It is not fitting to look back when the way lies over an abyss. One must simply unite for the sake of salvation.

**234**. If we enumerate all the heavenly luminaries, if

we measure the whole unrevealed Depth, we will not thereby ameliorate the present hour. With courageous heart one must cognize the painful darkness that draws near when the fires are extinguished. In the opinion of many, unity is an unnecessary anachronism. They presume that individuality is safeguarded by disunity; such is the logic of darkness. Yet sometimes amidst dangerous epidemics, by remembering simple expedients, people find salvation. Thus simple are the means of unification. They unequivocally smite the darkness. Thus, let the spear not slumber over the dragon.

**235**. Fiery affirmation takes place not in pleasant drowsiness but in storm and lightning. He who accustoms himself to feel tranquility amidst lightnings easily meditates about the Fiery World. It is necessary to think about the World of Light. Thoughts should be sent into its heights. Thus is it possible to participate mentally not only in the earthly battle but also in the battle of the Subtle World. Indeed, earthly destructions are as nothing, compared to the destruction of the Subtle World. A great number of the best intentions are dissipated together with hideous accumulations. At the same time the inhabitants become involved, particularly those who display activity. There are many of these, both in the lower strata and in the higher. The fire breaking through is sensed by all who have not accustomed themselves to the fiery state. Therefore, when I speak about thinking of the Subtle World, I am advising something very useful, and when I speak about thinking of the fiery worlds, I am advising something indispensable. The affirmation of fiery thought is already an acquisition of invincibility. As the links of a coat of mail are gradually strung together, so, too, the fiery plumage grows invisibly.

**236**. One can imagine an instant without the

elements of earth or water or even of air, but it is impossible even to conceive of an instant without fire. Extraordinary is the structure when that which is most fundamental remains invisible but ready to be manifested everywhere in the simplest way. Scholars do not wish to accept the element of fire in full, yet each division of it merely burdens the future.

**237.** Do you not think, when words elude you, as it were, that a considerable portion of your fiery energy has been directed elsewhere? One should not be astonished that fiery energy must be considerably expended when people are in widely separated countries. The fiery substance of musk can with difficulty make up for this expenditure. Thought about distant actions augments the sending of energy. One can think confusedly, as if in a drowsy state, and energy is hardly generated by this weak pressure; but the power of thought is like the lever of a pump, and the action of the pump's piston will produce a distant attainment.

**238.** One must understand how great is the achievement of preserving equilibrium in the midst of an attack; I commend this.

**239.** By means of his fiery nature man can discover subterranean ores and waters. This occult attribute has already become an accepted factor. Since such an application of fiery energy is possible, it means that there can also be many other manifestations of Agni. Combinations of fiery energy with sound, color, or with other fiery branches of the one great Fohat vouch for the regeneration of the entire world outlook. Let people simply draw near to the streams of fiery Uruvela. Everyone possesses the fiery energy to some degree. The applications of Fohat are numerous; not only people of the fiery element but even those belonging to the other elements can draw from the chalice of Fohat.

If the experiments of thought upon plants have shown remarkable results, then there can also be observations upon the effects of thought on a flame. Under a current of fiery thought, a flame can begin to approach or recede. The Egyptian Mysteries pointed out the special power of thought that has been sent through flame. In this advice was contained the recognition of the fieriness of thought. Thus one can turn the attention of people to the Fohatic spheres.

**240**. One receives communion from a Fiery Chalice; another swallows a goblet of inflaming wine. The first is enraptured in spirit, the second shudders in the flame and is destroyed. The first can receive communion endlessly; the second quickly reaches the limit of poisoning. Is not the solution in the spirit? Quality of thought employs the fire for Good. Drunkenness is deplorable, as a perversion of the sacred Fire. Least of all can Fire be coupled with egoism.

**241**. Is it possible for one incarnated on Earth to create mentally in the Subtle World? It is possible, especially if Agni is acting. It is possible to cultivate and improve plants. It is possible to create constructive forms; one can participate in a great number of improvements, provided they are not ugly. Urusvati has seen a tree planted by her. Thus it is possible to create from weak fragile forms something strong and lasting. So we prepare during earthly existence the future beautiful gardens. Thought in all its constructiveness also creates our own future happiness. Thus we proceed by means of thought beyond the limits of Earth.

**242**. Light out of darkness—this truth continues to appear to many as a paradox. These multitudes have not seen Light, and do not understand that Higher Light is inaccessible to the eyesight, either earthly or subtle; even its sparks tire the eyes. H. was enwrapped by waves of these sparks, and the eyes of Urusvati were especially fatigued. This enwrapment was necessary for Him, it was an example of mental sending to a great distance. Thus We send indications, but due to various tensions much is distorted. It can be affirmed that irritation requires tenfold energy, and such shafts of sparks can sever one's head. Therefore when I advise you to refrain from irritation, it means We are seeking the best results. Fiery energy surpasses all belief. People oppose this power and thus give rise to many calamities. The manifestation of enwrapment with fiery sparks depends upon many different causes. Fiery armor protects one from hostile arrows.

**243.** One must not approach Fire with covetous aims. A simple prayer about perfectment opens the best Gates. Likewise, a simple truthful attitude assists in cognizing the actual rhythms of the Cosmos. It is easy to substitute greed for cosmic rhythm, but the bond with Hierarchy leads to realization of Truth. Experience in the beautiful keeps one within the bounds of authenticity. When the earthly world is so rich, when the Subtle World is still richer, when the Fiery World is so majestic, then experience in the beautiful is needed. Only acuteness of observation helps to affirm beauty. It is a mistake to think that transitory methods of art can create a single basis for judgment. Actually, only the power of observation, which nourishes the third eye, provides a firm foundation for creativeness that is suitable also in the Subtle World.

**244.** Creativeness in the Subtle World differs considerably from earthly conditions. One is obliged to become accustomed to so-called mental creativeness. True, thought in its convolutions can produce very dim, flickering outlines. Stable forms depend not only upon the force of the will but also upon former observations. As minerals through a fiery process produce well-formed crystals, so, too, fieriness is needed for creativeness. Like everything else, it is accumulated gradually and it belongs to ineradicable accumulations, therefore it is never tardy in coming.

**245**. You value sagacity in co-workers, it is exactly so throughout the Chain of Hierarchy. Knowledge alone will not give the fiery alertness of mind accumulated by many experiences. What is possible and what is impossible in all situations of life cannot be written down. Knowledge alone is a deadly peril, but its application is a fiery art. That is why We so esteem ready sagacity, that straight-knowledge which whispers when one should not turn the key in the lock. He who has accumulated such straight-knowledge will not be a traitor, either consciously or indirectly. To give away the key not according to the level of consciousness means to act as a traitor. Not to notice wiliness or falsification means not to be discriminating. Discrimination only on the morrow is not worth much. Such perception will not prevent one from falling over the precipice—but how sensitive must be the accumulation of sagacity! In each school the development of fast thinking must be taught; without it how can one pass through the flame?

**246**. You have read about the fact that for seventeen years daily earthquakes have been taking place; this scientific information is not entirely accurate. For eighteen years Earth has been continuously a tremor. One must affirm all the details of the dates of the approaching fiery denouement. Indeed, in view of the growth of the waves of Earth's tremors, one should be alert and think whether all is in order. But the condition of the world is not helped by the seismograph needle. Even if at some time all the seismograph needles were to break, this would be of no help, and besides, what newspaper would publish anything about this breakage! In a word, events created by people have a greater significance than they think. Thus, count back the eighteen years and you will see a significant and highly abhorrent event.

**247**. The tremors of Earth become stronger; ask those who have a double pulse how much it is increased. Undoubtedly, all that is related to fiery energy has been augmented and intensified. People strengthen these regions by the order of their living and thinking. Nothing so irritates the fiery element as disorderly thinking. Formerly people were, at least sometimes, taught to think. Not infrequently scanning and memorizing the laws of life awakened the current of thought. But the awakening of cravings and of egoism can lead to disorderly thinking. Amidst these mere fragments chaotic fury is engendered. Why invoke destruction?

**248**. During the experiments with thought-transmission, it is possible to observe to what an extent thought coming from outside glides over the brain. One of the qualities of fiery energy is ardor in conformity with the nature of Fire. For this reason it is difficult to retain in the memory a communication from outside. One should not blame oneself for this fiery habit, but should observe the properties of Fire. Indeed, alertness of thought is of assistance, yet one cannot retain the fiery contacts under earthly conditions. It is not only difficult to remember thoughts from outside, but it is also difficult to separate several simultaneous sendings. And in such a case the thread of the Hierarchy is also of assistance, for a single strong striving attunes, as it were, the entire chord.

**249**. About one of the Rishis it was said that even

at the mention of evil he felt pain. One should not consider such a Rishi an idler, but rather be amazed at his dissociation from evil. Indeed, each one who realizes Fire feels evil with especial keenness as the direct antipode of his being. One must, I say, one must develop in oneself this counteraction to evil, the opponent of progress. One must, I say, one must recognize this boundary which impedes advance for the good of evolution. One may hear about the complexity of such boundaries, but the manifestation of Fire will reveal where is evolution, and where the decrepitude of decomposition. The Fiery World is a true symbol of uninterrupted evolution.

**250.** If for a moment we imagine space as consisting of layers of paper, and we subject it to the action of radio or television, then on each layer we shall find a perforated outline; entire portraits will be impressed on the spatial layers. Impressions remain on the strata of Akasha in exactly this manner. Sometimes we are ready to complain that for a long time we do not see what we would wish, but we do not consider that for various reasons an image need not be impressed in space. Images not made by human hand are carried like sheets of paper in a whirlwind; that is why one must become accustomed to the thought that everything is ineradicable. Only thus is it possible to become truly cautious and solicitous about one's surroundings. One must not think that it is possible to escape the law, which is expressed even in simple physical devices. It can easily be imagined how a portrait, spatially transmitted, may be intercepted at any point of its transmission. You know enough about physical teraphim; this means, then, that there can also be subtle teraphim. Therefore one must guard everything valuable, not only in the home but also in space. Protective aerial conduits can be created, but they swallow up a mass of energy. Thus, let us learn to really guard the precious concept.

**251**. Each physical apparatus has a perfect analogy in the Subtle World. Moreover, it can easily be perceived how simple it is to augment the power of an apparatus by invoking Agni. Thus it is possible to reperform a great number of experiments that turned out unsuccessfully. The experiments of Keely and even the apparatus of Edison remained imperfect for the Subtle World, because the energy of Agni was not applied; in one case because of a surrounding suspiciousness, in the other because of personal unbelief. It has been said that even a candle is not lit without faith.

**252**. It is difficult for people to realize that from each flight one may not return—so poorly do they picture reality to themselves. It is necessary to study the past in the records of alchemy and in chronicles. When an understanding of Agni was attained, this was reflected in science and also in problems of state. It must not be thought that Agni is only a factory inspector, it is the motive force of all the thoughts of humanity. It not only must be guarded but actually cherished.

**253**. It should not be thought that the calamitous situation of humanity can be improved if people do not keep in mind the threatening volcano and do not resort to psychic energy. The shifting of the Gulf Stream is only one of the many menacing signs, many others can be found nearer at hand.

**254**. To speak according to the level of consciousness of your listener means to be already on a lofty step. Various dogmas are especially harmful in that they propound a rigid formula regardless of the level of consciousness. How many negations, how much anger and confusion arise merely from disparity in the degree of consciousness! And not only the degree but the mood of consciousness is so often the deciding factor. Enough has been said about the harm of irritation, which beclouds the consciousness; but in addition to this principal enemy one must remember about all small distractions of thought. One must become accustomed to carry the fundamental thought of existence unobscured. Thus, when schoolteachers learn how to deal with pupils according to their consciousness, true evolution will begin. It is impossible to divide humanity merely according to age or class. We continually see how certain children are in need of adult speech, and elderly people, sometimes in government positions, can understand only childish expressions. Not for the latter children is the Kingdom of Heaven! The new consciousness does not come from mechanical formulas. Thus, one must learn to speak according to the consciousness of the listener. This is not easy, but it constitutes an excellent exercise in sagacity. Furthermore, this also applies to fiery occupations.

**255.** The fiery tension of space inevitably causes a particular fatigue of the eyes. It is necessary to interrupt the work of the eyes, closing them for a brief time. One can also make use of warm compresses, but closing the eyes for short periods is very helpful. A great number of new conditions arise during the Epoch of Fire. One must take these new factors into consideration in all conditions of life. The principal error is to take the external conditions of nature as something immovable. True, the moon may have appeared to remain static for a great number of generations, but nevertheless it was possible at one time to observe a substantial change in it. A lamp on a table falls over but once, yet the possibility of this always exists. Thus, one must not forget useful prophylaxis in connection with the tension of the fiery element.

**256**. People are always careful not to overturn a lamp. In this care there is a certain respect for fire. Fear of a fire is only a crude affirmation of respect. It cannot be doubted that people are not devoid of a special feeling of respect for the element of fire. The manifestation of this miraculous element has always caused a particular uplifting feeling.

**257**. Suspicion is in itself a provocation. A provocation may be a conscious one, but in the case of suspicion the provocations are especially disorderly. Apart from all the vital complications, suspiciousness leads to susceptibility to infection. How many epidemics are multiplied merely by suspiciousness! Karmic embryos of disease are provoked by suspiciousness. The border line between fear and suspicion is almost indistinguishable. A guard must be alert but not suspicious. Equilibrium is not created by suspiciousness. Courage seeks the cause but does not suspect. Therefore suspicion is primarily ignorance.

**258**. Much attention is now being paid to astrology. Even science at last perceives the cosmic laws. But it may be noticed that even with precise calculations inaccuracies often occur. One should know whence come these fluctuations. We must not forget that just now the planet is enveloped by heavy strata; chemical rays can be refracted by such a saturated atmosphere. The relativity of deductions results from this unprecedented situation. The same may be noticed in other domains. The claim of the fallacy of ancient calculations is due to unwillingness to pay attention to reality. People want everything to conform to their own understanding. You once saw how a crowd forced its way into a theater while the stage was already in flames. Thus it is in everything. It is true that the severed head of a dog may bark, but the human spirit becomes dumb. Such is irrationality and lack of balance! The time is dangerous; it is permissible to feel anguish.

**259**. Verily the *rapprochement* of the worlds is necessary. It is necessary, even in a small measure, to prepare the consciousness for this necessity. People must be prepared to encounter densified bodies in life without coercive magic; but for this it is necessary that the fiery heart cease to be an abstraction.

**260**. I have just watched a pupil of Bekhtereff experimenting with the transmission of thought to a distance, but he could not master even the simplest condition. He could not dissociate tension from the irritation that clogged his apparatus. While he thought that he was exerting himself, in reality he was only irritated, presupposing that nothing would result. While his thinking was theoretically correct, he could not separate his emotions. Moreover, pseudomaterialism, which assumes that everything is for everybody under any circumstances, interferes. Certainly, this may be possible after the evolution of two more races, but now it may be likened to an elephant's load on the back of a cockroach. The understanding of psychic energy is confused. Even though it be called a material hammer, let it at least be realized. The name does not matter. One can cite a mass of names, but crudity will not diminish because of them. The increasing coarsening of psychic energy is the most terrible epidemic.

**261**. In antiquity human hatred cast a small viper, but not a python. Do not measure evil by its length. Actually, a small viper corresponds more closely to evil, since proportionately greater destruction issues from it. Let us not rely upon external measurements;

evil seeks to undermine through minute entities. Likewise, disintegration begins with the smallest. One can observe how the essential nature of an entire nation is changed within one generation. Whole ages are not needed where the viper of treason has built its nest. It is astonishing how, beneath our very eyes, the dignity of a nation crumbles; but human minds usually do not grasp such a striking occurrence. A single rejected word may have lain at the basis, nevertheless, it resulted in treason. If we recall the events of the end of the eighteenth and in the middle of the nineteenth centuries, we are struck by the similarity to a recent event. Thus the character of entire countries is changed.

**262**. Recently one may have noted that people often catch radio waves without a receiver. Though this may be useful for scientific observations, on the other hand We are displeased with this mixture of currents. Let humanity become accustomed to transmitting and receiving thoughts. But it is not useful when the fiery substance is mixed with intruding coarser currents. True, such a manifestation indicates to what an extent the fiery element is already intensified in humanity, but it will not be of benefit if, unrecognized, it breaks into undesirable regions. Indeed, these outbreaks may reach such proportions that they can become destructive. I affirm that fiery epidemics can begin precisely from such disturbances. When I speak of equilibrium and goal-fitness, I wish to remind about the harmony of all life.

**263**. Each day the tension in nature and in men increases. Thus, one can imagine what occurs in the valleys, when even on the mountains special measures are needed. Verily, it is a time of disturbance; but you know the panacea.

**264**. "Me, me, me!" cries out the child, unwilling

to admit his elders to his occupation. Up to the age of seven, do not the mind and heart at times remember the principle of independent achievement on Earth? Later on the wise memories grow dim and often are inverted. "Let them, high and low, labor for me!" thus speaks the man who has forgotten about self-perfectment. But the child remembers and defends his independence. When another child whispers, "How can I manage to reach it?" he is ready for new experiences and conquests of the spirit. But it is not enough that such words of children are uttered—they must be noticed and appreciated. Fiery attention should record these calls and vows of the Subtle World. A small child states, "At last I am born." In this affirmation of striving for incarnation the Subtle World is evidenced. One can cite many instances when not only small children but even newborn babies unexpectedly uttered words of enormous significance and afterwards lapsed into their normal state. One must develop in oneself a fierily manifested memory and solicitude for one's surroundings. Thus one gathers the most valuable information.

**265.** Wherever the truth is manifested it will remain as such. One should eject from oneself all that hinders the acceptance of the manifestation in its complete reality. One must impel oneself to such honesty.

**266.** One should not laugh at Fire being the higher element. Easy laughter and jests only demoralize one's consciousness. Finally one loses sight of the boundary at which solemnity and striving begin.

**267.** If we recall various evidences of perspicacity in children, we can hardly insist upon a mechanistic cell theory. Only later do people lose the perception both of the past and of their destination. How often adults have been saved by children! How often children have not dared to express their feelings! A false timidity is created by the surrounding ugliness. A refined and exalted spirit grows numb before the festering sores of prejudices. How often do adults forbid all improvisation, forgetting that this is the song of the spirit! Even if the technique be imperfect, how many beautiful seeds can be implanted through such utterances of the heart!

**268**. Various grimoires anticipate raps of invocation. Truly, even in such low formulas the truth remains that elementals respond more readily to summoning raps. Yet the law is the same everywhere. You know how much We oppose all magic. But even in an appeal to the Hierarchy of Light there remains the significance of the call of prayer. One should remember that even earthly forces do not respond unless addressed. Just such a current, quite material, is formed during a conscious appeal to the Hierarchy. One should not assume that Fire is not essential during such invocation, since the living fire is the best purifier. But when the fire of the heart is ablaze, no substitute is necessary.

**269**. Freedom of choice is predicated in everything. No coercion whatsoever should obstruct the path, but it is permitted to give a torch to everyone on a long journey. Enlightenment alone can help one to comprehend freedom of choice, therefore enlightenment is the affirmation of being. From the earliest years every school should provide instruction in linking reality to the essence of that which is predestined. Only thus can we link our existence with self-perfection. Freedom of choice, enlightenment, self-perfectment, are the paths of Fire. Only fiery beings can independently perceive these abutments of ascent. But everyone must be led through these gates, otherwise destructive disturbances arise which, together with the chaos of the elements, throw the planet into tremor. Thus, unbridled human confusions are added to the agitation of the elements.

I consider it necessary to reiterate about the confusion which crushes all inceptions of evolution.

**270.** As a rule, the man who is saved does not want to recognize his rescuer. He who has received Fire strives to rush away, without thinking that darkness may engulf him.

**271.** A fire is not kindled under water. Achievement is not created in the comfort of a hothouse. In the midst of human burdens let us ask ourselves, Is this not already an achievement? In the midst of oppression let us ask, Is this not forcing us toward the gates of achievement? In the midst of explosions let us ask, Have we not sufficient strength within us to ascend by ourselves? Thus, let us examine every manifestation as to whether it leads to achievement. Thus, let us note everything that moves us toward achievement. Who can foresee precisely what counterblow will put new circumstances into motion? But without a blow, matter will not be brought into motion. These blows upon matter are called "hearthstones of achievement." Only those who understand the creative substance will realize that what is said is not merely encouragement but the just assertion of a law. One may turn the law into a misfortune, but it is correct to apprehend the usefulness issuing from the foundations of being.

**272.** Each receptivity is already an acceptance of Fire. Tension of energy is the transformation of an undifferentiated element into active vibrations. True receptivity is always positive, because the fiery energy then acts directly. Each unlawful deviation and destruction arouses the so-called black fire. It has a peculiar analogy to venous blood. Phlebotomy had its reason. The black fire could be discharged by it. Fortunately the luminous Fire does not call for such coarse measures. The more naturally the Fire is kindled, the more beneficial it is. Hence the conclusion that the fire of love is the most perfect. You wish to protect the Hierarch, and you do so not from fear, not for gain, but from love. The substitution of fear or covetousness for love results in black fire. The result is the same in the case of any other unworthy substitutions. Every fire is magnetic; therefore one should so cautiously avoid the magnetism of the black fire. It does not transmute the particles of dense emanations, but acts just reversely, thus encumbering space. This can be especially harmful in the case of blood relationships when the dense unconsumed particles are so easily attracted and can overstrain already weakened organs. Thus, it is impractical to kindle the black fire.

**273.** The study of reciprocal intercourse among people is true social science. The relations between man and man studied in sociology do not reveal all interrelations. Sociologists do not study the manifestations of spiritual reactions. They leave this to psychology. But this science, in addition to being superficial, usually studies separate individuals, whereas it is necessary to study the expressions of sociality, for the spiritual influence is unusually powerful and its contact with cosmic processes leads to the solution of many problems. One should assiduously compare crowds and also learn how to compare their actions with nature's resonator. One should not overlook these powerful factors. It is not enough to know the effect of a volley of cannons; this is too elementary. It is far more important to know the effects of a crowd's glances or its shouts. One should realize that these waves reach remote shores by way of all the fiery currents. Thus, one can discover the causes of many unexpected occurrences, but this demands observation.

**274.** Who would believe that the Chalice of a Yogi

can send out salutary currents for a great deal, both far and near? These radiations are very painful, like needles pricking from within. The Chalice cannot refrain from sending its accumulations for the welfare of the near ones. It is unwise to regard these transmissions of benefaction as painless. When both the dense and subtle principles act, there must be tension. But the spirit is ready to overcome these tensions. One must understand that such transmissions strengthen the Fiery World. Cooperation with such degrees of Fire is not easy!

**275.** One should pay attention to folk prophecies in which cosmic manifestations are predicted. Very often one may find accurate calculations in them. However, there may be many other circumstances.

**276.** If a hurrying traveler should inquire the time, there could hardly be a heart so cruel as to tell him a deliberate lie. In the very striving a fiery convincingness is contained. Indeed, striving is the very force that saves one from the blows of hate. Thus, when We pronounce the great concept, Agni, striving is understood in all its ardor. In humanity's conception the Fiery World is growing, together with the achievement of thought. But do not try to convince of the Fiery World a heart that is ignorant of Fire. Such coercion will only lead to the black fire. If we could count the number of servants of darkness created by various coercions, we would be terrified by the enormous total. One must possess the utmost sensitiveness in order to understand when one can turn the key the second and third time in the lock. Neither dogma nor chemistry can say when the sacred word *permitted* can be pronounced. But the fire of the heart knows when karma and the consciousness of a brother will not be overburdened; for the manifestation of Agni must not burden.

**277.** Everyone agrees that books should not contain too much preliminary material. But even average builders agree that the site of the construction must first be cleared and the necessary materials assembled. You yourselves know what it means just to clear the site—one must raze veritable jungles of envy, doubt, and all kinds of rubbish. One must apply all tolerance and magnanimity in order not to be bent under the load of weeds. Of course, all the forces of darkness and ignorance will revolt with especial vehemence against Fire. Therefore each book about the successive steps of life will not be brief. Let the last part of such a book appear separately, otherwise everyone will wish to read the end before the beginning. This habit is especially pleasing to the servants of darkness. Thus they create a quicksand for the weaklings.

**278.** The physician should not be surprised to observe that symptoms of obsession are assuming the proportions of an epidemic. They are far more numerous than the human mind imagines. Moreover, the varieties are highly diverse—from an almost imperceptible eccentricity up to violence. I commend the physician for noticing a connection with venereal diseases. Truly, this is one of the channels of obsession. It can be said that the majority of those suffering from venereal disease are not strangers to obsession. However, in one way the physician has proved too optimistic—although venereal disease facilitates the entry of obsession, its cure does not lie in an eviction of the obsessor. Thus, also, irritation in extreme forms may invite an obsessor, but one must not expect that the first smile will eject him. A complete science is contained in such observation. The physician is correct in wishing to visit not only insane asylums but also prisons. It would not be out of place to visit the stock exchange also, or the deck of a ship in time of danger. One can observe chronic, protracted or temporary symptoms. Likewise, the perspiration can be observed. Many characteristics will gradually become evident to the observer. Among them, details of the Subtle World will be traced. One thing, however, remains incontestable—the ejection of the obsessor does not depend on physical methods. Only Agni, only the pure energy, can oppose this human calamity. I repeat the word calamity, because it is commensurate with the extent of the epidemic. A great number of physicians will regard Agni as a superstition and belief in obsession as ignorance. People so often endow others with their own qualities. But, at the same time, obsessors of all degrees will be troubled by these investigations.

**279**. More than once have We pointed out the desirability of flights into the Subtle World. But conditions may arise of such tension as to make Us suggest caution. With the best intentions, flights may become intolerable to someone. On returning to the physical body the subtle being is somewhat fatigued, and each malicious assault can result in harm.

**280**. The physician must also be warned to be cautious with the obsessed. When approaching the obsessed, one should remember not to hold even the conjecture of obsession too definitely in mind. One must not forget that an obsessor is highly sensitive to thoughts, once he suspects that his presence is discovered. He can express his malice in many ways. By destroying an obsession one can make many enemies, therefore one should conduct one's observations without personally disclosing the fact.

**281**. Among fiery manifestations, radiation from the fingertips during work is very instructive. Around the writing hand waves of light can be seen. Moreover, they change according to the content of the writing. Thus, one can observe a highly important manifestation—the visible participation of Fire and also the variation of Agni energy in accordance with the inner quality of the work. Of course, you have noted not only waves of color but also luminous formations which arise during the reading of a book. These messengers of Light can come from outside as well as from within, but both serve as a proof of the activity of the fiery energy. Many are able to see these stars, but they do not know how to focus their attention. This brings us again to the same point—spasmodic impulse bears no more significance than sleep, as far as its ultimate effect on the work is concerned. Only concentrated attention and perseverance without discouragement will lead to the discernment of the manifested laws. Let none think that the possibility has not been given—rather, it has not been accepted.

**282**. Without doubt there exists a link between the hand at work and the Chalice, which reveals itself through radiation. And if such a link is perceived, one may be congratulated upon one's ability to observe. I equally value observations of the battle between Light and darkness; the stars of Light and darkness are quite apparent and denote a cosmic battle. One can foresee how in the course of time an astrochemical basis for many manifestations will be found. And each record of them will be of great service in the future.

**283**. Also tell the physician that not all obsessions are necessarily dark ones. There may be influences from the middle spheres, which, in the belief of the obsessors, are directed for good, although no especially good results will be derived. The obsessors are of such low degrees and the vehicles within their reach are of no high development, thus, duality of thinking, imbalance, and a lack of self-control result. There are many such people, who are called weak-willed; in fact, the two wills weaken each other. One can cure such persons only by giving them the work that they prefer, but in very intensive measure. The obsessor becomes irked, remaining without an outlet during such concentrated work, for every obsessor seeks to express his own ego. Thus, the physician can observe different types of obsession, but, in principle, such epidemics are quite inadmissible in the human advance toward perfection. Moreover, the concept of the Guru greatly helps to safeguard from obsession. In the case of a weakening of will, the Teacher offers his surplus force in order to bar the intrusion of the alien dark influence. Naturally, the Teacher with a high consciousness is able to determine sensitively when his help is needed. Indeed, such guidance has nothing to do with coercion.

**284.** Fiery striving can facilitate all diagnoses, for nothing else can determine subtle demarcations, which even lack verbal definitions. Not without reason has it been said, Let us rise to the fiery level; words are no longer needed there.

**285.** It is indeed instructive to observe the fiery convulsions of the planet, especially when you know about extraordinary influences. One can point out the movements of Fire just as one can follow the thoughts of people.

**286.** The Agni Yogi is not only a magnetic focus but he also improves the health conditions of a locality. Thus, the Raja Yogi and the Agni Yogi take upon themselves the currents of space. It is not an exaggeration to state that Yoga restores the planet's health. One must hasten to realize the significance of spiritual perfectment. Only through such realization can one ease the strain of the Yogi's task, in which everyone can burden him, but only few can help. One should attain at least the step of simple respect for the unusual. No one cares to reflect how easily he may cause suffering by his negative malicious attack. Each ignorant person is comparable to a servant of darkness.

**287**. True, Armageddon is not wanting, yet even the dark force itself at some time yields a store of new cunning devices. Let us not complain because of the many, many attacks. It cannot be otherwise. The ability to become accustomed to danger is a powerful weapon against enemies. Verily, people are in danger every moment. It is a great delusion to think that everything rests in safety. Maya appears to men under the guise of tranquillity, but precisely the Yogi senses that the cross of existence stands immutable. Only the acceptance of the cross and the ascent of the Mountain where there are even five-legged calves, only such valor will carry one over the abyss. Let us not forget that I ordained caution, because it is a quality of valor.

**288**. The Teacher rejoices when collective labor is possible. Rejection of collective labor is ignorance. Only a lofty individuality finds within itself the measure of collective concepts. So long as the personality fears collective work, it is not yet individualized; it still remains in the stifling atmosphere of selfhood. Only true discernment of the indestructibility of freedom permits adherence to collective labor. Only through such true mutual respect can we attain the realization of harmonious labor—in other words, attain active good. In this good is kindled the fire of the heart; hence each manifestation of harmonious labor is so joyous. Such labor augments the psychic energy unusually. Let the work be carried out at least in short united labor; even if for brief periods at first, it must be in complete accord and intent upon success. In the beginning, fatigue because of disunity is unavoidable, but later the coordinated collective force will multiply the energy tenfold. Thus, even in small nuclei one can thrust forward the prototype of world progress.

**289**. Sunbirds do not descend to Earth. In this myth is indicated the separation of the Fiery World from earthly conditions. One can see that men have paid special reverence to the fiery element since ancient days. Indeed, with what solicitude must one regard each fiery manifestation! In the midst of the most ordinary life one can discern the sparks of the higher Fire. This means that around each such spark a purified atmosphere grows; therefore it is especially abominable to extinguish these gleams. They flash out unexpectedly, but the extinction of such lights produces consequences of particular instability. It has been said truly that it is better not to be born than to multiply the abominations.

**290**. Labor serves as the best purge of all abominations. Labor generates the potent factor of sweat, which has even been brought forward as a means for the propagation of man. Perspiration has been analyzed very little; it seldom has been studied in comparison with man's personality, and it has been little observed in relation to the various elements. Even an inexperienced observer will notice the many different varieties of perspiration. It is actually easy to notice that a fiery nature is not given to a quantity of perspiration, and, in any case, it alkalizes it. On the other hand, earth and water natures are strongly saturated with perspiration. Thus, it can be observed with what wisdom one of the earliest evolutions of man was indicated.

**291**. One should not be diverted from the various stages of human evolution. Much may appear strange from our point of view, but let us bear in mind that all conditions have relatively changed. Then we shall arrive at an aspect which, though alien, is not too strange. It is fallacious to imagine all the lives in the worlds according to our contemporary understanding. We so easily forget yesterday, and so meagerly imagine tomorrow, that many of our judgments are like autumn leaves. It is fitting to feel one's insignificance before every cosmic law. However, fiery wings are bestowed for the approach to the Fiery World.

**292.** The trouble everywhere and always is that as soon as circumstances improve somewhat, a dark hand tries to cast small shaggy balls in the way. One can distinctly see how small harmful fissures appear. But in a furnace where the pressure is great even a small fissure allows the escape of destructive gas. Amidst life, one can witness experiments in higher chemistry. Hence it is so important just to observe.

**293.** Healing through suggestion has been called fiery striving. True, this method of healing is now being developed more extensively. Therefore one should avert possible harm from ignorant application of the fiery energy. Suggestion can arrest pain, but if those who employ suggestion do not know the origin of the illness, these suggestions can be likened to harmful narcotics. It is another matter when suggestion is applied by an experienced physician; he not only alleviates the reflex of pain but also traces the flow of the illness and can suggest to the corresponding organs that they resume their normal functions. A wise physician will also not neglect astrology. One may laugh all one wishes, but a scientifically cast horoscope will aid in diagnosing sickness itself and determining contributing circumstances. One should pay full attention to astrochemistry and understand the power of suggestion. If suggestion utilizes fiery energy, how deep and powerful an influence is exerted by Fire! One must do away with the custom of narrow command and forbiddance now used by hypnotists. Only a knowledge of the organism and of all circumstances permits the physician to apply his command to all the affected parts. The weakened organs can be considerably restored by guiding and coordinating them with the fire of the heart. Every physician must develop within himself the power of suggestion.

**294.** It is quite senseless when a physician allows an ignorant hypnotist access to his patient. A crude force cannot follow the complex course of the disease. It is not a question merely of putting the patient to sleep, all conditions should be correlated and the complex channels of the disease traced. Each word, each intonation of the suggestion has a fiery significance. Therefore, only an enlightened mind can encompass the laws and methods of suggestion. Only such a mind will realize the complete responsibility for influencing the fiery energy.

**295.** You know that during suggestion one should not wave the arms or stare at the patient. In general, it is not necessary even to look into the patient's eyes, but one should project the will from heart to heart. Only afterwards should one proceed in applying one's will from the center, in the needed direction. It is absolutely useless for the patient under suggestion to know what is taking place. In fact, the preparations for suggestion often set up an undesirable counteraction. Besides, although the patient may believe that he is ready to submit to the treatment, his Manas will resist the intrusion. The longer both consciousnesses are mutually balanced, the more potent the suggestion will be. However, the experiment should not be announced in advance; each treatment should take place unexpectedly. But physical conditions must be favorable. The temperature should be average, moderate, without the irritation induced by heat or cold. The air must be pure, and it is advisable to have a light aroma of roses or eucalyptus. One should arrange inconspicuously that the patient be comfortably reclining in an armchair. A bed is less suitable. Everything sudden or noisy should be shunned in order to avoid the possibility of a shock. It must not be forgotten that during suggestion the subtle body is in a state of great tension and attempts to leave the body. Therefore, one should with all possible caution forbid its leaving the body. Naturally, all commands should be mental and not oral. Western hypnotists scoff at the idea of a mental command; they think that words and fingers can dominate the will. But let us leave to them their occidental blunders. In certain primitive tribes the patient was smitten on the forehead with a club. Such an act also subjugated the will. But where there is the Teaching of the Heart and of Fire the methods must be different.

**296.** Of course there are people who will say that a blow with a club, being a direct method, is therefore permissible, but that fiery action is something concealed and inadmissible. By such reasoning each one who thinks about good is already dangerous, but the murderer is only a reflection of the social order. Not a few people think in this manner and in so doing obstruct all that is subtle. But the club is no longer useful; the subtlest solutions and respect for the human heart are necessary.

**297.** Gypsies usually accompany remedies with an incantation, in the belief that only thus will the remedy be effective. And so Our Himalayan traditions are maintained through many generations of migrants.

Truly, if we compare the effect of medicines taken willingly or with repugnance, the difference will be astounding. Even the most potent medicines can produce almost contrary effects if they are accompanied by a corresponding suggestion. One can write a significant book on the relativity of physical influences. One can gather facts from various fields to prove that among the decisive factors the physical are the least important. Thus, step by step, one should trace the movement of Agni. One need not enter at once into complex formulas, but can proceed from the striking evidences of each day. If nature healers understand wherein the dominant principle of success is contained, an educated physician should discern even better the determining factors. Upon this path the past and future will meet.

**298.** Agni is eternal! The fiery energy is imperishable! Folk sayings often speak of eternal joys and sorrows. The indestructibility of joy and sorrow sent into space has been observed very scientifically. Many bear the sorrow of another, and many grasp at joy that does not belong to them. Thus, one must always remember about eternal sowings. Thought, if not powerful, can be engulfed by the currents of space; but the substance of sorrow or joy is almost as indestructible as the fiery seed. It is useful to impregnate space with joy, and very dangerous to strew the heavens with sorrow. But where can one find the store of joy? Certainly not in the bazaar, but near the ray of Light, in the joy of Hierarchy. The increase of sorrow is one of the causes of fiery epidemics, but when physiology shall teach men about the debilitating consequences of sorrow, the quest for joy will begin. Gradually the rock of joy will be affirmed and an exalted solemnity will begin, recognized as the most healthful factor. Not without reason have We pointed out the benefits of the presence of healthy people. Joy is the health of the spirit.

**299.** One must develop the ability to understand an alien mood. This is not thought-reading, but straight-knowledge of the nature of a neighbor. It is easier to observe what is in the distance when we know what is close by. Many stand upon the threshold of such straight-knowledge, but are prevented from understanding their surroundings by a spasm of selfhood.

**300.** Fleeting pilgrims—thus are called those who are cognizant of the great paths. Only through a realization of the brevity of the earthly path is it possible to comprehend the grandeur of Infinity and learn the process of perfecting the spirit. Security has no existence whatsoever, and the illusion of security is a most pernicious specter. Yet, without relying upon the physical world, one should learn to value every crumb of it. Let each movement of Fire recall to us the power that maintains the balance. If the planet is equilibrated by the inner Fire, each being also will find support in the fire of the heart.

**301.** One need not be surprised at flashes of light before one's closed eyes. The prophets said, "O Lord, I behold no darkness!" This is not a symbol of devotion, but a scientific evidence of the kindling of the centers. One constantly finds references to these lights. One should seek for them not only in antiquity but should also inquire about them among the blind and children. A poet could write a song on how heaven reveals itself to closed eyes.

**302.** It is useful to take photographs not only at different hours but also during diverse cosmic tensions. When, if not during the moment of tension, can one espy the spots of absolute darkness? When, if not during the imbalance of the elements, can one obtain the most complex impressions? Our own fluctuation is reflected upon the film, but one can also secure impressions of various subtle manifestations. This can begin with the simplest conditions, because it is necessary to work in varied circumstances.

**303**. Dreams about the future are widespread. Prophecies are disseminated by the thousands, and people in various countries are becoming accustomed to definite dates. In this way the course of evolution is being affirmed. So, too, the awesome dates are being called to mind. One might say that never before has humanity had to so cast its lot. It is impossible to violate free will more than is now being done. You yourself see how the dates are being brought to mind in the most unusual ways, but blind are those who do not wish to see. You yourself also see how difficult it is to establish a solemn unity, even as a salutary remedy. Yet you also see how a great many destructions may be mitigated. Where there would have been a blow, only a slight shock occurs. But do not rest in the belief of a secure existence. Everything is unstable; the Ladder of Hierarchy alone is firm.

**304**. People love to discuss evolution and involution, but avoid applying these concepts to themselves. Not following their own evolution, people attract similarly insignificant satellites from the Subtle World! The Subtle World is really striving toward the earthly one, but in full conformity. Consequently, if people would strive toward evolution, they would attract evolving beings. Thus, the betterment of world conditions would be in the hands of humanity itself. Thus, each striving for the Good creates a response not only in the Subtle World but also in the Fiery World. If for some reason such striving remains unexpressed, it nevertheless remains in space in full measure. The potential of Good is like a pillar of light. A carpenter, shoemaker, or physician can think equally of the Good. Constancy and steadfastness in Good is already a conquest. Some may regard the time spent in the Ashram as imprisonment, but with the development of the spirit it will be the most salutary of all sojourns. You know how time flies, and in this flight one becomes accustomed to Infinity.

305. Of course, an outflow of energy can even cause dizziness, especially when the transmissions are projected to remote distances; then a kind of inertia sets in. Gravitation is felt so strongly that it is better not to be in an upright position.

306. One can observe in daily life much that pertains to the customs of the Subtle and Fiery Worlds. Humanity can be divided into two types: one never leaves dirt behind, and when preparing to depart brings everything into order and cleans everything up lest someone else be burdened with the rubbish; the other does not take any consequences into consideration and leaves heaps of dirt behind. You may be sure that the second is far from the Fiery World. You may be equally certain that the first is of a fiery nature and is a purifier, like Fire itself. One should also observe the way a man passes by small wayside stops. One who is aware of his mission hurries on, though he is well-disposed toward everything he encounters. The other contrives to devise some confusion at each stop, disturbing the surroundings. The first is experienced, having passed through many incarnations, and understands that a night's lodging is not his Father's house. The second cannot discern true values and is ready to tarry at each chance bazaar on his way. Thus people constantly reveal their natures. Only an experienced

traveler knows that a night's lodging is not a destination and understands how carefully one must treat things which may be of use for the caravan that follows. He will not use up all the firewood, but will think of others. He will not pollute the well, because of its usefulness to others. Thus, one can observe where is Light and where is darkness.

**307.** Can one imagine people as thinking only of that which is useful? Of course one can; harmful and undisciplined thoughts are primarily useless. One can accustom oneself to useful thoughts, and such an exercise will be the best preparation for the Fiery World. The habit of thoughts for Good is not attained quickly; still, it leads to fiery realization. Thus, not in the manifestation of a special world, but through the quality of daily labor do we approach the Fiery World.

**308.** Self-perfectment is Light. Self-indulgence is darkness. One can so build one's life that each day will, as it were, be the end. But one can so illumine one's life that each hour will be a beginning. Thus one can rebuild one's earthly existence beneath one's very eyes. Only in this way will the questions of the future and the understanding of fiery perfectment become perceptible. Daring should be found to reconstruct one's life in accordance with new accumulations. To die in the bed of one's grandfather is to be relegated to a medieval status. We even advise that these beds be taken to a museum; this will also be more hygienic. However, we should not limit tomorrow by the measurements of yesterday; if we do, how can we approach a comprehension of the Fiery World, which was like hellfire to our grandfathers. And now, when due reverence is tendered to Light and the grandeur of Fire, we can have spiritually a very rich tomorrow.

**309.** For two weeks you have felt the subterranean

shocks. Imagine how Earth is developing a state of mobility. No human ingenuity can stay the elements, but if you have a clear conception of the Subtle and Fiery Worlds, no earthly convulsion can veil the inalienable, radiant tomorrow.

310. From the East, the White Eagle—thus We reveal a new consciousness. Nothing is possible without the East. The history of mankind was created either by the East or for the East. It is impossible to imagine the immensity of the structure of culture, whose Temple is so vast.

311. Advise the young scholar to collect everything regarding Fire from the most ancient teachings. Let the Puranas of India, the fragments of the Teachings of Egypt, Chaldea, China, Persia, and absolutely all teachings of the classic philosophy not be overlooked. Of course, the Bible, the Kabbalah, and the Teaching of Christ, all will yield plentiful material. Likewise, the assertions of the most recent times will add to the valuable definitions of Agni. Such a compilation has never been made. Yet can one advance toward the future without gathering the signs of millennia?

312. Evidence from the most recent researches should be valued. When people begin to soar into the highest strata and penetrate into subterranean caves, synthetic conclusions may be expected. Do not neglect observations on the effects of the lower strata of the atmosphere. In fact, one should take into consideration literally the whole of relativity, which can only enrich one's deductions. It is necessary that amidst all this relativity we find uses even for half-burned slag. Wherever Fire has been active, everything can provide valuable observations.

313. No one can rightly form an opinion about cosmogony without having studied the fiery element.

It would be comparable to an architect's beginning to build a stone structure without having studied the nature of stone and the resistance of building materials. But the contemporary state of minds is so remote from a salutary synthesis!

**314.** The subterranean tension is not over. We succeed in breaking up the shocks into light tremors. In general, one should remember this strategy of splitting up evil. Often it is impossible to avoid the accumulated tension of malice. Then, there remains only to split up this tension of darkness.

**315.** The Chinese method of healing by means of a puncture of the corresponding centers, of which you recently read, is not curing but only a temporary relief. The ancient Egyptians produced the same reaction by pressing upon the corresponding centers. And even nowadays cupping glasses and hot poultices are in the same category. Thus, throughout life one should eliminate irritation by means of corresponding complements. The Teaching of Old China also contained the process of healing by means of heightening the vitality. Precisely China has valued ginseng and a prolonged use of musk. Therefore, it is not to be wondered at if the latest medical research discovers aspects of the higher vitality. Likewise, one can notice the fieriness of the manifestations of vitality. May the best of physicians learn how to discern the fiery origin of the vegetable and animal lifegivers. Such experiments should not be deferred; when fiery epidemics threaten, let us not forget that like cures like.

**316.** Why wonder that the development of vision demands moderate lighting? It is quite clear that sharp light does not permit the increase of inner light. Yet only striving for self-perfection provides a solid foundation. Therefore, in ancient times the initiations into the Mysteries were accompanied by prolonged stays in darkness, until the eye overcame the obstacles of darkness by its inner sight.

317. Not only is human unemployment reaching dangerous proportions but the idleness of nature must also attract notice eventually. One need only note how quickly flourishing vegetation is replaced by dead sands. The creeping death of Earth's crust should be called suicide, not mismanagement. Sands, glaciers, landslides do not presage a brilliant future. It is impossible to hasten the healing of nature, even if people turn to a healthy direction of thought. It will require decades to restore to health Earth's destroyed crust. But for such especially beneficent measures human cooperation is needed. But do we see signs of such mutual labor? Do not destruction and discord prevail in human minds? Is not every effort toward unity met by derision? People do not wish to think of the reality of the future. We speak of the great Agni, yet scarcely a thousand minds dare to think about its undeferrability.

318. One should pay attention to impending events. One should realize that humanity is entering a period of continuous warfare. Such wars vary, but their sole basis is the same—hostility everywhere and in everything. No one reflects upon what a devastating conflagration is created when multitudes of people consolidate a circle of destruction around the entire planet. This is that very serpent which is more devastating than avalanches and glaciers. Do not think that this is a bugbear. No, each day brings evidences of destruction. The eternal skeleton does not slumber, but frivolity attempts to divert everyone's eyes from the conflagration.

319. Wars of arms, wars of trade, wars of unemployment, wars of knowledge, wars of religion—multiform

are the wars, and earthly boundaries have already lost their significance! Planetary life is divided by innumerable boundaries.

**320**. *Millefolium*, or "Thousand Leaves," was the name of an ancient decoction of wild field herbs. Its significance lay in the belief that the field flora is in itself already a collective panacea. Of course such a combination of plant forces is very noteworthy; for who better than Nature can match up conformable neighbors! The proportions and methods of adaptation rest in the hands of man. Verily, each symphony of vegetation astonishes one by its consonance. Creativeness is rich, both externally and internally, but, as a rule, people cruelly violate this precious veil of the Mother of the World. For the sake of plunder they prefer the bony grin of the death's-head on the sand. Political economy should be based upon an understanding of the values of nature and their wise use; otherwise the state will rest on sand. Thus, in everything one can study the golden mean, the very path of justice. People themselves are horrified when a disruption of the fundamentals takes place. They are disturbed by albinos; yet this is only a violation of the fiery principle. One can witness similar disturbances in all kingdoms of nature. They are not only an abomination, they are infectious and mutually harmful. One must continually return to medical counsels, but is not the fiery element a mighty healing power? Fire is the affirmation of life.

**321**. One must persuade people to conserve their own treasures. The most miserly person on Earth is often a planetary squanderer. The New World, if and when it arrives, will manifest love for the treasures of nature, and they will provide the best emulsion of vital essence. Multitudes will have to spread out from the cities into nature, but surely not to sand dunes!

In every part of the world oceans of sand have been formed. Similarly, the consciousness of mankind has crumbled into grains of malice. Every desert was once a flowering meadow. Not nature, but men themselves destroyed the flowers. Let thought about Fire compel people to ponder upon thrift.

**322**. Many desire to know details of the Subtle World, but many will be sorely perplexed. The entire perceptibility of the Subtle World is relative, depending upon the development of the consciousness. One can be enraptured by the light, or one may find oneself in fog. One can build beautiful structures by willpower, or one may remain on piles of rubbish. One can instantaneously assimilate the language of the spirit, or one may remain deaf and dumb. To each in accordance with his deeds. Each perceives in accordance with his consciousness. The Subtle World is a state of true justice. One can observe that a consciousness, even though simple, progresses if illumined by love. The bazaar-colored emotions of Earth-dwellers bear little resemblance to love. Love often remains unrealized. But in the Subtle World love is the key to all locks. For many people imagination is an unattainable abstraction, but in the Subtle World each grain of the accumulations of imagination is a path to possibilities. For Earth-dwellers, offense, bitterness, and vengeance constitute the bases of the bile and liver; but in the Subtle World, even for an average consciousness, these infamies fall away as worthless husks. Therefore We emphatically repeat about the fiery consciousness, in order that one be directed immediately into the higher spheres. One should indeed strive by all lofty means toward the fiery consciousness.

**323**. Your judgment is correct in regard to the need for an exodus from the festering cities and for a proportionate distribution of the population of the planet. If humanity is fundamentally a fire-bearer, is it possible not to understand how very necessary is the wise distribution of this element? It must be understood that the illness of the planet depends to a great extent upon human balance. One should not abandon vast spaces and gather in fratricidal congestion on infected and blood-soaked sites. Not by accident did the ancient chieftains found their camps on virgin sites. Today, science itself favors the normal peopling of free spaces. None will be forgotten or excluded, and the very forces of nature, called into cooperation, will render healthful Earth's diseased condition. Then only may one hope that labor will be valued, and that, instead of hired laborers, co-workers will be born. People's thinking will also undergo a reformation when the focus of thought is directed to an even distribution of labor over the entire face of Earth. One should regard this as a guarantee of the only solution. Otherwise people will only shake off the yoke, not finding the Truth that dwells in their hearts. Fiery is this Truth!

**324.** Certainly it may be asked why in antiquity the danger of overcrowding did not arise. In the first place, the population was comparatively small; furthermore, let us not forget the fate of Atlantis, Babylon, and other once congested places which lie in ruins. Humanity remembers only a few of these burial grounds, but the cosmic laws have acted more than once. Hence, one should not be astonished that cosmic tension is increasing alongside the infection of the lower strata.

**325.** When we speak of the Fiery World we should not avoid earthly solutions. The fiery state so greatly surpasses the earthly that the best earthly balance is required in order to permit communion with Fire. Many earthly conditions must be reconciled in order that thought may comprehend the fiery body. Let priests become more scholarly, and scholars more spiritual. Through these attempts, even though modest, there may be erected an important abutment for the necessary bridge. This concept of a bridge has been ordained since antiquity, but now it has become imperative.

**326.** Certain agitators hope that by continuously overthrowing everything they can insure their own property. These thoughts are highly indicative of plunder and dismemberment. It is quite inadmissible to think of attracting the fiery element for the purpose of plunder and destruction. I repeat, these are the ways of ignorance, which must be abandoned. Let him who has cut down a tree immediately plant another in its place. Let the gardener reap with one hand, sow with the other. The simple rules against plunder must be among the first lessons taught at school. The teacher must prepare the spirit for the most fiery assimilations. Only by constantly affirming the ways of the future can one prepare the warriors of the spirit.

**327.** Someone wished to know about the highest worlds, but he lived like a pig. Undermining the roots is not consistent with upward striving. For pigs—the pigsty.

**328.** The Teaching must primarily inspire one upward. Thus, it is easier to speak of Fire, which must be understood as the very highest. It is instructive to ask the smallest children how they picture Fire to themselves. The most surprising answers may be received, but they will be full of significance. Only adults consign Fire to a servile position.

**329.** Conciseness of formulas is the decree of Fire. One should become accustomed to the sacred conciseness. One should not regard it as easily attainable. In it are expressed goal-fitness, solicitude, reverence, and an astute power. Not a lengthy formula is sent, but its essence. One can concentrate power in a single word and thus multiply the effect. Not a torrent, but lightning, is the symbol of the command. Much inner work is needed to produce the most concise and most convincing. Hence, ancient conjurations consisted of short invocations. One may accompany such an arrow with a gesture of the hand, but such a gesture is not essential, although it may be a powerful impetus for oneself.

**330.** Music is needed for all fiery sowings. One should choose good music; it unifies our emotions. But one should not absent-mindedly let the music just pass by one's ears. People often have before them a great phenomenon, and yet they fail to hear the loudest and fail to perceive the brightest. People often isolate themselves completely from their surroundings, but fail to realize that precisely this state is very valuable if wisely induced.

**331.** It is the Teacher's duty to follow the quality of the pupil's thought. Not twists of the mind, but tendency of thought gives evidence of progress. This understanding of another's thought is not supernatural, but is derived from many movements and glances. With only a little attention the Teacher will perceive the fires of the eyes. These flashes are quite significant and give a wise physician the entire record of the internal condition.

**332.** One should not only look forward to the advent of the densified subtle body but one should strive with all one's forces to become conscious of the Subtle World. Not only is the Subtle World to be realized but we must be filled with daring so that we may gain a perception of the fiery forces. We should become accustomed to the thought that sooner or later we are destined to reach the Fiery Shores. Thus, let us learn to cast the largest net in order to obtain the best catch. Not only in dreams but actually in the midst of daily labor we must direct our thoughts to the distant fiery manifestations. Otherwise, upon finding ourselves in the Subtle World, we will still have difficulty in cognizing the fiery radiance. Not only the eye, but consciousness itself must become accustomed to light. People suffer most from an inability to direct themselves forward. A limited consciousness only looks back, and therefore often begins to retrogress. "The Kingdom of Heaven, the Fiery Kingdom, is taken by storm"—this truth was pronounced long ago, but we have forgotten it and have dismissed each daring aspiration. Many precious indications have been confounded. People have distorted the concept of humility, so needed in relation to Hierarchy. For their own convenience people have made naught of it. Indolence was not ordained, for one must strive with all daring and labor toward Fire, the Beautiful. There is no earthly object of such value that the Fiery World should be renounced for it.

**333**. All earthly senses, when transmuted, ascend to the Fiery World. Not only do sight and hearing exist spiritually but even taste has its new application. Without taste it is impossible to understand many chemical combinations. And in the process of creation all the senses are needed as means of correlation. Therefore, it is necessary to refine the senses while on Earth. With due reason a certain hermit made his daily food of herbs and leaves in order to refine his sense of taste. And when a passer-by asked his reason for this, he answered, "In order to love thee better." Thus, each subtlety is of use in the realization of the fundamentals.

**334**. As though we had been there, let us speak about the Subtle and Fiery Worlds. Let these very talks be subjected to special derision; nevertheless, consciousnesses striving in this same direction will appear. In this way we shall discover those to whom the heart in tremor whispers of the Fiery World, the World of Beauty.

**335.** Can knowledge of the future be regarded as sorcery? Can cognition of the inevitable be magic? Each religion, as a link with the Highest, finds words to express the ineffable transition into the Subtle World. The earthly consciousness retains possession of all its senses, which are found in the Subtle World though in transmuted form. The precise moment of transition into the Subtle World is accompanied by a sensation of dizziness, as during fainting or at the beginning of a fit of epilepsy. The sensations that follow depend entirely upon the preparedness of the consciousness, or rather upon the fiery ego. If the consciousness has been obscured or dimmed, the senses cannot be carried over into the new condition. In this case a kind of oblivion or drowsy roaming about occurs. This state is not a pleasant one. I do not, of course, refer to the dark state of criminals and the depraved—the nature of their torment is indescribable! But it is preferable to speak of the luminous possibilities. Thus, if Agni has been awakened during life through knowledge or heroic feeling, it will immediately accomplish the great transmutation. Like a veritable torch, it will indicate the way; like radiant helium it will carry one up into the predestined sphere. Though so imperceptible in earthly life, Agni becomes the guiding principle in the Subtle World. And not only does it light the way in the Subtle World, it acts as a guide to the Fiery Beings. Without Agni it is impossible to commune with the Light of the Fiery World. Lacking the manifested fire, the roaming spirits are stricken blind. We behold by

Fire, and we ascend by Flame. There are no other pro-
pellants, and therefore blessed be the Fire-conscious!

**336**. If each cell contains an entire universe, then
the prototype of the Creator is to be found in each
human being, throughout Infinity. How necessary it is
to learn to reverence the Holy Spirit! One may give It
the most exalted names. One may even suffuse one's
heart with It namelessly, when all names pour forth as
from an overflowing chalice. But defamation is inadmissible, for it severs the thread of Light. The affirmation of Guruship is necessary, as a natural step toward
the realization of Agni.

**337**. Why do the Fiery Beings seldom appear to
Earth-dwellers? For this also there is a scientific explanation. The Sublime One said, "Touch me not." Thus
simply was pronounced the essence of relation between
the Fiery World and the earthly one. To the earthly
senses the Fiery World is like a powerful dynamo. The
earthly body is consumed by contact with a Fiery Being;
proximity alone is enough to stop the heart of the incarnate one. A lighted torch should not be brought into an
inflammable dwelling. Even the most mundane physician knows how much electric force a human heart
can withstand, and the intensity of common electricity
is not to be compared with that of the fiery forces. The
manifestation of Fohat itself may not always be visible. How rarely, then, can the Radiant Guests appear!
Being undisciplined, people either become terrified or
try to touch, and thus are consumed. Let us not forget
that fear can burn away the heart. Even in white magic,
during positive invocations, the invoker encloses himself in a circle in order to protect himself from the fiery
currents. Of course, the heart that recognizes Fire can
gradually assimilate it.

**338**. It is difficult to turn from Earth to the Fiery

World. But it is equally difficult to approach the earthly spheres from the Subtle World. Such plunges may be compared to the work of divers. As the diver must wear a heavy diver's suit in order to resist the pressure of the ocean, so he who approaches Earth must also sheathe himself in a dense body. The state of the newborn babe is wisely designed, because it can thus gradually assume the burdens of Earth. More than one period of seven years is necessary to master earthly existence. Therefore one should carefully protect the children.

**339.** The dark ones do not slumber. They maintain a far greater unity with their Hierarchy than do the so-called warriors of Light. The dark ones know that their only salvation lies in darkness, but the fireflies flit about a great deal, argue much, and love their Hierarchy but little.

**340.** Follow Me. Strive to Me. Only thus can you understand the future. What could be preferred to the Forces of Light? One's faith can be renewed as an immutable force. Faith that does not guide one's entire life is worthless. I indicate the countries that have lost their path; the machine is still in motion, but without a regeneration of the consciousness there is nothing on which to exist. New consciousness can come only from the spirit. The new force can be strengthened only through knowledge of the higher worlds. The accumulation of such knowledge will strengthen life. One may reject the most essential if one fails to consider the future! One must accept all transitions as improvements. A single flight of thought can transport us across the abyss. Even that which seems most inevitable depends upon the quality of thought. The affirmation of thought can even alter the return to Earth. The Subtle World is regarded generally as a passive state, but it need not be merely passive; it can be active as well. If it has been said, "As in heaven, so on earth," this means that there, also, conditions exist for higher achievements. We should not judge only by average measures. If the average period between incarnations is approximately seven hundred years, there can also be spans of seven or even three years. Karmic conditions themselves must yield to the hammer of the will. Thought itself is the best fiery guardian. Thought is unconsumable! Even on Earth, a man suffused with faith and thought loses weight. Thought also leads to the higher worlds. When thrown off balance, a man requests a moment's respite. This respite affords an accumulation of will. Without will there is no faith. Thus We arm people with weapons of Light.

**341**. From the Subtle World earthly outlines are usually only dimly perceptible. The cause lies not only in the density of the earthly atmosphere but also in a reluctance to observe. He who desires to see, can see. Even in earthly twilights, one must strain the sight, in other words, infuse thought into one's vision.

**342**. During his journeys Apollonius of Tyana would sometimes say to his disciples, "Let us tarry here. This place is pleasing to me." From these words his pupils knew that a magnet was concealed there or that the Teacher intended to bury a magnet there. The sensing of magnets is accomplished by means of a particular current connected with the power of Agni. In the course of time science may investigate these magnetic waves, for they are not exhausted for centuries. Magnets have been set like milestones in places of special significance. When a ploughman carries with him a bit of his native soil, he recalls, as it were, the ancient custom of bringing a handful of earth as an irrefutable token. And now you also know how some commemorative soil was brought. Its destiny is not simple; an evil one wished to scatter it, but a benign hand intentionally concealed the treasure and it remained forgotten. Still, the thought attached to this offering exists and is more effective than one might think—thus thought lives on. An object magnetized by thought, verily, has power. Thus, without superstition, but quite scientifically, one should study the stratifications of thought—they are the work of Fire.

**343.** Societies for psychic research could be of importance, but they confine themselves to the lower strata. They are satisfied with necromancy, although they could regenerate the spiritual aspects of life. We do not condemn these societies, for they had to begin with the lowly and insignificant, but after half a century there should be evidence of some striving toward the higher worlds. However, this is scarcely apparent.

**344.** At times it is useful to sit calmly, directing one's spirit to Infinity. It is like a shower from the far-off worlds. We ourselves must attract the currents, otherwise they may glide by without leaving a trace. Thought attracts positive currents like a magnet and repels negative ones like a shield.

**345.** The Guru may ask his disciple, "What are you doing, what do you desire, what torments you, what gives you joy?" These questions will not indicate that the Guru is unaware of his disciple's state of mind. On the contrary, with complete knowledge the Guru wishes to see what the pupil himself regards as most important. Through lack of experience the pupil may indicate the most insignificant of all circumstances. Hence, the Teacher does not inquire merely out of politeness, but as a test of the consciousness of his disciple. Therefore one should carefully weigh one's replies to the Teacher. Not the so-called amenities, but a constant broadening of consciousness is the Teacher's concern.

**346**. The pupil must also remember about divisibility of the spirit. One must strive in the consciousness so as to realize the presence of the Teacher in spirit. Those who envision the nearness of the Teacher are not quite wrong. This is better than light-mindedly to forget entirely about the Teacher. Those who memorize the words of the Teaching are not so wrong. In school, passages of texts are learned by heart to strengthen the memory. So, also, when the Teaching burns within the heart, it is affirmed by brief irrevocable formulas. For some, it is easier to assimilate precise expressions. Do not prevent each one from following the path of his own karma. It is better not to force when one's individual fires are evident.

**347**. One desires the easiest way; another prefers the most difficult. One cannot speak, but stands firmly on guard; another is eloquent and flies after his words. Some can sense the most important manifestations, but others choose to dwell with failure. One could enumerate these differences endlessly, but only the presence of the fire of the heart will vindicate the characteristics of the personality. Thus, we shall not tire of repeating about multiformity. The gardener knows how to combine his plants, that is why he is the master of the garden.

**348**. It is apparent that people desire to have a change of existing conditions. A ruler asked that a contented man be found. Finally after long quests one was discovered—he was deaf, dumb, and blind!

**349**. Technocracy should be regarded as a device of the dark ones. The dark ones have often led people on to mechanical solutions, thereby hoping to occupy the attention of humanity, only to divert it from spiritual growth. Yet the problems of life can be solved only by the expansion of consciousness. It can be seen how mechanical hypotheses easily ensnare the hopes of humanity. Such also was the Maya of the ancients, which could be interrupted by the slightest shock.

**350**. Hygiene of thought must be applied on both the spiritual and earthly planes. One must carry out experiments, strengthened by fiery medicines, upon the processes of thinking. One should pay attention to the action of phosphorus or of the evaporation of eucalyptus upon thinking. One should verify the extent to which thinking is improved by musk. One should gather all data in regard to various resinous oils. Finally, one must remember all the combinations that are closest to the activity of Fire. These experiments should be carried out with persons of strong fiery thinking. Such experiments will remind one not only about vitamins but also about Agni. The efforts of physicians to concentrate not only upon internal remedies but also on the reactions of the sense of smell will produce the needed results. People are gravely sick. The dark forces endeavor to seduce with all kinds of narcotics, but the narrow boundaries of life are not broadened by stupefying the intellect. Just now spiritual vigilance is needed. One must grow to love this vigilance as a state fitting to man.

**351**. Many small circles are scattered throughout the planet. The black lodges know what to do. But the servants of Light, by their disorganization, often even harm each other. The black lodges are not approached by strangers, but the servants of Light, through good nature, or rather ignorance, often are ready to embrace the most dangerous traitor. One must eject indifference, which paralyzes the best forces. Truly one can become exhausted not so much by enemies as by the indifference of friends. How is it possible to understand fieriness when one is indolent and indifferent?

The qualities of Fire are the antitheses of indifference. One must beware of the oppressiveness of such inert people, although occasionally one can put them to shame and at least rouse indignation in them. A death-like withdrawal of the spirit is a departure from life.

352. Let us not be grieved at the sight of indifference; it only proves the conclusion that it is inadmissible to remain in such a disgraceful, wretched condition. Even in an hour of exhaustion We still do not discontinue the work of unification. At times one cannot even bring together people who are quite close to each other. It matters not; let them remain temporarily in separate homes, but let them at least refrain from quenching the fires. Thus, one must be vigilant that fires be not extinguished.

353. A certain Guru remained out of sight in his cave. And when his disciples asked him to show himself, he replied, "Foolish ones—is it not for your sake that I have hidden myself? For I do not wish to cause discord among you by my appearance. But when you accept me as one who does not exist, perhaps your own fires will burn the more intensely." Even through such means does the Guru show concern about the kindling of the fires so that the heart may be aflame!

354. Very often the question has arisen as to which thought is the more effective, the uttered or unuttered one. Indeed, it may seem that the application of verbal formulas might add strength. People attracted by externals imagine that a framework of words will enhance the effectiveness of the thought. This, however, is but conventionality, and words will not help the essence. The wordless thought is far more powerful, manifesting a purer degree of Fire. One can observe that an unuttered thought remains entirely free from the condition of constraint brought by language. It approaches

the fiery tongue and it multiplies its own power. We send fiery thoughts; they are fierily understood. This understanding may be called straight-knowledge, but its origin may be called the language of Fire. We receive, as it were, a radiogram from the Subtle World, but from its higher, fiery spheres. The Fiery World is primarily within us, if only we discern its abode! Thus, when one doubts whether communion with the Fiery World is possible, one should remember its presence everywhere. However, a current must be established through the heart and not the brain. One can find contact with the Subtle World continuously, but the Fiery World requires an especially good frame of mind. Verbal husks will alienate rather than bring us closer to the Fiery World.

355. Rhythm or melody? Correctly speaking, it is rhythm which creates vibrations. As you know, the music of the spheres consists primarily of rhythm. The Fire is in the rhythm, but not in the context of the melody. Of course there may be happy coincidences when melody becomes rhythm. One should thoroughly understand the connection between rhythm and Fire.

356. Doubt is the main entrance for the dark ones. When doubt begins to stir, the Fire becomes low; and the front door swings wide open for the black whisperer. One must augment harmony and find joy even in a hen laying an egg. Thus, in great and small, we outdo the enemy.

357. There are many who would like to ask certain questions but are embarrassed. For example, they would greatly like to know if, on approaching the Fiery World, their health will suffer. In answer one may recall a philanthropist who discontinued his almsgiving for fear of infection from contact with the poor. Of course he was not a true philanthropist. Likewise,

he who fears the Fiery World is no Fire-bearer. Hence, let us regard the Fiery World as something primordial, inalienable, manifest in courage and joy of heart.

**358.** Pythagoras forbade all raillery among his disciples, because it, above everything, disturbs solemnity. He who greets the sun with a hymn does not notice the small spots. In this command is contained the affirmation of the Beautiful. Let the dark ones retain for themselves the fate of mockery. Those who need jesters will leave no memory of themselves among the wise. His insistence on the solemnity of hymns reveals Pythagoras as a Fire-bearer. Let us take an example from such Fire-bearers, who have traversed their assigned earthly path in beauty.

**359.** They will say, to quarrel is forbidden; to deride is forbidden; to betray is forbidden; to slander is forbidden; to strike another is forbidden; to be arrogant is forbidden; to serve one's selfishness is forbidden; to exercise prerogatives is forbidden—what kind of life is this? Let us add—to leave dirt behind one is also forbidden; for each one who leaves dirt behind will have to carry it out himself.

**360.** And still another question secretly troubles certain people. They want to know whether the Teaching hinders the reading of the Sacred Books? There is no need for concern. We especially advise the attentive reading of these Scriptures. We constantly direct the attention of people to the need of familiarizing themselves with Books of Genesis. Is not the Fiery World mentioned therein? Mentioned so beautifully and concisely—"We shall not die, but change" and "As in heaven, so on earth." Such principles could only be pronounced by an Initiate. These Sacred Books can provide a wealth of information about the manifestations of Fire. Hence, one should urge the assiduous reading of these Scriptures. So, too, the chronicles of the lives of the saints can bring an understanding of the Fiery World. The affirmation of these manifestations after many centuries must inspire the questing scientists. I repeat, it is sad to observe the separation of science from the highest foundations of Existence. In connection with history, at least, scientists are duty-bound to pay attention and respect to the Tablets of the past. Yet, not only scientists but even artists nurtured upon imagination avoid concentrating on the treasures of the Scriptures. As if such knowledge were inferior to other knowledge! But one thing is amazing—that those who question Us about the Sacred Books find no time to read them despite Our advice. He who is aflame in heart will not tarry because of an unsolved question.

361. Those who plan their diet for a long time ahead act unwisely. Being fuel, food should be determined primarily by requirements. But these requirements are manifested in accordance with cosmic currents. The manifestation of certain cosmic currents may almost eliminate the need of filling the stomach, or the contrary. During a tension of the currents food is especially harmful. It can cause illnesses of the liver and kidneys, and intestinal cramps.

362. You have read about the epidemic of hearing voices. The organism acts like a radio receiver. Such acute sensitivity could have been of use, but the trouble is that while certain precise cosmic dates draw near, human consciousness lags far behind. Therefore, instead of a beneficial result, there is a harmful one, contributing to obsession. Many such abnormalities occur also in other domains when the consciousness, strangled by mechanization, drowns in madness.

363. During a difficult period, a solemn attitude

is essential. One should not think that if one remains alive, the period has not affected him. One should be far-sighted.

**364**. One should discern which qualities become more pronounced through realization of the Fiery World. Among these, justice is especially evident. It is impossible in words to convey this quality, which, when straight-knowledge is evidenced, is regarded as the greatest. Beyond earthly laws, the just ones know where the truth is. The law leads to many injustices, but he who is conscious of the Fiery World knows where the truth lies; in spite of the obvious he senses reality. Thus, the fiery consciousness transforms life. Fiery martyrdom also bestows the higher knowledge. So, too, we can discern other qualities of the spirit which grow under the fiery shower. Moderation without Fire becomes mediocrity, but the Golden Path intensified by Fire is the best exemplification of moderation. Similarly, courage without Fire becomes recklessness, but courage resplendent with the fires of the heart becomes an impregnable wall. Indeed, patience, compassion, and friendship will take on different colors in the fiery Light. But only according to action, and through testing, can the Teacher ascertain the degree of fieriness. Words are the least suitable for such assurances. How many words cleanse the thresholds of prisons, but few are the jailers who can boast of being just. Also, how many words there are about patience! Yet the first failure produces the most intolerant cannibals. Of course, one need not explain how verbal courage turns into great cowardice. But he who wishes to approach the Fire must watch all his motives.

**365**. Mountains of scientific deductions are piling up, yet it is difficult to find people who are not shackled thereby. The Greek philosophers knew these

147

shackled souls. They understood how limitedly man can act when he has been left on a small bit of ground. He is like a stork on one leg! Such conflicts would be difficult for a stork, who knows his nest in a certain tree and stands on one leg. But the knowledge of Fire demands two legs, in other words, two natures.

**366.** I have a long list of people who are harming themselves. How can one draw their attention to all the rejected opportunities? The least rejection can generate enormous consequences. The time will come when the list will be disclosed, and the astonishment will be great.

**367.** One should remember about harmful objects. People are sometimes willing to acknowledge a certain significance in teraphim fashioned for the purpose of influencing people. But, after all, many objects carry upon them accumulations of influences. Not rare are the objects made in an hour of hatred, fatigue, terror, or despair; they will carry these sendings with them into the world. And if they fall into the hands of an owner who is under the same astrochemical conditions, they will act in accordance with the message with which they have been suffused. Sociologists are trying to improve working conditions. This is right, but in addition the spiritual level of the workers should be raised. It does not matter whether they create great things or small, the poisonous saliva can saturate them equally. For natural magnetism there is no need of special black magic. Black fire fills every evil heart, therefore let us be very observant in regard to objects. One may recall that Apollonius of Tyana never touched objects that were unfamiliar to him. First he looked at them carefully, especially when they were ancient. When one of his disciples wanted to put a ring on his finger, the Teacher warned him against touching poison. A deadly poison was discovered concealed in the ring. And Apollonius added, "Such poison is less deadly than the poison of the heart." One should not regard the sayings of the sages as remote symbols. Often they have a literal meaning, which must be remembered and applied. We do not go to a shop to purchase clothing infected with smallpox; yet this infection will be only a one-thousandth part of the contagion present. How often have I stated that the accumulations of thought are far more virulent than poisons! Just as fire deposits a patina upon a vessel, so is the fire of thought irremovable when it saturates the surface of an object. Among purifiers eucalyptus is useful, for it contains much fire. All living fire is also useful. Much infection has been destroyed around bonfires.

**368**. Why, even in the Subtle World, do many perceive so little of the Fiery World? Their eyes are poorly adjusted. During the periods of earthly incarnation they paid no heed to the Fiery World; they derided it; they denied all the higher fires; they refused it recognition and were ashamed of every thought about the fundamentals of Existence. With such denial they crossed over into the Subtle World. Could their eyes perceive a radiance which does not exist for their consciousness? Each receives in accordance with his merits. And these merits are not difficult to attain, if only they would not be blocked by negation. The Subtle World grants its gifts in accordance with the consciousness. But if the snout is bent groundward, will not a boar be the next attainment?

**369**. You explained quite correctly the curing of the case of tuberculosis, known to you. In fact, many cases of disease, especially among women, come from the kindling of the centers. But this conflagration can be quenched by giving a useful direction to the

consciousness. It is possible that the fiery consciousness had been knocking for a long time, but the sparks
of Fohat penetrated the region of the Chalice without
being utilized. It is in this way that the conflagration
starts, and tuberculosis is the most common result
of unassimilated Fire. To assimilate in consciousness
means also to assimilate physically. This connection of
consciousness with the body is especially noticeable
in the example of Fire, which causes a quite apparent
physical deterioration if the Fire is not realized. Therefore, during illness, especially catarrhal ones, it is useful to perform a fiery pranayama. This pranayama is
very simple—the usual inhaling through the nose and
exhaling through the mouth while directing the prana
to the seat of the disease. But for intensification of the
action one should keep in mind that the Fire of Space
is being inhaled and the consumed Ur, exhaled. Thus,
Fire is again the remedy, and the physician can alleviate the condition of the patient by assuring him of
how easy it is to attract the basic energy. Fortunately,
sickness strengthens one's attitude toward faith, and a
seriously ill patient will accept the reality of Fire more
readily.

**370.** The state of sickness increases the work of
the spirit. The physician can successfully advise many
things that will provide a beneficial course for the ailment and strengthen the consciousness of spirit. It is
very important to strengthen a certain state of spirit.
To this end, during rituals and incantations certain
vociferations were used to accentuate, as it were, the
moment of the descent of power.

**371.** The intensified assimilation of fires demands
a certain tranquility. It is impossible to absorb the
higher energy while atop a volcano. Therefore it is

necessary to affirm in the words of Solomon, "And this too shall pass!"

372. The epidemic of tetanus belongs to the fiery illnesses. It can be asserted that such an epidemic can spread as widely as cancer. The condition may be alleviated by mountain air, but the chief requirement will be the assimilation of the fiery energy. Any shock can cause either cancer or tetanus; this indicates that the organism may be fundamentally unbalanced, so that even the slightest shock induces disease by opening all entrances. He who spoke of the treasure of consciousness was a great physician. One should urgently introduce fiery prophylaxis. Today you have heard of cancer, tomorrow perhaps of tetanus, the day after, cramps of the larynx, then bubonic plague, after that a new brain disease; thus a veritable chorus of terrors will thunder out, while people ponder about the cause. Of course, they would rather ascribe it to gasoline than to the action of Fire, which is neither understood nor accepted by them.

373. The fiery understanding of obsession is called "Urumiya." Man is not the only one to possess this straight-knowledge; certain animals close to man sense this dreadful state. Horses and dogs in particular sense and resent the proximity of obsessed persons. In ancient China there was a special breed of dogs, highly prized, which was very sensitive and useful in detecting the obsessed. In ancient times it was also a custom to exhibit the horses and dogs before guests, observing at the same time the reaction of the animals. Many envoys were put through this test. One should observe that cats also sense obsession, but usually quite inversely. Obsession induces happiness in them. For example, when a cat senses an obsessed person or his impelling presence, it does not hide, but walks around

mewing happily, whereas a dog bristles up and either tries to hide or to attack such a person. One ought to develop Urumiya in oneself, not only for protection but also for the purpose of expelling the obsessor. Very often a single conversation about the significance of Agni begins to act upon the obsessor. Fearing fire, the very mention of the fiery energy angers him and forces him to retreat.

374. Urumiya also relates to the science of Fire. The mastery of directing Fire lies not in the field of mechanics but in the realization of higher energy, acquired through experience in the Subtle World. A new arrow will not fly by verbal command; fire is needed, for which space does not exist. True, even powerful arrows can be repelled by the black fire when there is a coincidence of actions. Then it is better to wait or defend oneself.

375. The seed of the spirit and the divisibility of spirit provide the explanation regarding the monad. The seed of the spirit is indispensable to life. The divisibility of spirit makes possible both the enrichment and the dissipation of the monad. One can consciously divide one's spirit for the good of the world and send forth its separate parts for achievement. From this, only enrichment results. But ignorance may dissipate the treasure and remain, together with a dormant seed. From this, soullessness results. Actually, the parts of the spirit dissipated in ignorance may become obsessing agents, and then, woe to the sleeping heart! Thus, in order to avoid returning again to the divisibility of spirit, let us remember that the seed of the spirit can sleep or can be radiant in vigilance. Only by this light is the magnet of the heart created, which attracts to its bosom the released parts of spirit. There is a vast difference between setting free and losing. Thus, one

can remember that the slumbering seed of the spirit, though it maintains life, admits all the qualities of soullessness.

376. Also, let us make an end to the confused conception of a group soul. The spirit of concordance is expressed with especial force in animals before individuality has been actualized. But it is incorrect to call the concordant soul a group soul. Translations and commentaries have produced this confusion. Plato's conception of twin souls not only was closer to the truth but was expressed beautifully. Thus, let us not use this erroneous term *group soul*; let us replace it with the term *spiritual concordance*. Also among men such concordance is a valuable achievement; it builds individuality. Let us not complicate what can be readily understood. Before a long journey it is necessary to provide oneself with only the most essential. It would be unfortunate to load oneself with elaborate laces and forget the key to the gates of our Father's house. Our Father is not in need of laces and furbelows. Remember the simplest paths of the Light of Agni. Of course, read books, for one should know the paths of former thoughts, but for the future provide yourself with the lamp of Agni.

377. The tensions are many, and one can learn to rejoice at achievement. Achievement is impossible in a state of depression. Depression is death, like a purse full of holes! Through depression the most precious spills out, and it is therefore correct to call depression "death." As a man arises from sleep for labor, so does he open the door to achievement. We must light the fires with special brightness when we walk toward victory. Remember this especially in the days of oppression. It is nothing other than the bowstring for the arrow.

378. The pure heart senses where there is tension,

and will succeed in surmounting oppression and the enemies.

**379**. One should speak about the Fiery World even to very young children. But first one should tell them that a void does not exist and that there is no loneliness. Thus one can approach the subject of Protector and Guide. Children will become accustomed to the thought that nothing is secret. Such a foundation will provide them with a real protection against fear. It is especially harmful when parents, in ignorance, try to convince the child not to be afraid because nothing is there. Such a seed of negation can cloud the child's entire life and break down its consciousness. The child is fully aware that everywhere something exists. It sees many images, even fiery ones. It is visited by unknown children, who come to play, and adults. Ignorant physicians will try to drown this perceptivity in bromides—like binding wings with lead. But poisons will not help! Only a sensible explanation of reality will bring health to children. One should listen equally attentively to each fragment of truth. The lama says, "One should pray each day, otherwise it is better not to pray at all." And fundamentally you know that this is so. Actually, one should preserve the higher vibrations, while not losing the connecting rhythm. You know the value of constant rhythmic work. You know to what an extent such great exertion opens the Gates.

**380**. Since Hatha Yoga demands certain bodily exercises, the question may be raised as to whether such exercises are also needed for other Yogas? Neither Arhats nor Great Spiritual Toilers practiced these. Verily, theirs are the trials of the spirit, which not only subdue the body but take the place of all exercises of the flesh. Only the avowal of spirit can replace all else.

**381**. Among the minor narcotics beware especially

of bromine. It is an extinguisher of the fires, yet is very often used in various compounds. Valerian, on the other hand, kindles the fires. Treatment with narcotics is like curing by use of snake venom. The Atlanteans used snake venom, but one can imagine of course how often such treatment was fatal. For public health one must take care that foods should not be contaminated. Over-fermented cheese and other foodstuffs filled with the poison of decomposition must not be used. Fire requires pure fuel.

**382**. I do not hide the fact that the pressure is great. One may remain silent about it, but it is better for the already tempered spirit to be aware and to send forth thoughts for the Good. Worthless is the sophistry that is satisfied in uttering, "My small thoughts are useless." Every thought is needed, if it is a thought.

**383**. It is difficult to dissociate within oneself the three fundamental principles. Of course, the fiery fragments can be disconnected. Should this be so? Only submergence into the darkness of chaos pushes aside the entire Fiery Image. Thought about the three principles can enrich one's conception of the three vehicles, but it is one thing to begin to think and quite another to continue and to develop one's thinking. The cosmic aspect of Being would seem a simple thought, yet what assiduous and consecutive effort must be applied to give it beauty. In connection with guidance you can notice one and the same condition in every case. It is not sufficient to direct the pupil, one must lead him to an attainment. Even within a household can one be certain that an errand will be executed thoroughly? How often a man goes to make a purchase and returns with his pockets unexpectedly empty! You already have seen many who, after starting out judiciously, turn away from the path and set fire to all their acquisitions.

The harm of such burnings is great, not only for oneself but for those linked to one by karma. One can imagine how dreadful it is to renounce an already assimilated grain of Truth! Such a destructive rending results usually from chaotic thinking. Such co-workers are useless even for market errands—setting out to buy a turban they surprisingly can buy a single slipper. Therefore, only right and unwavering thinking can overpower the darkness of chaos.

**384**. Let each wavering put us to shame! How dangerous it is to stumble when one is carrying fire!

**385**. An aviator, having attained a record altitude, is still filled with dissatisfaction. He then resolves to try for greater heights. Dissatisfaction is the gateway to Infinity. Dissatisfaction should be valued to the full extent. Pleasure is neighbor to contentment, whereas joy is wings to Infinity. The fiery Teaching must preserve each kindling of the fires and guard against all extinguishers. Satisfaction is the sign of mediocrity and ignorance. Not satisfaction, but joy in eternal labor is the destiny of the great and ascending one. Nowadays fools may laugh when We speak of eternal ascent. Even the grave will not spare the fool from Eternity. Only a puerile brain could fail to understand that the earthly garment is not consummation. The fires summon to the uncognized, and even the blind see these lights. Do not fail to ask the blind about the fires. Some of them see fiery signs and understand their connection with the heart. Thus, the calls of dissatisfaction lead to the Fiery World.

**386**. Among the prophylactics against cancer and other fiery ailments one may advise valerian. I often speak of this tonic and preventive remedy, but any prophylaxis must be systematic—every evening without fail, like the daily course of the sun.

**387.** System, rhythm, have a determining significance. In biographies one can perceive how rhythm has strengthened the mind and Fire. In fact, at the present time rhythm is much spoken of, but it is not applied in life. Thinking is very chaotic and life is disorderly. The ancients in their pranayama exercises introduced a certain rhythm, but now everything is permitted, and man is the slave of everything. The Yoga of Fire should be another reminder about the significance of man.

**388.** It is very bad to cross over into the Subtle World filled with the black fires of malice; this results in blindness. Besides blindness, such malice deprives one of means of communication, in other words, of the language of the spirit. When We speak about the inadmissibility of malice, We offer the best advice; for malice is not a human attribute, it is the lowest form of ignorance. Through malice man degrades himself to an animal state, with all its consequences. Therefore, if a man filled with malice passes into the Subtle World, it will be especially difficult for him to rise. If all kinds of passion impede the ascent, malice, like a red-hot iron, burns away all accumulations. The beings in the middle spheres of the Subtle World will not find a way to perform a purification until the self-blinded can find a fragment of broken spiritual consciousness. The advice about good will must be repeated often to various people. Let children also hear it.

**389.** Good will is not weak will. Quite often people, having deprived themselves of one attribute, have lost many other needed qualities with it. One should not confound shameful obsolete survivals with valuable achievements. Thus, malice is unworthy, but indignation of spirit is that uprising of elements which is found in the highest Teachings. Spiritual battle has nothing in common with malice. Thus, Light pierces darkness, but not through malice.

**390**. Blindness in the Subtle World is dreadful. Imagine yourself entering a half-darkened house, in the corners of which lurk indistinguishable images, all intermingled, and surrounded by indistinct spots. Even where no particular monsters exist, he who is blind and malicious will see horrible shapes. Actually, instead of Fiery Beings, he will vaguely discern two or three sparks which will have no meaning for him. Thus, one should lift oneself away from earthly concepts up to the far-off worlds.

**391**. People often harm themselves by refusing even to think of the Subtle World, or by believing it to be something inconceivable. One must conceive the Subtle World as the most perfected state of our worthiest feelings. Only thus can one prepare oneself for a better abode in the Subtle World.

**392**. Let us turn once again to the consequences of malice. When a half-blind mole gropes his way about the underground of the Subtle World, he may stumble into discharges of Fohat. These strong discharges, which are like lightning, are very painful. You have seen the electric armor of the spiritual battle. The striving of the psychic energy shakes the entire being. One cannot touch or even approach such a living apparatus. In conformity with such tension the entire surrounding sphere is charged. Destruction and extreme pain will repel each dark one who approaches. Thus, it should be repeated once more that malice plunges one into darkness, and darkness is full of dangerous surprises.

**393**. Sometimes in the hour of danger the Teacher gives protection, taking the danger upon Himself. He covers, as it were, the massed darkness with His hands. At such times one must observe particular caution. A powerful tension is near. During this time it is best to feel a special gratitude to the Teacher. Above all, this feeling, coupled with solemnity, preserves harmony and the right vibration with the Teacher. The shield of Light is not always at one's disposal. The ignorant assume that the world owes them a living, but the rational know how difficult it is to build out of chaos, and so bring their stone for the structure.

**394**. Only the foolish fall into despair. Every hour brings its lesson, and therefore one must be grateful for each experience. Night permits observation of far-off worlds and remote distances. Likewise, each hour of the day is filled with possibilities for observation. One must be grateful for such accumulations. Science seeks a solution in the glands, but does not yet dare to think about the fiery energy.

**395**. One should observe cosmic manifestations in connection with life on Earth. Many analogies will be apparent. I praise those who observe what others overlook. The present time is severe. One can read in various Puranas about dates. If some scientists can calculate eclipses and earthquakes, other scientists can calculate other dates—the transition from Kali Yuga to Satya Yuga has been described with considerable accuracy, and the gravity of the time has been indicated.

**396**. When I indicate the beneficialness of gratitude, I do not mean that someone is in need of it, but that in itself it contains the chemism of bliss. One must analyze the chemism of various emotions; such observations will help in finding psychic energy. Not vitamins so much as the fiery energy must occupy the imagination. The revelation of the essence of human existence cannot be regarded as something occult! One should attract many minds to these researches; they will also observe in passing other useful peculiarities of feelings.

Thus, one should first establish the direction of evolution. There cannot be two directions of progress. There can be but one true direction, and all other efforts will be errant. This should be remembered, because many confuse individuality with the general stimulus of the epoch. If a given epoch must strengthen in the consciousness the power of psychic energy, no machine can screen the imperative advance of the world.

**397**. The ability to discern the true direction is a great and fiery quality. One can understand that such a quality is not easily strengthened. It demands not only discussion but the most attentive study of life. No one believes that one can leap, at one bound, from animal consciousness to straight-knowledge. Animal instinct is the germ of straight-knowledge, but great is the abyss between a dog that senses its master, and a man who is aware of the Fiery World! To sense the Fiery World while in the earthly body is already enlightenment.

**398**. Furthermore, one should understand it broadly when I speak of caution. The most dangerous thing is to strive in only one direction. One may save one's leg but break one's neck. Therefore preconceived judgments are most harmful for striving. People readily follow a preconceived plan and thereby bar themselves from a better destiny.

**399**. Evolution is independent and voluntary, this is a fundamental law. It is not only the basic elements of karma but also the Fiery World which constitute a manifestation of conscious evolution. It is impossible to force people to evolve spiritually. A sleeping heart cannot be forced toward good. One can point out, one can set milestones, but to break the consciousness means to kill the root of the future tree. Millions of years may seem long, but neither years nor centuries exist. People have divided existence into seconds and have drowned themselves in zeros. Therefore the psychology of the Subtle World is so important, since there hours are not needed and only results are important. People are often indignant at the ordainments of the Teaching, exclaiming, "Why does not the book give the final formulas?" But such a demand proves an ignorance of the foundations. The Teaching gives the precise direction and kindles the fires along the entire path of labor. One can proceed by these beacons. One may find solutions already cosmically ripe. One may hear exact hints, but the spirit must by its own will combine them into a mosaic. To affirm the path is the Ordainment of the Great Architect. As in legends, we must put our ears to the ground lest we miss a single step or whisper. Though people read much they apply but little. Yet the dates are so close!

**400**. People do not think about dates, they rely upon the mechanism of a clock. Of course, Cosmos is filled with mechanics, but among prime movers the first place is occupied by Agni.

**401**. He who said that the flashes of light are nothing but directed thoughts was not far from the truth. Indeed, spatial thoughts are like electrical discharges and can produce considerable light effects. Colored sparks also depend upon the quality of energy which evokes these discharges. We can project thoughts which can not only create luminous signs but can also produce bodily sensations. The transmutation of thought into sensation only proves that thought is energy. Thus, one should become accustomed to thought-energy, from early childhood. But for this the school must teach about the substance of spirit. One can observe to what a great extent humanity has departed from spiritual principle in the last few years. Many books that should have directed people precisely toward the spiritual life, on the contrary, failed even to attract people's attention. But it cannot continue thus. By all methods one must remind people of the essence of spirit. The existence of numerous sects is of no help, and leads people into aimless wanderings. The nature of Kali Yuga is characterized by a division of the entire organism into its component parts. But the Blessed Mother arises at dawn in order to gather these scattered parts of the one Being. The Mother of the World attracts the attention of nations and awaits the Star of the Morning.

**402**. Unexpectedness paralyzes all human senses. Hearing, sight, smell, and also touch are lost. But this is not the result of fear, only of turning away from a preconceived path. Actually, of all the elements fire offers the greatest amount of unexpectedness. People limit their consciousness to merely a few formulas of Agni. Therefore, all other varieties of the element of fire are simply not contained in the consciousness. This means that there is much still to be assimilated, and the unexpected can thus be turned into the expected. One should also deal similarly with hitherto unfamiliar manifestations of life. One should arm oneself spiritually in order that nothing in the Subtle World may surprise one. Many hope to meet relatives and a Guide; even films, devoid of spirit, have disclosed impressions of such meetings more than once. But in all worlds it is best to rely upon one's own consciousness and strength. Therefore one should eliminate every possibility of shocking the narrow consciousness. One must free oneself from being shocked by the unexpected. There are numerous unexpected concepts, forms, and combinations which make the consciousness shudder, but the more we admit and imagine, the less we are bound. Thus, develop your imagination on a world-wide scope.

People refuse to believe that the unexpected, in other words, ignorance produces a paralysis of the nerves. Though it be ever so brief, such a reaction arrests the work of Fire. Wherever possible, one should accustom oneself to the concept of unexpectedness. This advice should be remembered especially.

**403**. The man who asserts that religion obstructs his understanding slanders religion and thus blasphemes against the spirit. Contentment is no adornment.

**404**. Perhaps the seventh vitamin is Fire. It has often been clearly stated that pure air provides far more essential nourishment than city air. But by purity one should understand a particular fiery saturation. People in the mountains can live longer without food and without needing sleep. The nourishment of spirit, or Agni, can satisfy them without the need of heavy foods. Studies should be made of the nourishment by prana on heights.

**405**. The idea of having at least a half-hour daily for thought is good. I do not mean some special concentration. It is useful to think about the best aspect of everything that is taking place. Even small signs reflecting the best in life afford a glimpse of Light. They also stimulate the flow of gratitude and magnanimity. Such fires are equivalent to a dose of musk. Thought about the best generates aspiring tension of the nerves. The nerves should also be given work, but only Good will strengthen the nerves.

**406**. Magnetization of water has now been virtually abandoned, yet not so long ago it was used for purposes of both light and darkness. The significance of such magnetization is apparent, and indicates once again the fieriness of such a process. As a precautionary measure a goblet containing an unknown beverage was covered with the hand, in the belief that the skin would reflect symptoms of poisonous ingredients. Also, for magnetization, iron and lithium waters were used, but all sulphuric admixtures were avoided. In the most ancient writings there are references to the transmission of thought through water and chrism. Milk was not used for magnetization because of its organic constituents. This was an error, for the milk of healthy cows is well suited for this purpose. But in ancient times people feared rabies and preferred to avoid magnetizing milk.

**407**. The Arhat possesses the ability to prevent his feelings from becoming blunted. This rare ability is acquired by Him only through fiery tension. This may be termed an adamant asceticism. It attracts the hearts of the people. He about whom you recently read knew these intense poignancies of feeling. Everyone who approached Him felt his unfailing freshness of heart. This continuous acuteness is attained not by a special technique, but by a simple opening of the heart. He never pitied himself, and this trait was not an intellectual one, but had become his second nature. Yet, because of the deadening influence of daily routine, how many priests have lost that which they had accumulated! Daily routine is the great testing stone. It opens the Gates of Eternity and affirms Fire.

**408**. The Great Architect builds eternally. It is senseless to suppose that certain parts of the Universe are completed and remain static. A great deal is made of the term *evolution*, but people have absolutely no conception of this process in its actuality. There has been much argument about the social structure, but it always has been presumed that human society exists in something inflexible and finite. The stories of the Deluge and of the glacial period are regarded almost as merely symbolic. And it is not proper even to speak of Atlantis, despite the testimonies of the Greek writers. One can see how the human consciousness evades everything that threatens its established comfort. Likewise, the concept of evolution is turned into an abstraction, thus not disturbing the consciousness of the petrified heart in the least. But does not the heavenly vault evoke thoughts about eternal motion? Only through such evolutionary concepts can one absorb the beauty of the earthly pilgrimage as the sojourn for ascent. The very briefness of the path should not disturb one, on the contrary, it should give one joy, as does the rotation of the sun. It is urgently necessary to expound to what extent evolution is incessantly in the hands of the Great Architect of the Universe. One should feel that the planet is in space, just as seamen know that the vast ocean is beneath their ship. At first seamen are terrified by this suspension over an abyss, but reality and experience accustom them to this truth. Every inhabitant of the planet is on a similar ship— below him is the abyss. The seamen cannot depend entirely upon their ship and scientific calculations, if they could there would be no shipwrecks. Astronomy knows a few heavenly bodies, but it does not know the starting point of the comets, and it does not anticipate the gigantic meteors. Only upon their obvious appearance are people notified. The destruction of entire worlds is sometimes noticed, but more often it occurs without attracting any attention. Astronomy is a night watchman! But what about the events taking place by day? Thus, we observe only approximately half of that which is evident. How much that is unexpected is concealed from the sleeping heart!

**409**. Record all unusual events. Only by such records can one preserve many remarkable manifestations; otherwise they vanish in the dusk of indifference.

What if your most precious biographies had not been set down? Now you would not know them, and many inspirations would not have been kindled in your hearts. Thus, do not be ashamed to write down, however briefly, that which seems to you of special significance. Do not weigh whether it is small or big, but judge it by its unusualness. Indeed, unusualness will yield many observations of the Fiery World. Each spark of it is in itself significant.

**410**. Who can boast that he has attained the full measure of striving? Verily, no such madman exists. Each heart understands where the benign path of fiery acceleration lies. The blessed striving must be frequently called to mind in a human way. How beautiful it is to be constantly aflame! There is no dungeon such that the fire of the heart cannot illumine it. Thus, be aflame with beauty!

**411**. The language of the spirit is essential for the Subtle World. Its essence lies in the subtle nature, but it is possible to become accustomed to it even while in the earthly state. Such orientation is a useful fiery test. The school must discover the resourcefulness of pupils by a test of giving one word, and later on comes the task of understanding at one glance. The latter experiment will be closest to the Subtle World. In addition one can develop a sense of relativity by addressing one's interlocutor according to his nature. Thus, in an earthly conversation each one adopts the best language for his companion, taking into consideration his state of consciousness. Every schoolteacher knows how multiform must be his language in order to make friends of his pupils. But besides the school, in any home one learns to discern the thoughts of the mistress of the house. Thus, in the midst of daily life, characteristics of a subtle order are manifested. One has only to take note of them, to penetrate into them, and to expand these observations. But for this, one should be imbued with reverence for the future and learn to love the principal factor of the Subtle World—Agni. I insist on the expression, "to love fierily," only thus can one assimilate this element which is so difficult for Earth. Our discourses should first of all lead to an understanding of the Subtle World and, as its apotheosis, bring one fearlessly to the radiance of the Fiery World. We rejoice when, amidst the earthly sojourn, the dimensions of the Subtle World are established. Through this, we bring Earth to a closer cooperation with the far-off worlds, in other words, we participate in the process of evolution.

**412**. Nowadays negations are the order of the day; yet no one will cross into the Subtle World without fear, unless he purifies himself by bathing in the sphere of straight-knowledge. Not long ago such a way of thinking would have been called poetic and no one would have paid any attention to it. But now it is already understood that the formula of synthesis will be of great help. At a time of hasty departure the farewell to travelers consists of one most urgent word; therefore, We send the word—Agni.

**413**. Thoughts are like mushrooms in the forest; they must be gathered. When one goes for mushrooms, one does not look for nuts. Thus, at each hour one must know what is most immediate. Let us assimilate varied manifestations, but let us remember the immediate and find the short path to it. This will be Adamant.

**414**. I affirm that at present one should gather all one's strength and courage. Throughout the entire world the forces of darkness are attacking. Is it possible that the good forces will be found fighting among themselves? The manifestation of heartache actually arises from the thoughts being sent. The physician may call it spasms of the aorta, without taking into account certain important external causes. Can one see only the effects without discerning their causes?

**415**. Truly it is difficult to understand why persons serving the same goal disparage each other. Straight-knowledge, even in a small degree, should be developed. But mutual disparagement is one of the most shameful sins. I know of no better definition of it than sin, so destructive is the work of mutual annihilation. This can be explained as a certain aspect of obsession, but shame to those who, after having approached the knowledge of the fundamental principles, stoop to such a base state. Let the belittling and the destroying ones ponder upon their own consciousness. They are far from the fires of the heart.

**416**. "Be silent, O strings, that a new melody may come to me," says a hymn of the Greek Mysteries. Such rebirth of spiritual harmony is not a "void," as it is sometimes called. To open the heart does not mean to devastate it; on the contrary, when the last reverberation of the chord dies out, let the striving of the spirit immediately become more acute, in order to reach a more exalted harmony.

**417**. One should often evaluate quietude, which can fortify the fires. One can imagine an astral whirlwind that can shake even the staunchest flame. This agitation does not come from within the flame itself, but from without. Hence, we must be very cautious, for the pressure is great.

**418**. People often experience an unexplainable state of exultation or depression. They attribute this to their stomachs rather than to the approach of good or dark forces. Yet these manifestations occur frequently and can be intense. People often experience a touch or pricks. They ascribe such manifestations to cobwebs or dust, but it never occurs to them that the entities of the Subtle World may thus contact them. Similarly, people often hear movements and rustling, but they think of mice or centipedes in order to drive away all thought about manifestations of a distant world. The same people will complain that the Subtle World does not manifest itself. But subtle movements are not like blows of a hammer! As with everything else, the approach of the Subtle World should be acknowledged and fearlessly studied. We must not condemn that to which we did not even give attention. Yet if some people are so fortunate as to behold a Fiery Being, they will think first of all about a demon. Such is the corruption of the contemporary consciousness! Such crass ignorance is called skepticism, critical judgment, or erudition, when it would be far more accurate to call it plain stupidity.

**419**. The spiritualization of thought is a true fiery quality. It is like the tempering of the blade in preparation for battle. It is one thing to have a fleeting thought, which, however useful, only skims over the consciousness and is quickly dispersed in space. But it is of much deeper significance when the thought is firmly enveloped in the heart. One can regard this process even from the physical point of view alone. Therefore it is useful at the inception of a thought to give oneself the following command, "I will place this thought upon my heart!" This advice will give much discipline to the thinking beginner. Moreover, whatever is consciously deposited in the heart remains in the Chalice.

**420**. Sparks and other manifestations of light produce much of the connective tissue with the Subtle World. One can even notice streams of sparks issuing from the mouth and eyes when the fiery tension is strong. It can be asked whether these are electrical phenomena. In answer one must say they are rather phenomena of Fohat, which are related to the energy of the Fiery World. Thus, those who have eyes and ears not clogged with the dross of ignorance can observe much not only of the Subtle but also of the Fiery World. One must not, in self-depreciation, think that for us on Earth the Fiery World is inaccessible. Teachings relate that certain persons of no especial learning instantaneously and directly approached the most Fiery Summits. Every religion speaks of such assertions.

**421**. Vows of the most diverse nature have been sanctioned by various teachings. Each vow is quite useful from the standpoint of discipline. It is difficult for people to believe how necessary for future achievements are such exercises of discipline. A vow cuts short many paths of dissoluteness. Indiscriminating and irresponsible dissoluteness results in the most deplorable consequences in the Subtle World. It is like a child's playing with fire. One should keep constantly in mind the danger of dissoluteness. In the Subtle World it is difficult and painful to begin tardily ridding oneself of dissoluteness. It is better to test oneself here by various useful vows. People often find themselves in ridiculous situations when they take vows zealously only in time of danger. The ancients showed a better understanding of this in their vows in the Name of the Most High, thus strengthening their exalted and solemn state of mind. This was not superstition or bargaining with the Higher Forces, but the transport of a spirit which had attained a new freedom.

**422**. You were right in recalling the useful Burmese custom of reminding those who are seriously ill or dying of their best deeds. Even from a medical point of view such reminders undoubtedly are beneficial. As to the spiritual side, they of course prove how many wise customs still exist among the most diverse nations. These customs are born of a profound knowledge. They prove the connection with the present world, vitally indicating how attentively one should regard the customs of nations.

**423**. Equally wise reminders can be found in songs. The Koreans sing about three travelers who beheld heaven. One saw it as granular, the second saw it as if in drops, and the third beheld it aflame. But the first had dust in his eyes, the second had caught a chill, and the third had a bright and warm night's lodging. Thus did people understand the three essences and wisely characterized them. One traveler was not afraid of the Fiery Heaven, and Fire guarded him amidst the darkness.

Earthly fetters obscure the eyes, and the Subtle World makes a wayfarer tremble if he has not cognized Fire.

**424**. A man ought not think that nothing has occurred anywhere during the day just because nothing has happened to him. On the contrary, when the constellations are adverse, scorpions may emerge from unsuspected holes. A tiger may roar, but scorpions can sting silently. Let us gather in thought around the Teacher.

**425**. One should direct one's entire consciousness into the future. It is seldom that one finds within oneself the courage to admit the undesirability of turning back to the past. The evidence of daring yearning for the future indicates that the spirit is ready for fiery cognitions. Only such an enlightened consciousness will continue its thought-creativeness also in the Subtle World. Only such irrepressible thought-creativeness and striving for distant flights will afford the fiery approach. All the terror of the legions of darkness cannot overcome an intense striving to the future. Though the dark ones approach, Light will not lose its guiding power. So, also, useful deeds are necessary to help our near ones. One should not consider these beneficent counsels as moral precepts beyond the pale of life. They sustain us, directing us along the shorter paths.

**426**. The ability to draw a circle around the area covered by the dark and crawling ones can help in affirming one's dauntless outlook. One can stave off the approach of the dark ones by repeating My Name as a Mantram. Thus, we can understand why humanity is responsible for uttered words. If the utterance of a benign concept results in a calm state, the opposite will irritate, worry, and demean that which exists. People saturate the world with the most malicious words; will not rivers of evil flow from them? One must have lost respect for human dignity not to acknowledge that the consequences of evil speech are terrible. It is said continuously that malevolence bears fruit after a century. The historian can verify the harvest from such black seeds.

**427**. Not many aspire to Our conscious life, but fortunately the minority creates. Hence, Our Abode will not be disturbed by crowds of dark ones. They will say that they have had no instruction, but none of them have any desire to study, even if it takes only seven years. People are loath to face long periods, because they do not know how to think about Infinity.

**428**. Slander is especially harmful for the slanderers themselves. This truth should be remembered by people who have bad habits. A thought corresponding to reality forms a vehicle for an elemental. Everything worthy, austere, vital, gravitates toward creative thought, and will beneficently sustain its creator. But the devices of slander will attract brooding elementals, who, failing to find a vital foundation, will precipitate themselves upon the slanderer. Therefore, when I warn people not to succumb to the vileness of slander, again I do not advance a moral precept but point to very painful consequences. It is most disagreeable to find oneself in the Subtle World in the midst of raging elementals. Terrible is such a maelstrom filled with the fragments of one's own malicious thoughts. All these creatures clutch at one and hang on, acquiring an actual physical weight. Thoughts, like drops of energy, attract small elementals. The character of these germs of the spirit is most varied: depending upon their substance, almost imperceptible embryos can achieve, under the nurture of thought, diverse manifestations. They can form the basis of minerals and even of plants. But one can imagine quite clearly how those thoughts that are void of any vital bases litter the lower strata of Earth. Meteoric dust is imperceptible to the eye, but it results in very substantial sediments. Hence, one can imagine how vast the dust of thought is and, being the effect of energy, how very substantial! The consequences of this debris of thought cause the illness of the planet.

Sowers of evil and slander, can you realize what a suffocating dungeon you prepare for yourselves? Evil thoughts will find their sire. Such a dark sire cannot escape from his own engenderings. Despite everything, someone will probably think this an invented scarecrow rather than acknowledge that thought is eternal energy.

**429.** Mind has been symbolized by the sign of Fire. Fiery thinking is the descent of knowledge from the Fiery World. Such a descent marked the great epochs, called the Days of the Mother of the World. Even in the history of Earth, one can trace several such epochs. Will not the future bring such a Day of Light if people shall realize the uselessness of evil?

**430.** The inhalation of fire is practiced by certain yogis and is a purifying action. One should not understand this literally. One cannot inhale flames, but fiery emanations are useful. For such inhalation, the yogi chooses a quiet place, keeping his spine erect. Before him the yogi makes a fire of deodar wood, or, if deodar is unavailable, twigs of balu, so arranged that the smoke does not reach him. Then the yogi performs the usual pranayama, but in such a way that the emanations of the resin reach his breathing. There are two results—first, a purification of the body; second, the strengthening of the Agni energy. Nothing so helps the kindling of Agni as the properties of deodar. As you know, insects cannot endure the strength of deodar resin. You also know that imperfect entities cannot approach a fire of this wood. Usually, deodars prefer a volcanic soil to grow in; in this way a significant kinship is manifested. Volcanic soil in general merits study, along with its vegetation. Not only has the inhalation of fire been practiced by the yogis but also lying on deodar planks so that the spine comes in contact with the heart of the wood. Various records of antiquity indicate how ardently people have sought the fiery element. Experiments are necessary in order to understand the value of deodar. The significance of Fire should be remembered in order to understand volcanic soil.

In the south of India sandalwood has also been used for fiery inhalation.

**431.** It can be observed that the manifestations of the Subtle and Fiery Worlds are unexpected. What, then, does it mean that by expectation we often, as it were, impede a manifestation? By this is proved the difference between physical and fiery energies. Physical energies often underlie so-called expectations.

They begin to fall into forced ideas, and thus, instead of helping, obstruct the subtle approach. Through their effort of expectation people unconsciously begin to prescribe even the form and place of the vision, and thus harmful cross-currents are bound to result.

**432.** It may also be asked, Why do visions coincide with special moments of life? Is this the result of a Guidance that is aware of the approach of the crucial hour, or is it due to an exalted spiritual attitude, which permits one to see what otherwise would remain unseen? It is both. But besides our own state of consciousness, certain cosmic currents approach which transform the earthly strata. Undoubtedly, not only astral chemisms act upon us but also certain higher energy, the origin of which is infinite. Neti, Neti, the Ineffable, guides us, and often we are touched by the Highest Power.

**433.** How is it possible to ascertain the verity of the Teaching? A multitude of good words may cover up something mediocre; but Truth, we know, does not fear examination. On the contrary, when observed, Truth draws nearer and shines forth. Therefore, each investigator of the Teaching may be advised, "Approach with all force; observe by thorough measures; investigate by all methods; cognize with all daring; reveal indefatigability, and be aflame with each discovery of Truth." The Teaching cannot be fallible. It cannot deviate from the paths of usefulness and good. One should not believe only in assertions. Faith is the realization of Truth, tempered in the fire of the heart. The Teaching is infinite, otherwise the very concept of Infinity would not exist. One should strive toward Truth. Truth does not reject—it directs. In the Teaching there can be no distorted concepts. Regard the path of the Teaching as the affirmation of that which is beyond doubt. One should not approach Truth along a meandering path. One must proceed by testing each word, each statement, and each dictate. If the Teaching is a true one, each step to it will be enlightening and broadening. Disparagement, denial, abasement are poor guides! More than once you will hear from a speaker the conceited remark that the only correct Teaching is the one known to him. It is then good to remind the conceited one about the grandeur of Infinity, of the millions of years of life on Earth, of the billions of worlds—let him meditate upon the vastness of Truth and the soundness of its fitting recognition. One could agree with the method of skepticism if only something would result from it. As a rule it corrodes the creative principle. An indefatigable spirit is needed to advance along a constant progression. Only such expansion and containment will bring real tolerance toward anything that is futile, this is learned through relativism. Thus, say to him who has doubts about the Teaching, "Test it, be aflame in your heart, and broaden your spirit!"

**434.** The realization of the Teaching as a necklace of Light provides a precious thread upward. Let the billions of worlds stay the disconcerted from the danger of rejection.

**435.** Falsehood and darkness fill the end of Kali Yuga. One must realize this in order not to lose one's strength. It is impossible to avoid the dark days, and only a knowledge of their cause will give one the patience to survive them. People do not want to simplify the path to Truth; and encumbrances like technocracy only serve to reveal the dark chains of lower matter. Blasphemies, in all their virulence, also reveal the darkness of negation in contrast to the realization of Light. You can read about these signs in the Puranas, therefore the fulfillment of all the other predictions can be anticipated. We all must now adapt ourselves to the fiery element—this also is affirmed in the Puranas. I consider that it is time to call people to the understanding of Be-ness.

**436**. Whence come the waves of sudden joy or anguish? They are regarded as unfounded, whereas causes underlie everything. I advise you to record such waves, which otherwise might be forgotten. With each move every man produces a significant experiment, yet he lightly rejects these flashes of cognition. Joy and anguish are not without cause, and records of these moods will remind one when earthly communications bring confirmation of them. The fiery mail is confirmed by earthly messages. Of course, many causes, not only earthly but also from the Subtle World, may not reach us, but still one can perceive significant coordination between events and feelings. Thus, experiences are accumulated which constitute a convincing whole. Verily, man's greatest experiments were performed in the laboratories of life!

**437**. Let us write down, and tell the physician, about obsession. Indeed, there may be cases where the obsessor gains such control over the body of the obsessed as almost to dislodge him. One can also encounter cases where the obsessor is so empowered by the vital force of the obsessed that the expulsion of the obsessor will cause death. He has so usurped the psychic energy of the obsessed that the latter loses his vitality upon separation. Therefore expulsion must always be carried out most cautiously. At first one watches the diet of the patient and observes his psychic energy. If a decline of vitality is noticed the weakened heart must not be strained. Expulsion is generally easiest during an attack of fury. The aroused energy helps to overcome the possible decline of heart action, which might otherwise end in complete prostration.

**438.** As with everything, fiery self-disinfection is the best prophylaxis. Precisely Fire protects against obsession. Precisely Agni is the panacea for cancer, tuberculosis, and all other diseases. But until people assimilate the significance of Agni, one must have recourse to vegetable and mineral expedients. The simplest, most natural, and most essential property of everyone seems to be the most neglected. You know to what an extent those who remembered about psychic energy escaped many illnesses. You saw it and became convinced. During the approach of fiery energies it is necessary that people be not ashamed to acknowledge the fiery principle in themselves. This will be the cultivation of Agni.

**439.** It is even impossible to imagine humanity's future direction if it does not purify itself through Fire! Striving toward the Fiery World will afford the first glimpses of Agni. Many ignominious actions will fall away like husks, at a single thought about the Fiery World. No sermons from without can enable one to attain that improvement of health which is created by a single spark from within. But it is difficult to impel the consciousness according to a higher measure. We will tirelessly urge the consciousness toward this first gleam of enlightenment; what follows will be much easier.

**440.** The bringing of fire is the ancient symbol of the purification of the spirit. The seed of the spirit itself cannot be defiled, but a ship can become covered with barnacles, which hinder its course. The Fiery Mother understands when the necessity of cleaning the seed approaches. The new sowing can be accomplished only with pure seeds. One must help when the time comes for the Sower to go out into the field.

**441.** The final dates are often accompanied by spatial ringing. This ringing proves that the current of energy is like a string that reverberates upon contacting a countercurrent. Indeed, each such ringing indicates tension. During such ringing one should first of all reject all futile thinking, in order the more harmoniously to unite with the guiding current. Perhaps earthly events produce such tension. Perhaps also the events of the Subtle World are approaching, and one must be ready to receive them. But when the ear is open to the ringing of the far-off currents, then the consciousness is also expanded for the appraisal of events. Thus Agni works and transmutes all that exists.

**442.** One of the most difficult qualities is to be able to refrain from divulging that which is not predestined to be divulged, in order to avoid inflicting harm. The example of Aeschylus is instructive. The elements precipitate themselves upon him who forces them out of the state of conformity. It is impossible to save such a light-minded traitor. You know that similar betrayals are committed in small matters as well as great, and many of them not from malice but from thoughtlessness. It does not matter how the cage of a savage beast came to be open.

**443.** The most difficult yet indispensable discipline is comprised in actions for the good of the world. It is not easy to watch oneself in order to reject egoistic thoughts and actions. But when the entire personality is consecrated to the world, discipline is not only easy but is even not felt. To find a starting point for renunciation means to construct a straight path to the Fiery World. The affirmation of personality with all its astrochemical implications is not egoism, which stifles the aspirations toward ascent itself. Egoism is of Earth. It does not exist in the Fiery World. Its remains in the Subtle World are like heavy chains. It is not difficult to perceive how the meaning of egoism ends with the earthly state, it is not applicable to the subtle ascent. Earth-dwellers, finding themselves in the Subtle World, are especially amazed at the absence of egoism in its higher spheres. Nothing so greatly helps to put an end to earthly accounts as the liberation from egoism. Being conscious of the Fiery World reveals in the simplest way how worthless are the tortures engendered by egoism. The Light of the Fiery World acts as a great disinfectant. The crystals of Fohat are so greatly concentrated in this radiance that each approach to this power purifies our psychic energy. I consider that self-discipline directed to the General Good is the most immediate means for great achievements.

**444**. Let the tormentors think that they torture you severely. Let them even revel in these thoughts, but let them at times think what it means to harm their fellow man. It is not easy to free oneself of such millstones about one's neck!

**445**. The Teacher must remember that each one carries his own load. It is impossible to make all equal. One cannot demand the same speed from all, and one must encourage each one who knows how to bear his burden. It is not easy for the Teacher, and no one should think that an Arhat rests. When we approach the preordained dates, is it possible to imagine a pleasant respite in the earthly sense?

**446**. It is correct to surmise that improvement in the chemical influences of the luminaries does not eliminate established causes. Much may have been sown, but lightning does not destroy all the crops. Thus, one should not leave off sowing, nor should one lean too heavily on a staff when walking rapidly. The ability to proceed is a habit retained from former experiences.

447. The chakras, the fiery wheels, call to mind the countless circles of conception and completion. One can picture how the equilibrium of the worlds is founded upon fiery chakras. They contact and interpenetrate each other, and form inseverable links. Similarly, one can imagine how the chakras of man determine his fiery nature and bring the human entity into the totality of other fiery formations. People already have at their disposal rays that are not recorded upon the flesh; so, also, rays will be discovered that can capture the fiery centers on a film. This will demonstrate how the chakras of man correspond to the fiery formations of space. The figure of the fiery man merges into the rhythm of space. Thus, it can be physically demonstrated to what a great extent is everything that exists subject to the one law of rhythm. Of course, to succeed in such instructive experiments it is necessary to develop the fiery chakras in oneself. They exist in every organism, potentially, but soulless beings cannot project on a screen even a faint glimmer from the extinguished fires.

448. One should not think that actions as such are lower than the feeling of love. One should sharply divide rhythmic actions from egoistic actions, which do not respond to the rhythm of Cosmos. Egoism is self-isolation or revolt against cooperation. Even great minds often failed to discern where was the egoism of flesh and where the action of lofty cooperation. How can the chakras glow in the presence of egoism of the flesh?

449. I affirm the futility of communications with the middle spheres of the Subtle World. They only

irritate the entities there by various reminiscences, and the earthly fluids disturb them. Moreover, people learn nothing from them. The rhythm of space is expressed in the higher spheres.

**450.** It is difficult to imagine that the records about the Fiery World can have a place in the midst of such a battle! There is no human imagination that can picture the chaos of the cosmic battle! The continuity of the battle is beyond the strength of human nature. People cannot even grasp consciously how the encounters of such powerful energies are taking place over and above daily life.

**451.** The approach of the fiery and subtle beings is characterized by a tremor of the heart and a sensation of cold or heat. But, then, if we are continually surrounded by beings of the Subtle World, why do we sense them only occasionally? Herein is comprised the law and the quality of thought. If these beings approach us—in other words, think of us—we sense them not only with our fiery centers but even physically. It is customary to speak of the hair standing on end from fright, but this is not fright; it is a particular reaction of energy, somewhat similar to electricity. At the basis of such a feeling also lies thought. Not suggestion, but the qualities of thought give rise to these feelings. Even a physical glance makes a man turn his head. How much more powerfully, then, must the fiery energy of the higher worlds act! It means that there is before us an entire series of useful experiments and observations as to how and on which centers the fiery energy of the Higher World acts. One should note also that a sensation of cold is experienced at times, and likewise one should observe whether a similar sensation is felt near an electrical machine in motion. The study of external reactions to thought must occupy the attention of scientists.

**452.** Not only do thoughts themselves produce physical manifestations but condensation of the energy which is sent produces powerful reactions. You definitely know about the sensations from the manifestation of light. The oppressive feeling from the black stars or the feeling of calmness from the blue ones is quite distinct. You also know that such sensations do not emanate from you, but are received from space. The world of thought is the heritage of the future. Investigations of thought also will lead to psychic energy. One can begin the observations from various points of view. Therefore I direct your attention to different approaches to the same subject of light-bearing thought.

**453.** The Yogi of India says to the scientist studying the question of self-preservation: Truly, it is high time to study the fiery nature of man. It should have been understood long ago that it is not only the will but the fiery energy which surrounds man with a salutary veil. One should indeed study this in laboratories, but such laboratories must be different from those dealing with soil fertilization. It is high time for scientists to realize that for subtle experiments subtle conditions are needed. Likewise, it is time to recognize that these conditions are not created through mechanical disinfection. Each experiment requires fiery spiritual purification. In fact, much may be achieved amidst nature and in temples where the emanations are not so defiled. But in ordinary laboratories, which are not even ventilated, and where the dust is full of poisonous deposits, little can be achieved. Not without reason did healers ask before healing, "Have you faith?" And then the result was especially successful. But not only was the healer evoking faith, the kindling of the fire of the centers was also needed. When the fiery chakras began to rotate, considerable purification took place. Thus, let the physician pay attention not only to the will but also to the basic psycho-fiery energy. Let him remember that the surrounding atmosphere has a tremendous importance. It would seem unfitting to call attention to this, yet after millions of years of earthly existence, people still pay as little attention to the quality of their surroundings as they probably did in the times of the cave dwellers.

**454**. More than once during successful research work progress has been interrupted by petty difficulties. Among these difficulties repugnance, so called, has a special significance. It arises from many conditions, both external and karmic. It is difficult to describe in words this feeling which shuts, as it were, the fiery centers, thus depriving them of power. Undoubtedly repugnance is akin to fear. But for ascent one must overcome repugnance. In ancient Mysteries there was a special ritual for the conquering of repugnance.

**455**. One may stress further that people should not be astonished that they themselves must place the final stone in the mosaic. This law is the more just since usually there is scarcely the desire to set even the first given stones. Much has been given and much is not applied. It has been stated clearly that many mechanical formulas must be reanimated by fiery energy. But, as before, people call this occultism and fear even to think about such experiments.

**456**. Walking on water or sitting upon water, like walking on fire, are remarkable proofs of thought-power. Let us recall, for example, how sitting upon water is achieved. True, the body has to be purified by a strict vegetable diet and a transport of the spirit. But in addition one should know how to swim and to float upon the water, in order the better to protect oneself from the serpent of doubt. Selecting some shallow, quiet waters, the yogi prepares a light wooden support on which he sits, so constructed that the water reaches to his waist. Then he concentrates by means of the rhythm of paranayama and lifts his thought toward the supremely Ineffable. Thus several days can be spent, alternately resting and again drawing near to this spiritual exaltation. And when the thought frees itself from earthly attraction the human body loses its weight. Thus the yogi rises upon the water and the wooden support floats away. But should the thought remain at the original level the position of the body will remain unchanged. In addition one may notice luminous emanations of the body, which, according to an ancient saying, link man to heaven. The only deciding factor in these experiments is the quality of thought. It is impossible for an impious man to sit upon the water, just as immunity from fire cannot be attained without a certain rhythm and exaltation. Who can determine how much time is required for a preliminary discipline of body and spirit sufficient to attain such an apotheosis of thought? It should be said that the degrees of patience, perseverance, and determination vary infinitely, and, besides, certain influences of cosmic conditions are also very necessary. Nor should one laugh on hearing that the conditions are more favorable around full moon.

457. There is a parable about the trial by difficulties, in which it is shown that people always try to choose the easiest way, whereas that which seems easiest turns out to be the most difficult. Examples both amusing and tragic can be cited. It is justly pointed out that the cleverest person may enumerate to himself all

the details of an easy achievement, but forget just the one which turns out to be the most difficult. By body alone we cannot escape fire and water. One should remember about flaming thought.

**458.** If people could only realize how much they lose mentally, when they could be continuously acquiring! But darkness does not permit the imagination to flourish. However, it is difficult to remember about imagination when we are already in the Subtle World. There we must apply it, not generate it.

**459.** It must be understood that every success is based on the quality of thought. One should understand that We can vouch for success when thought flies to Us.

**460.** One should not laugh at the fact that certain yogis make use of a bamboo reed or a roll of papyrus during levitation. Certainly it is possible to achieve similar results without these physical aids. But if someone requires a feather in his hand for levitation let us not deprive him of this small assistance. The essential is not to be found in the feather or in the roll, but in thought, in fiery energy. There are many symbols which can evoke energy, and everyone can look for the nearest conductor. Thus, the gypsies require water or melted wax, but the essence lies in their psychic energy, which is very strong in this race. It is easy to derive instructive observations from them. Unfortunately, one must watch carefully their scrupulousness. Very often the increase of energy, which is an atavistic accumulation, is connected with a mediocre consciousness. But the physician and scientist must investigate all possibilities. Similarly, many northern races can provide interesting material, especially in Norway, Karelia, Scotland, and among the Eskimos. Of course, even primitive glimpses of this energy are useful to the scientist.

**461**. Meteoric microbes should not be surprising. The assertion that life is in everything merely expands the horizon. If a microbe can come flying out of space, then how many other new observations are to expected! The very fieriness of space affords new conclusions about Fire as a vital substance. One must urge the scientists to live in greater harmony, lest precious observations be dispersed through hostility and denial.

**462**. Why is it so difficult to correlate observations from the different fields of science? The time is approaching when complete accord between scientists from the most diverse branches of science will be required. It will be necessary to combine new rediscoveries of ancient cultures with mechanical and physical observations. Skeletons of giants will be found together with objects which will require the most manifold observations. And finally, the ancient knowledge of the firmament will be needed in connection with strange changes on our planet. Sound unity is needed, in order to expand the horizon of new investigators.

**463**. How can one explain the imbalance between heat and cold? One should not fear to speak about the fiery waves; through them one can be reminded of the fiery peril. Many are the current predictions which, coming from entirely different directions, point to the same dates. It is not by accident that strangers begin to repeat the same words. However, one should refrain from fishing in a puddle of denials.

**464**. Torpor, as well as repugnance, must be overcome. Many fail to take notice of this pernicious fellow traveler. Yet one can clearly trace how not only some unknown causes but seemingly the most innocuous everyday objects intercept the current of the fiery energy. Not only repulsion but a certain kind of unnoticeable torpor arrests the tension of work. The most common object obscures, as it were, the receptivity of brain and heart. Sometimes the pattern of a fabric, the rhythm of a song, the flash of a knife, the tinkle of metal, or a multitude of similar fragmentary emotions throw us out of the usual trend of aspiration. Whence comes this torpor? When and where were these reverberations and flashes perhaps decisive factors in our existence? Let us not deny the cumulations of the past; this is one more evidence of past existences. One should regard these recollections very soberly, and even record them as an exercise in observation. But one should not be spiritually encumbered by these fragments of the past. One may also encounter objects which can give impetus to one's striving; one may rejoice at such companions of bygone paths, but even they must not engage our attention too long. Forward, forward, ever forward! Each moment of torpor is a loss of progressive motion. How often it has been said that motion is a shield against the hostile arrows! Thus, proceed fierily. Let your fire be a beacon for your companions. One should remember that one must give light through thought.

**465.** One should abstain from derision as from the most noisome vermin. No mockery fails to turn back upon us. The most inexorable boomerang is the humiliation of one's neighbor. It can be said that Fire is covered by a veil of dust when in the proximity of mockery. One should take serious account of the meaning of abuse and mockery. Mockery causes stoning to death. And the mother of mockery is meanness.

**466.** The epidemic dryness of the throat indicates not only dryness of the atmosphere but also fiery tension. There is a heavy accumulation of many signs, but surprisingly little attention is paid to them. On the contrary, with the superficiality of ignorance, the strangest explanations are given of them. The shallowness of these explanations indicates that people prefer to remain with their illusions rather than deal with reality.

**467.** He who dies through his insistence that there is no life after death actually furnishes a typical example of the independent action of psychic energy. He practically commands himself to cease living and achieves the results of his command. There are many similar cases, but no one pays attention to these striking examples, which are open for general observation.

**468.** The manifestation of the loss of cooperation makes people quite helpless. The loss of concordance of rhythm destroys all possibilities of new achievements. You yourself see what difficulties are engendered through disunion. Such a state is very dangerous.

**469.** The beauty, light, and splendor, of the Fiery World are affirmed by each approach to it. Moreover, a special rapture is awakened by the feeling of unity. The fiery light leads to a mutual attraction, in other words to a true unity. The flesh, on the contrary, gives the impulse for each disunity. This property of the physical world impedes the embracing of the transport of unity upon this dusty and foggy surface. Therefore, one should direct one's thoughts the more to the Fiery World, in order to reinoculate oneself with the feeling of unity, already depleted. One should recharge, as it were, the magnet that has remained unused. The knowledge of how to utilize a magnet is necessary even in daily life. Likewise, the potency of Fire that has been left unused merges into the depths and becomes inaccessible. One must call it back by all the best recollections of it and by the worthiest imagination. Verily, for the fiery splendor a purified imagination is needed. One should understand that the dense forms cannot give any idea of the Fiery World. But an instantaneous illumination can remain forever as an ineffable feeling based upon unity.

**470.** One can note in all Teachings that under common terrestrial symbols are concealed the great concepts of the Fiery World. Must a city be necessarily terrestrial? Or must a cow necessarily call to mind only terrestrial herds? Or need milk be only from earthly kine and serpents only of Earth? One can find a great many such reminders in all Teachings. The reason for this lies both in the indescribability of concepts of the Fiery World and in the fact that writers and readers knew the stipulated definitions, which have been forgotten in the course of time.

**471.** When, after brilliant epochs, people fell into the horrors of flesh, the best terms were forgotten or were transferred to other concepts. One should not forget the earthly vicissitudes, and one should profit by these examples. The mechanical concepts are basically so ineffectual that one should prayerfully turn to the seed of the spirit, which glows brighter than all the electric lamps. One should not regard the reminder about Fire as a mere fairy tale. Many among you will think of Fire only as a torment of the conscience. But the Fiery World is cognized through joy!

**472.** Poor is the master craftsman who does not make use of all the riches of nature. For the skillful carver, a bent tree is a precious treasure. A good weaver uses each spot for the embellishment of his carpet. The goldsmith rejoices at each unusual alloy of metals. Only the mediocre craftsman will deplore everything unusual. Only an impoverished imagination is satisfied with the limits set by others. The true master develops great acuteness and resourcefulness in himself. The blessed spell of his craft frees the master worker from discouragement. Even the night does not bring darkness for the master, but only a variety of forms of the one Fire. No one can entice a master toward aimless speculations, because he knows the inexhaustibility of the essence of being. In the name of this unity, the master gathers each blossom and constructs an eternal harmony. He regrets the waste of any material. But people far from mastery lose the best treasures. They repeat the best prayers and invocations, but these broken and unrealized rhythms are carried away like dust. The fragments of knowledge are turned into the dust of a dead desert. The human heart knows about Fire, but the reason tries to obscure this evident wisdom. People say, "He was consumed with wrath; he withered from envy; he was aflame with desire." In a multitude of expressions, precise and clear, people show knowledge of the significance of Fire. But these people are not master artisans, and are always ready thoughtlessly to scatter the pearls they themselves so need! One cannot understand the human prodigality which destroys the treasures of Light. People do not deny themselves a single opportunity for negation. They are ready to extinguish all fires around them, only to proclaim that there is no Fire within them. Yet to extinguish fires and admit the darkness is the horror of ignorance.

**473.** You notice how much stronger are the lights of space than the radiance of sunshine. In darkness, it is difficult to estimate lights, but by comparing them with the light of the sun one can have an idea of the splendor of the Fiery World. It must be understood that earthly eyes cannot bear the supreme radiance, therefore We prepare them for the Fiery World by sparks and lights. One should not, like a pig, keep one's eyes directed only toward the ground.

**474**. You notice that at times We do not pronounce names, but replace them with symbols. Referring to a warrior, We imply the collective concept of all warring forces. Thus, one must not burden people even by pronouncing their names.

**475**. Communions in spirit constitute a considerable part of earthly existence and doubtless belong to the fiery nature. Not only do they occur during sleep but during our waking state we also feel many reflexes from such communions. No one, not even the coarsest person, would dare to deny that at times he has felt certain contacts or thought-suggestions from outside. The Teacher may point out that such contacts may be received from many sources either along the line of the thread of Hierarchy, or from the Subtle World, or from earthly inhabitants. It is very characteristic that a thought coming from the outside is forgotten quite easily. Not without reason did the ancient wisdom advise drinking a draught of cold water after such thoughts, as though a molten substance were in need of cooling to retain its form. This ancient advice is not without foundation. Thought coming from outside seemingly sets the centers aflame and should be engraved, as it were, in order that it be transformed into conventional energy. The same applies to dreams and visions. We not only receive fiery impulses from outside, but our subtle body exerts its entire fiery essence in order to condense the perceptions and intensify the conviction. It can be observed how the fiery perception collects all the most characteristic details. At times one is surprised at the degree of observation and the easy flexibility of the fiery eye, as compared to the earthly one. One can write down many dreams and sensations which will reveal the sharpness of the collected details. Often the fiery creativeness condenses details. It does not lie, but combines all the homogeneous parts. Therefore We strongly advise that close attention be paid to the fiery sensations; in them lies truth—molded by Fire, the genius. It may take decades to perceive through intellect what fiery illumination effects almost instantaneously.

476. The fiery consciousness affords that invincible optimism which leads to Truth. In its essence Truth itself is positive. There is no negation where Fire creates. One must accept the conditions of the world according to the level of the fiery consciousness. The conditions of life often impede the fiery consciousness. It is difficult to be reconciled with the conventionality of the garb of constructiveness. Dealing with many details in the course of life impedes the fiery receptivity. But for him who has even once contacted the Fiery World, all the husks become negligible. Thus, one must be guided along the higher level, not being disturbed by the imperfection of one's surroundings. As for those who are not good, all good measures must be applied. Fiery realization is not selfhood.

477. It is quite natural that the fiery perception will precede an earthquake, which is in itself the result of fiery tension and discharge. The hypothesis that meteors cause earthquakes is too narrow, there are many causes which produce destruction in the firmament.

478. Fiery breathing exists, because the fiery body is alive. Seldom is it possible to observe the flashes of fiery breathing in the earthly body, yet a purified body can sometimes feel such sighs. They may be felt either in the crown of the head, in the heart, or in other centers; one can feel something like an expansion of these centers, as it were. This can even cause

dizziness or nausea, because the physical world cannot easily adapt itself to such a manifestation of the Fiery World. Among the causes of enlargement of the heart may be included fiery breathing. Often the heart expands, but loses the rhythm and thus cannot contract normally. In levitation fiery breathing is of great importance; it takes the body out of physical conditions. Here again we are concerned with thought as a fiery product. You yourselves know that during levitation the body loses weight. You must also remember that the thought about levitation did not occur—it was only the entire being striving toward Hierarchy. Yoga constantly advises: "Think only of the Highest, so far as your consciousness can encompass. Imagine this Highest to be the best Aspect. Imagine this Highest to be in the Ineffable Light. Strain your consciousness as if toward something completely tangible. Manifest the best disposition. Gather all treasures of the Good, for the Voice of the Silence said, 'In good we ascend!' " You see once more how clear were the ancient counsels, for application in life. One can constantly advise scientists to reread attentively the ancient Teaching.

**479.** Who would believe that the human organism reacts not only to planetary disturbances but also to currents of the entire solar system? Yet it would be unwise to deny this and deprive man of cooperation with the far-off worlds. Our task is to remind men that as the highest expression of the manifested world they can be centers for uniting the worlds. Only by inculcating this thought can men be directed toward true advance.

**480.** To hold back humanity from higher thinking is similar to murder. This is not exaggeration, for coarseness and the lowering of the level of thought lead ultimately to disillusion and annihilation. Thus, when it is stated that a thought of Light is like a pillar of a temple, it may be understood that fiery illumination bestows eternal life.

481. The conditions of the world have not improved. Not without reason are you full of expectancy. The abscess is coming to a head. We are on vigil, and he who is with Us is saved. But to be with Us means to know the Teaching; to know, means to apply.

482. In Tibet horses are fed on leopard flesh in order to make them fierce. The Kshatriyas of Rajputana depend upon a meat diet to maintain their warlike spirit. These two examples alone show the significance of meat-eating. People do not slaughter a vast number of cattle from a sense of refinement. Like troglodytes, they are ready to devour bears. One must realize that the mass slaughter of animals is carried on in full consciousness. People know that vegetables or fruit give more vital energy than a cup of blood, yet they prefer being served with bloody meat, greatly relishing this coarseness. There is no other name for this frenzy of blood consumption. People are perfectly aware that a handful of wheat or barley is sufficient to sustain life, but their animal instinct tries to drag their minds back to a bestial state. Do not beasts try to tear each other's throats? Does not darkness impel people to the lowest actions? Let us not forget that mass killings, whether in war or in the slaughterhouse, equally pollute the atmosphere and violate the Subtle World. It must be realized that every conscious killing shakes the entire surrounding atmosphere. Moreover, these actions strengthen the forces of darkness and chaos, breaking the rhythm. One must avoid disturbing the Subtle World in any way. We can allow a diet of vegetables, farinaceous food, and milk, also eggs, the very freshest and in a liquid state. You know how repulsive the very

sight of meat becomes to the organism accustomed to a vegetable diet. Thus, in practice one must accustom oneself to refinement and remember that even an elephant increases his strength through plants alone. One should not think that people eat meat because of poverty. With the least effort one can obtain a vegetable diet; besides, many very nourishing herbs and roots are not utilized. One could learn much from certain animals, they know far more about natural foods than man, the meat-eater. Do not be concerned if the lover of blood scoffs at vegetable food; only remember him, because he is from darkness. Many are indifferent to meat and are compelled to it only by ugly home conditions. We do not mean them. We deplore the conscious vampires and necrophagi. Hence, be simpler and more refined in your diet.

**483**. Let the thought-creativeness of the Subtle World remind us of what kind of amplifier is revealed to us. Verily, he who passes over in righteousness multiplies the righteousness, and he who passes over in evil becomes a source of evil. Thus we can multiply our energies without limit. It is therefore our duty to refine our organism in order that it be a worthy receptacle. And these actions can be performed in palaces as well as in huts. Only consciousness of the grandeur of the revealed Fiery World leads to the path of unity.

**484**. In regard to the question of nutrition, it should be noted that it is necessary to have some raw vegetables or fruit each day; raw milk is likewise preferable if the cow is known, and also bread of a somewhat coarse flour. Thus one can obtain sufficient vitamins without increasing the obvious superfluity of food. Hence, one should not burden oneself with the thought of food, because such thought often obscures many valuable strivings. He who has found the balance between physical and spiritual demands already stands at the border of understanding the Higher World.

**485.** Testing the quality of thought in relation to various physical circumstances will give one a fiery understanding of many things. If we compare the thinking of a miner in a deep shaft with that of an aviator at the highest altitude of his flight, we will find a remarkable difference in the trend of thought, in both method and intensity. It would be worthwhile to observe the thinking of a bent reaper and that of a horseman. Thoughts of one and the same order are reflected quite differently in them. Physical conditions act like an accompaniment to the melody of the spirit. During construction, one must exercise one's entire imagination in order to find the consonances of so many diverse conditions. The fiery collective consciousness of peoples presents an instructive spectacle.

**486.** When I advise caution I have in mind varying conditions. The state of health is bound up with many cosmic causes. Thus, one should not look for causes only in colds or indigestion. The chemism of the luminaries is analogous to substantial doses of medicines and mixtures which can perceptibly affect the organism. Similarly, nervous pains may be traceable not only to obsession but also to reaction to the currents of space. Why be surprised at the large number of nervous diseases? More than once have I indicated the horror of such epidemics. They are contagious and under many forms have one common basis—precisely, affliction of the subtle body. Now one can understand once again why it is so necessary to study the fiery energy without delay.

**487.** Historic acts of great significance were often carried out in accordance with directions given in visions. The Invisible Government has pronounced its decisions more often than people suspect. The Higher Beings or departed relatives bring the message of imminent dates. One can only deplore the concealment of such visions and visitations, that is, unless secrecy has been enjoined. The fiery seal upon the lips is very lasting. However, one may disclose the truth to posterity in memoirs that will sustain many hearts. You yourselves already know of an entire succession of historic events which were based on warnings and indications. Thus, one can note a series of events from antiquity to our days which were seemingly links of one guiding thought. It is right to collect these fiery revelations; in them will be disclosed an entire interworld system. One must probe historical facts deeply, in order still more consciously to understand the wisdom of the construction. I advise the recording of all known historic events that took place or were connected with higher visions. During such work many more facts will be found, because a striving thought is like a magnet.

**488**. Many are familiar with a vague inner tremor having apparently no visible cause. No one will consider that he may be touched by the current of some powerful thought. Perhaps his receiver is not attuned to this rhythm, but the energy itself shakes his solar plexus. Thus, many fiery sensations glide over people's bodies, as if asking to be noticed.

**489**. Warnings should be given in schools that until the thirtieth year not all the centers are ready for higher manifestations. It is necessary that the youth should know how wise it is to prepare the body and spirit for the labor of ascent. It is necessary that teachers be leaders in life. It is necessary that the abstract become real and strengthen all of life. Many pure spirits are ready to join in conscious labor, but they seek for the right approach. Let teachers bear in mind that the path of negation is most destructive.

**490.** It cannot be doubted that the expenditure of inner energy is far greater during mental than during physical labor. This statement should be laid in the foundation of culture. Also, it is time to realize that vitamins and many other substances gain force only when coming in contact with the fiery energy of man. Let this belated discovery also testify to the power of human fiery energy. Striving along the path of discovery of the qualities of human psychic energy will provide the structure of life. One should attentively observe the degree to which man himself transmutes even the most powerful substances. Let us compare the effects of medicine taken with faith and medicine taken with repulsion. We have often witnessed how, under the influence of suggestion, a medicine had an opposite effect; how water acquired the most powerful properties of medicinal compounds. But it was not an outside will that produced these transformations. The will only directed the fiery energy, and in the furnace of Fire the transformation took place. It must be understood that we ourselves affirm our power through the understanding of fiery energy. One cannot express it more powerfully than to say that man is created in the image of the Highest; thus the presence of the higher energies is indicated. But it has not been said that man can make use of these energies only by means of artificial exercises. Energies are inherent in human nature; this means that they must act under the natural conditions of existence. Thus, we return again to the structure of life. If magic denotes artificiality of conditions, it is indeed unsuitable for the regeneration of life. The natural cultivation of the spirit and realization of the Fiery World will be the simplest solution for the aspiration of mankind. It is also said correctly that luxury is the antipode of beauty. Luxury is a form of magic, but where there is beauty no magic is needed.

**491**. Mediocrity arises from the failure of man to realize his inherent forces. Mediocrity is contagious; it exists for generations; it kills the being on the threshold of life. In mediocrity is affirmed a general condition in which the personality and human achievements are annihilated. Constructiveness is especially abhorrent to mediocrity. In fact, to mediocrity the Fiery World is a most frightening bugbear.

**492**. There are many events, but you must learn to discern amidst this multitude of dissenting voices the one plan for achieving the New World. A great many people prefer not to realize that they can take part in world construction. Let them carry stones for the Temple—invisible to them.

**493**. You have heard of many earthquakes and of innumerable meteorites which fall upon Earth, but earthquakes are recorded rather relatively. In certain zones they are recorded with extreme accuracy, but oceanic tremors remain only approximately recorded, although they may prove to be particularly dangerous. Likewise, there is approximation in connection with the fall of meteorites. It is true that many meteorites fall into water, but the fall is conditioned by magnetism. Thus, iron and other metals attract meteorites, especially when the deposits are in their natural state and are not void of cosmic magnetism. The conditions of cosmic magnetizations are successfully expressed in the so-called metal and water diviners. The existence of such people has been known since ancient times. Fortunately, contemporary science does not deny these facts. Thus, science has already established one of the properties of fiery energy. But it is most remarkable that these people sense precisely the subterranean waters and metals. Such a diviner will not react to a tank of water or a house constructed of steel. This magnetism is directed along the fiery channel and responds primarily to the natural state of a substance. This is also the core of all fiery communions. Naturalness and directness constitute the essence of fiery energy. One may never think of Fire, one may never perceive Fire, and thus shut off one's access to the Fiery World. I repeat that in the Subtle World it is difficult and painful to cognize Fire if in the earthly state at least some way of approach has not been found to the Higher World. Wisely it is said, "He who wishes to go to his ancestors will go to them." But by this only the lower state is defined. Why be deprived of the predestined beautiful spheres?

**494**. Exhaustion and hunger provide examples of the power of fiery energy. Compare a man dying of starvation who is aware of his inevitable end and a man who uses hunger as a cure. Note how long the second will preserve his strength and how quickly the first declines. Only fiery energy which is brought into play sustains the second, who wishes to be cured. Also note an experiment with fatigue—the one who can bring Agni into action does not feel any fatigue, but he who notices his fatigue droops. People call such actions "autosuggestion," but on what does this autosuggestion work? It calls forth fiery energy; it sets into motion the stilled wheels of Fire, and they alone bring such victories to the nerve centers. Earthly food can be reduced to small portions; the body will not require more when Agni is aflame. One should not think that such fiery transports are peculiar only to certain Rishis. Everyone who is conscious of the power of Agni can quite naturally draw upon this inexhaustible energy. The main thing is to begin with small things, watching one's inner impulses. No special laboratories are required to check oneself in various circumstances of life.

**495.** The Teacher knows how to understand the essence of the disciple's character. Unfit is the Teacher who wants to equalize all disciples; in this he demeans himself and commits an irreparable misdeed, violating the karma of those who have come to him.

**496.** Justice is primarily observation. One should take into consideration all the qualities of the disciple and estimate the extent to which he is able to assimilate new advantages. Each lack of assimilation of an advantage leads to horrible distortions of life. The criterion will be the development of fiery energy. A man aflame in heart will never become a parasite. Such an understanding of parasitism will redeem the entire trend of thought. There will be no parasites, there will be no idlers.

**497.** The history of denials reveals that men have rebelled most of all against manifestations of the Fiery World. This may have been terror at facing the unknown. Perhaps it was the usual revolt of ignorance. Perhaps it was the reflection of chaos being suggested to our mind as disparagement of everything. But one thing is apparent, in all domains of life people have tried to deny everything connected with fiery energies. The number of martyrs to the Fiery World exceeds the number of those who suffered for Truth. Parallel with the history of martyrdom one must write the history of denials. One must investigate, in the domain of religion and also among scientific discoveries, how every inch of fiery understanding has been gained by fighting ignorance with the greatest courage. Nothing has required so much self-sacrifice as the affirmation of the Fiery World. Even the most ordinary manifestation of light calls forth an explosion of suspicion. The most obvious manifestation will be explained in the most absurd manner. Precisely, Fire as the highest element is a most difficult realization for the human consciousness. In addition to ignorance there are many causes for this. People who have surrounded themselves with darkness will cross over into the Subtle World in darkness. Fiery glimpses are so insignificant to them, and the desire for ascent so unimportant, that Light remains inaccessible. So they walk about in darkness, fighting against the Light.

**498**. The fiery eye projects a ray of light if it focuses its attention upon a significant object. Even though this ray is not always outwardly visible it nevertheless attracts the attention of those nearby by its magnetism. Such magnetizations pertain to the Fiery World. This is not suggestion affecting the will, it is magnetic guidance, quite in keeping with the laws of the common magnet. Thus do the great laws permeate life, and it is fortunate when they are directed toward Good.

**499**. Is not fear of Fire caused by the fact that only its destructive aspect is apparent to the physical eye, whereas its fiery creativeness is not realized in the physical state? One must with especial conviction disclose to people that by reason of their very nature they have a unique path to Fire. Can the physician who has an aversion to his patient be a good physician? Or will the warrior whose spirit trembles with fear be victorious? Hence, we shall set before us the highest task, and in this way we shall not notice the steps of transition. Each element primarily precludes fear. To overcome fear momentarily does not mean to eradicate it. We must not be like small children, who are courageous today but may tremble with fear over an empty phantom tomorrow. Nor must we be like the pampered ones who seek daring adventure today but on the morrow will bury themselves in downy pillows. Let us not be under the threat of tomorrow, for of all the elements precisely Agni will not tolerate fear. We must comprehend Agni not as a destroyer but as a creator! In these two aspects of Agni lies the true touchstone of our nature.

**500**. It is especially difficult to explain to people that in the midst of days of extreme gravity there may be no outstanding events, and that the most propitious astrological dates may even be accompanied by misfortune. People will regard such comparisons as indicating the absurdity of astrological laws. They forget that the harvest is gathered after the sowing. Perhaps the best astrochemical currents can relatively lessen the scope of effects, but each effect has its inexorable cause. Therefore, in the midst of grave days one must exert extreme caution, solemnity, and magnanimity.

**501**. Think of Fire with the greatest benignity. One must coordinate one's spirit with the tension of the element. It can be seen that in different places the fiery tension is manifested differently. Only utter ignoramuses fail to notice this manifestation.

**502**. Waking dreams represent the action of fiery energy upon the Chalice. These are not forms of illness; they act as messengers of the approach of fiery energy. The circumstances of the Subtle World begin to reveal themselves similarly. They may proceed beneficently, but during a condensation of the fiery atmosphere they can cause insanity. The best cure lies in explaining the cause of this manifestation, in other words, in a cognizance of Agni Yoga. Obvious need compels Us to offer Our Counsels for wide application. Until quite recently the possibility of epidemics of waking dreams would have been regarded as absurd. But now, even the average physicians in hospitals are confronted with the necessity of studying the mass manifestations of such unusual symptoms. Likewise, other incomprehensible symptoms of the new conditions of the organism will begin to disclose themselves in life. Is it possible that people do not wish to prepare themselves for the new conditions? Such ignorance recalls the story of the child who had the faculty of seeing in the dark, but whose mother asked a physician to cure the child of this peculiarity. The evidences of the work of the fiery centers have become more frequent among people. It is unwise to reject these gifts which will furnish the solution for the immediate future.

**503**. Prevision of events represents a very important scheme of our fiery perceptions. Sometimes one may foresee proximate and even daily actions; but often, as if over a long distance current, we are able to perceive the most remote events. Many causes condition such irregularities. There is no harm if the fiery prevision warns us about tomorrow; and there will be no gap if the distant future arises before the third eye. The fiery force knows no distance; it is like an observer on a summit who sees where the paths on the earth below meet. Since the Universal Government foresees the distant future, our weak eyes can catch glimpses of these fiery decisions. With what solemnity and thoughtfulness one should receive these illuminations! One should not discuss them immediately and in the earthly fashion; one must cherish them as an entrusted sacred treasure!

**504**. Precisely—"Vanquish the godless!" One can rejoice when this decree is both understood and applied. One must have a well-developed consciousness to comprehend actual godlessness and to understand the weapon of Light with which darkness is struck. One can rejoice when darkness intensifies the light. Even darkness itself creates invisible light. It has been said that for the Yogi the moon shines by day and the sun by night. Gather about yourself so much Light that there can be no room for darkness.

**505**. Freedom from fear will not come through convincing oneself in each separate instance. On the contrary, such suggestions drive the feeling of fear inward, permitting it to return with full force at the first opportunity. Moreover, the terror will increase in proportion to the pressure of the artificial suggestion. Imprisoned fear is a very dangerous convict, and it is essential to rid oneself of fear—so declare all Teachings. Fear can be eradicated by comparisons. Point out the terror of facing ferocious beasts to the man who is threatened by fire, and he will say, "I would know how to escape wild beasts, but how can I escape this blaze?" Thus, collect all the possible causes of fear, and one after another they will fall away like dry leaves. Likewise, one should call forth complete relativity in order to become accustomed to the boundlessness of the Fiery World. The attraction to the earthly crust creates the illusion of security; this explains the attachment of human beings to the earthly world. It is quite true that precisely here one should absorb many feelings and lay a foundation of receptivity, in order to tread the fiery waves more easily. For this reason earthly specialization is not as valuable as the qualities of receptivity and containment. It is not surprising that the dividing lines of the strata of the Subtle World do not coincide with those of conventional classifications on Earth. One may find oneself in the Subtle World among the most unexpected assortment of neighbors. Such a surprise threatens only those who cross over with a load of earthly survivals. But he who has refined his spiritual criteria will find the fulfillment of his expectations.

**506.** One may rejoice when the beauty of the outlines of the Subtle World is apprehended. One may convince people that thought-creativeness can mold not only personal forms but also those capable of attracting and enrapturing the best hearts. The ability to create by means of thought is also developed on Earth; but how lofty will be such creativeness when people shall realize that they are creating not for Earth, but for spheres of supreme grandeur!

**507.** Let us be like arrows striving heavenward from a fiery bowstring. In each earthly object let thought find the spiritual essence which will create a beautiful vision in Infinity. Thus, let us be ashamed to send vile thoughts into the World of Beauty. Each day should reveal a prototype of beautiful enhancements. People are ashamed to speak vile words into a loud-speaker. Why, then, should one fill space with vile thoughts? Let the fact of the world conflagration remind one again about the quality of thought.

**508.** Yes, yes, yes, the seeds of good remain in the spirit, but not sufficient attention is given to them. People remember about accumulations; but, not having preserved their spiritual understanding, they strive to accumulate earthly objects. In the depths of their spirits men know about flights into the Infinite, but, having forgotten the significance of the far-off worlds, they wander aimlessly about on the earthly crust. One should not speak against earthly objects, which are products of creation; one should not speak against travels, which can be the highest schooling—the entire earthly existence must be comprehended from the level of the Higher World. Can one perform only useful actions in earthly life? Of course one can. It is easy to imagine an entire life as a continuous stream of usefulness to others. *Santana* is not a meaningless rolling of stones. It is like a stream feeding the adjoining fields, like a brook bringing cleanliness to the hearth, like rain making the sown seeds come up. Thus, one need not be a special sage to imagine a life useful in all domains. When the fiery waves shall compel people to seek safety in the towers of the spirit, they will regret with loathing each useless incarnation. In consternation they will try to gather crumbs of positive thinking. What is the use of offering advices not to dissipate precious energy! One must think about the approach of very unusual times. Neither cruelty, nor robbery, nor treason, nor falsehood will help one to withstand the fiery waves. Not shame so much as suffering will compel quests for salvation.

**509**. The ability to discriminate between the great and the small is forged in the same fire of the heart. Do not think that writings bring only great things. One must discern the source of these writings! There are not a few false, though attractive statements that are concocted about the destruction of the world. One should call forth one's observation, to discern how the reptiles of darkness crawl in to defile the thinking. Dirt does not come from light.

**510**. I speak again about understanding the hour of achievement. I shall not weary of reiterating that one must think loftily in order to rise above the dust.

**511**. He who thinks of modesty and humility is by virtue of this neither modest nor humble. Natural virtues do not require forced considerations. Much vanity has originated from such forced pseudo-modesty and pseudo-humbleness. In all qualities connected with fieriness, directness is needed. If a man has not acquired reverence for Hierarchy, no command can make him feel the beauty of this striving; external conditions will shatter the seed of striving. It is a great fallacy for people who have begun to think of the Supreme to alter the outer conditions of their lives. A shoemaker known to you could have abandoned his craft, but he preferred to affirm himself in the rhythm of the past in which his highest thoughts had been generated. This is not inflexibility, but a due regard for the precious rhythm already established. One can observe that external conditions can give the impulse to thought. This consideration is very useful during fiery achievements. A musician does not part with his instrument even when traveling. The reason for this lies not only in mechanical technique but, consciously or unconsciously, the virtuoso thus preserves an already established rhythm. Continuity of work is needed for the coordination of the centers just as much as is pranayama. But an experienced workman does not ponder over the use made of his work. Work for him is food; he cannot live without it. Let the physician cite examples of this. In connection with Agni, disorderly, unrhythmic work is especially harmful, and it is necessary that a rhythm should become habitual without forcing. Then one may expect Agni to become indeed a self-acting armor. The quality of self-initiated action is a fiery achievement. It does not come from outside, but only together with the broadening of consciousness. Without the affirmation of consciousness, self-initiated activity cannot be established.

Courage does not come by order. It grows from within, giving the sensation of being the core of the spiral. If courage once takes root, nothing can eradicate it. It is beautiful to realize the existence of a process whereby qualities may be acquired which grow like a mighty tree.

**512.** The fire on the mountain indicates the tension

of the atmosphere. Not without reason do people call these fires "messengers." The tension reveals itself in a silvery light. Many will deny even such an obvious manifestation. Many may mention hallucinations, forgetting that such actual details as the illumination of a cloud could not be imaginary. It is astonishing to see that even the simplest manifestations of a fiery order may be denied. Nor could the motion of the fire be foreseen in an illusion. Truly, these fires are messengers.

**513.** A neophyte asked a Rishi who spoke to him about Agni, "If I constantly repeat the word Agni, will I have any benefit from it?" The Rishi answered, "Of course. You have been so far removed from this concept that even through sound your nature will cling to the great foundation of Existence." In the same way We repeat about the various qualities and analogies of the great Agni. May the people accept this sound in the Chalice! Let them be so saturated with its reverberations that they accept it as inalienable to them. If, during the transition between existences, they even pronounce "Agni," it will be of help to them, because they will not be hostile toward Fire. The Subtle World will help to sensitize the understanding of the higher principles, but they cannot be approached with hostility and denial. The aim of the first book about the Fiery World is to affirm and accustom people to an understanding of Agni. Let them see how diversely Fire has been understood, from ancient times up to the present contemporary understanding. May the sparks of these fires of the heart recall to mind many mysterious manifestations and the recounting of legends by the old people. One must absorb into one's consciousness an attractive constructive image. One should admit it as one's own possession which will lead to the heights. Therefore, even the repetition of the sound, Agni, is useful.

**514.** Humanity truly represents, as it were, the cement of the planet; it helps to hold together the parts threatened by chaos. An unpopulated world easily disintegrates. But man must not pride himself on this mission, he must feel himself to be a guard on watch. Verily, only he who is fortified by the armor of Agni can the more fully consummate his destiny. Agni must not be in a state of inaction. The element of fire is the most active, most speedy, and most spatial, and it is manifested in the midst of the tension of thought. Does not man preserve the planet by thought? The most precious substances are created by thought. Compare breadth of thought with insipidity. I attest that people can gather a treasure of thought, which, in rhythm with the Cosmos, will create the New Era.

**515.** Nations hope to make up for the lack of Agni by crude violence; but no force, crude and low, can kindle the Fire of Light. One can observe an unprecedented obduracy coincident with the decline of Agni in the hearts of men. Is it not apparent that no force will assist one in finding psychic energy? Moreover, all violence, personal as well as national, retards men's discovery of psychic energy. This means that instead of urgent cooperation for discovering Agni, people employ force for the destruction of the planet. This is deplorable and unworthy!

Let them not ask for My Manifestation where hatred and lack of understanding prevail! We are on Great Vigil!

**516.** Some people must memorize useful counsels, whereas others know the fundamentals of life in their hearts; both kinds need a Teacher. The first must learn, but the latter should affirm themselves. Some understand the best means for human relations from their earliest years, whereas others must pass through a tiresome schooling in order to avoid destructive actions. Both need the Teaching as a reminder of the conditions of existence. It is astonishing to what a degree some remember instances from their past lives, whereas others have completely lost all memories of their former accumulations. A karmic cause does not completely explain such a marked difference in the understanding of life. Truly, the deciding factor in such understanding lies not in the circumstances of former lives, but in the acceptance of Agni. People call such wisdom a talent, but it is no special talent to keep Agni alight. Only the kindling of the centers produces uninterrupted vigilance of consciousness. Even a partial manifestation of Agni already preserves the accumulations inviolate. Agni is no violator, but our friend. It must be explained that the ascent of the spirit is indeed a manifestation of Agni.

517. One should not be distressed by writings that reflect human hatred; the darkness is vast! One can evoke the most radiant forces, yet the dark ones will obscure even the best manifestations. The dark ones can only obscure. If they are asked how to improve things, they will become wrathful, for their goal is not to make things better, but worse. One can see how evil forces penetrate into life under various guises. One should not comfort oneself with the idea that the dark ones cannot approach; they will utilize every grain of dust to cover themselves. Where they themselves dare not approach, they toss in a scorpion. The dark ones have many inventions. Therefore one must become accustomed to great vigilance.

518. Healing through the currents of space is especially effective for the nerve centers. Therefore I advise

that the organism be guarded from organic injury. The nerve centers, like fiery vessels, will readily accept the transmissions of Agni. But one should not obstruct such reactions, especially by irritation; like a shield of death it blocks all channels. You already know how I have warned of the fatal danger of irritation in life. Such embittered outcries are borne across the ocean, and he who is more magnanimous must realize his responsibility. Precisely, magnanimity will protect from irritation.

**519.** It is truly amazing when a mechanical giant attempts to strike the fiery heart, but instead carries the stones for his own tomb. This example is often repeated, but on each occasion one should rejoice over the victory of Agni. People plead for a miracle, but numberless miracles are all around them. They have merely to cleanse their eyes of irritation.

**520.** The vulnerability resulting from injury to the aura is terrible. One can imagine how one breach in the aura leads to the mutilation of its entire structure. Drowsiness, which can be noted when the aura is rent, originates from the consistently increased activity of the fiery energy when directed toward external radiations. During the process of restoration, the organism, and especially the heart action, is in a state of depression. For this reason I deem caution necessary in one's actions as well as during the counterblows. During the battle why should one burden the hearts of friends? One could perform numerous experiments revealing how the violation of the radiations has actually been reflected upon the heart. People accept with reluctance advice about observing caution in regard to their own radiations; but even prior to their being photographed, science is already aware of the existence of these radiations from every object. One should have full respect for the human organism and understand that each shock harms the astral body primarily. Besides, if organisms have worked together for a long time in unity, they can injure each other even more severely. And such injury will be not only of each other, but also will be reflected upon others near to them. One should therefore most assiduously eliminate all conflicts. One can visualize a dark legion which makes an onslaught upon each break in the aura. It is dreadful to feed such vermin with the inner layers of radiations. The protective net alone blocks the attack of the dark forces. Each breach in the aura also threatens one with obsession. Let us therefore be even more cautious.

521. A sigh was formerly regarded as a response to God. Concentration of the fiery energy produces this spasm. Notice that murderers and sinister criminals do not sigh. This tension occurs in connection with higher emotions. One could write a book about the sigh, and it would be shown to be very close to prayer. All the benevolent reflexes can be singled out in the same way. There is no reason to regard them as moral abstractions; it is better to accept them as foundations of health.

522. Does having no cares befit humanity? Some confuse having no cares with reliance upon Hierarchy. They hold that because they have been incarnated here someone must be made responsible for them. But the Great Service is great solicitude. One cannot imagine a day or an hour when a man may be without care, that is to say, can dispense with thinking. Thus, care must not be regarded as an arid burden, but rather as a distinguishing quality of man. Among the privileges of the Bodhisattvas, solicitude for everything that exists is the gem of their crown. Likewise, solicitude should be welcomed as the kindling of Fire. Not petty

reflections, but a most solicitous thought strikes sparks of light from the heart. It is unwise to avoid cares, for one must make haste with the fires of the spirit. Those who fear cares reveal but meager accumulations. The experienced wayfarer says, "Burden me with care when I enter the Beautiful Garden." Man, who has received the gift of thinking, has accepted not the least of these responsibilities. It has been said that the smile of a rich man is of slight value, but the poor man who has retained his smile will become the companion of God. So does the folk understanding value a smile amidst cares. My advice is that you realize that the number of cares cannot be lessened. Only thus do we realize that joy is a special wisdom.

**523.** Nothing can confuse the traveler who already has caught sight of his home. What, then, can impede the consciousness striving toward the Fiery World? Nothing can prohibit a man from setting himself the greatest task. Only thus can care be illuminated and thought be filled with solemnity. Only thus can the real values be elected, enabling one to go toward Hierarchy without hindrance.

**524.** To doubt the evidence of the Fiery World means to arrest the momentum; therefore do not look back. Let the movement develop a progressive flow of attraction, like a current. As a falling object can develop a terrific speed, so can an advancing movement generate a magnetic force which draws one in the designated direction. One does not go far by growling, but fiery thought will carry one over the unexpected. Know how to observe the growth of consciousness. Certainly it is more difficult than observing the growth of hair or grass. But the haystack indicates the growth of the grass. So, also, the consciousness can yield precious stores.

**525**. The welfare of nations is molded around a single personality. There are numerous examples of this throughout history, in the most diverse regions. Many will attribute this evident manifestation to the personality itself. But thus think the short-sighted; those who are far-sighted understand that such synthesis is nothing but the manifestation of the power of Hierarchy. Actually in all such manifestations the Hierarchy selects a focus upon which a current can be directed. Besides, a personality of this order possesses a fire, realized or unrealized, which makes the communion easy. But also indispensable is a certain quality on the part of the people themselves—trust in and recognition of the power. Therefore, in different matters I so often reiterate about authority. This quality is needed as a link of the fiery machine. You yourselves see how nations progress by affirming a leader. You yourselves see that there is no other way. Thus, the link of Hierarchy must be realized. One should not be short-sighted.

**526**. Of course you have noticed the state between sleep and waking. It is especially remarkable that at the slightest movement a sort of dizziness is felt. But in a comfortable position one can feel a decrease in weight. This state is no illusion. In fact one can check the change in weight on scales. The dizziness itself is the effect of the predominance of the subtle body. The ancient Teaching says that as man returns to his earthly body, he senses momentarily the quality of the Subtle World. One can feel the same condition during ecstasy of the spirit and at the beginning of an epileptic fit. But the decrease in weight of a medium occurs differently; then external elementary energies participate. The manifestation of the Fiery World is especially close to us when the fiery body transforms our sensations amidst earthly conditions; therefore we

216

can affirm that the conditions of the three worlds can also be manifested in earthly life.

527. One apparently simple manifestation merits attention: when ten men test their prowess separately they will find that the sum of their individual efforts is less than the total of their joint effort. This mysterious something is the crown of cooperation. Again we touch on the fiery domain. Only a combined rhythmic effort summons the fiery reserves. Is not such a calculable strengthening a proof of fiery energy? Let scientists collect even the most minute data about the manifestations of fiery energy. Let them observe this something not as a mystical but a real and growing concept.

528. Why was the fire of lightning considered by the priests of Egypt to possess special magnetism? Was it superstition or knowledge? Why is the knowledge of the priests regarded as so very well-founded? Yet the facts, proved by research, confirm the fieriness of these teachers of Egypt. Was it not by experimental methods that the Egyptian priests arrived at the magnetism of the fire of lightning? One can imagine a specially condensed state of fiery energy during such powerful discharges. Of course, such tension may be perilous, but, properly directed, it can produce a purification of energy.

529. A common error of people is to cease to study after leaving school. The Pythagoreans and similar philosophic schools of Greece, India, and China furnish sufficient examples of continuous study. Truly, limiting education to the prescribed schooling indicates ignorance. Obligatory learning is only the entrance to real knowledge. If we divide humanity into three categories—those who are altogether unschooled, those whose education is confined to compulsory

217

schooling, and those who continue their education—the number of the last will prove astonishingly small. This primarily shows indifference toward future lives. In their decline of spirit, men are indifferent even to their own future. There should remain a record that in the present significant year it is necessary to remind people about that which was useful a thousand years ago. In addition to elementary education one should further the education of adults. Several generations exist simultaneously on Earth, and they are all equally indifferent in striving to the future which they cannot evade. Such negligence is astonishing! Learning has become an empty shell. Yet for a simple holiday people like to dress in their best. Is it possible that they do not think it behooves them to secure an attire of Light for the solemn Abode in the Fiery World? One should rejoice not in bigotry, not in superstition, but with an illumined mind, and not only at the schools for children but also at the uniting of adults for continuous learning.

**530.** It is right to repeat about the sickness of the planet. It is right to understand the desert as the shame of humanity. It is right to direct one's thinking toward nature. It is right to turn one's thought to the task of cooperation with nature. It is right to recognize that to plunder nature is to squander the treasures of the people. It is right to rejoice at nature as the refuge from fiery epidemics. He who does not think about nature does not know the Abode of Spirit.

**531.** Human energy must come in contact with Cosmic Fire. Human energy is deeply immersed in the dense strata, and each piercing of these strata brings lofty enlightenment. Fire burns away all dross.

**532.** When the thought is striving forward and encounters the current of a hostile sending, a terrific shock results, which reacts upon the heart. I have already told you about the terrible hostile arrows. Besides these sendings the constantly increasing tremor of Earth also heightens the tension of the centers. Such a condition is unnatural, and only persistent striving toward the Fiery World will give humanity a different trend of thought.

533. Let us not rely upon the thought that nothing will overtake us. Such a conviction has a double-edged meaning. It is good to feel one's foundations, but each ignoring of the forces of the enemy is also unwise. It is better to assume that the enemy will approach and that fearlessness will sustain us in full strength.

534. Long ago I mentioned that a garden of offenses is unfit. One must show an understanding of the complete unworthiness of offenses. An offense is the most impeding state. It is like a hidden abscess. Buddha himself when noticing some kind of offense immediately sent away the disciple, saying, "Go and bathe in cold water."

535. The root of a thought, or its motivating cause, must be made evident to a refined consciousness. It is impossible to know all thoughts, because in the kaleidoscope of human fragmentary thoughts one becomes dizzy, and the mere scraps of unstable thinking are of no use. But it is useful to sense the motivating cause of each expression. Such fiery affirmation comes with the kindling of the centers. Man is beginning to know the purpose of words. The external expression is not important to the sensitive observer. Sometimes the speaker himself finds it difficult to determine the primary reason for his own words. But a fiery heart knows how the spoken formula was born. No grimace or gestures will lead the third eye into error. Such straight-knowledge is not obtained easily. Many

generations each add their mite to the consciousness. Understand that the affirmation of Fire is achieved by many incarnations. The root of thought will provide the way to the realization of other roots.

**536.** One can realize only with difficulty how greatly needed for the earthly plane is subtle construction. But many structures of the Subtle World are, as it were, actual teraphim for the future of Earth. Often the completion of such subtle teraphim is even more essential than the earthly structures. In them is laid, as it were, the root of constructive thinking. Therefore We rejoice when the prototype is already completed. Of course, one can rejoice only at a successful prototype.

**537.** The convulsions observed represent a significant manifestation. A refined organism mirrors the Macrocosm, and first of all reacts in striking concordance with the motion of the planet. A convulsion of the planet cannot fail to be reflected upon the fiery body. Not only earthquakes but all of the hidden internal convulsions of the planet will not pass unnoticed by the fiery heart. Furthermore, as a planetary convulsion is accompanied by pressure upon the poles, so the convulsion of the body may be accompanied by pressure on the Kundalini and the third eye. Energy can also stream from the extremities, just as there can be a contraction of the earthly crust during an internal convulsion—truly, man is a microcosm.

**538.** The perversion of human understanding has gone so far that a man infected with the imperil of irritation or malice is sometimes called a fiery being. Even malice people sometimes describe as inflamed. But since Agni is a connecting, all-pervading element, it is actually the principle of equilibrium. The human spirit has recourse to this element during ascent; even in a mechanical ascent use is made of the fiery principle. It should be explained that the inflammation of imperil in no wise corresponds to purified Agni. People themselves try to implant in their consciousness a disparaging meaning of many great manifestations. Indeed, it is a good exercise to occasionally spend a day without disparaging.

**539.** Thought about unity with Hierarchy is also an excellent purification. When all the reptiles of evil crawl out of their holes, there remains only striving upward. Let us then assemble all the expedients of equilibrium. Let us not think of weariness, which comes from yesterday; let us look to a morrow which is not filled with disparagement.

**540.** Anxiety is inevitable when the confusion of minds evokes the tremor of the lower strata. Let us not be concerned with these manifestations; we would be dead if we did not feel the present chaos. On the contrary, we should draw special strength by adhering to Hierarchy. If we assume that there is another way, we will be rent by the elements.

**541.** Earth still harbors the good robber and the cruel devotee. One would suppose that people, as the highest elements of Earth, would evolve far more rapidly than other elements of the planet. But a strange phenomenon is taking place—rejecting the ethics of spirit, people have encased themselves in a spiritual inertia. It seems that even the climate changes more rapidly than the human consciousness. Many inventions have appeared on this planet more than once. Bygone nations knew much, but the quality of thinking has progressed very little. And still people talk a great deal about a new race and a new humanity. But no Golem is to be the prototype of the new race. The quality of thinking will differ from that of past ages. The art of thinking must be completely and consciously regenerated, but without understanding the three worlds it is impossible to raise thinking to a new level. He who does not yearn for self-perfection will not think on a planetary scale. He who considers discussion of the Fiery World as superstition or paganism cannot revere the Image of the Saviour. One need not wonder that people become accustomed to honest thinking so slowly, for throughout their many incarnations they have been bereft of the best images of the heroes of mankind. People have continually seen that it was precisely the heroes who were tortured and killed before their very eyes. By such thinking one does not arrive at the concept of the new man.

542. In more ways than one it is possible to determine by experiment how the spirit helps even the development of muscles. I do not speak of Hatha Yoga, in which physical exercise is emphasized primarily. In other Yogas physical exercise has no such significance, but the spiritual development gives the muscles a special tone. Take two athletes—let one develop along physical methods alone and the other realize the power of the spirit. How much more will the latter excel!

543. Why should evil sometimes seem to be the victor? Only because of the instability of good. By a purely physiological method it can be proved that domination by evil is short-lived. Evil emerges together with imperil, but can at first produce only a strong flash; afterwards it begins to deteriorate and gradually destroys its own progenitor. This means that if Agni is even partially manifested, it will not cease to increase. Thus, when imperil begins to decompose, Agni, on the contrary, acquires its full strength. Therefore I advise that the first attack of evil be endured, in order to leave evil to its own destruction. Moreover, during the duel between evil and good—in other words between

imperil and Agni—the latter will grow proportionately, as imperil putrefies its possessor. Thus should one observe the duel between the low and the high, but only a mature consciousness can encourage one to withstand evil. It is useful to remember this and to gather not only strength but also patience, in order to conquer that which is in itself doomed to annihilation. I affirm that the truth, "Light conquers darkness," has even a physiological basis.

544. But who, then, will help gather useful examples? One can enumerate them, but too few physicians take the trouble to note, among the cases under their observation, the action and significance of Fire. I do not advise Our physician to make all experiments and observations on himself. He may become exhausted through overfatigue. He has a great number of examples around him.

545. The heart may ache when Hierarchy is commented upon in an unworthy manner. The heart is a center. Hierarchy is also a center. From the most cardinal, all is transmitted to the Supreme, and vice versa. When people are ignorant of something, they should not defile what is beyond their grasp. They should have enough humaneness to understand where the Ineffable begins. One cannot hope to continue to cast stones at the best Image. Some nitwits, filled with conceit, think that everything is permitted them. But when they lose their teeth, they should not be amazed but should look nearby for the causes.

546. To give is a divine attribute. The inexhaustibility of giving is found in varying degrees in all of nature. But fire is the element in which giving is most apparent. The very principle of Fire is transmutation and constant giving. Fire cannot exist without the sacrifice of giving; likewise the fiery seed of the spirit

exists through giving. But the sacrifice is a true one only when it has become the very nature of a man. A mental and compulsive sacrifice is neither natural nor divine. Only when sacrifice becomes an inalienable attribute of life does it become inseparable from the consciousness. Thus, by its qualities Fire teaches us during ascent. Let each one who wishes to attain cognizance say to himself, "I will be like Agni." One must grow to love fiery sacrifice as the closest means of communion with the Fiery World. Without this self-sacrificial striving it is not easy to rise above the claws of evil. Like Fire, which is elusive, the consciousness becomes mobile when united with Agni. One must approach sacrifice not by the path of despondency but by that of fiery splendor. One cannot define Fire by any other term than splendor. Likewise, the Fiery World cannot be thought of as other than a manifestation of grandeur.

547. It can be sensed how at times the fiery sendings collide against a wall of darkness. Only in particular cases of the attack of the dark forces does this impediment become possible. During such an attack should one exhaust the reserves of Fire or should one choose another direction? You already know that the swelling of darkness is of short duration; therefore it is better to choose immediately a different direction for the transmission. The stronghold of darkness is like a cardboard bull; one has only to know its character.

548. If you feel special drowsiness or weariness, do not try to overcome it. It is best to be very careful with the store of fiery energy. Who knows how much and how often precious energy is sacrificed for the sake of those who are quite unaware of it? Though they assert that no fiery sendings exist, they themselves eagerly devour other people's strength.

**549**. Spatial thought engenders a certain substance which in a vortiginous movement becomes a generating center for various inceptions. It would be beautiful to realize that human thought contains such a powerful substance; still only the most lofty and intensified thought produces an energy that is sufficiently powerful. But a small thought—unrealized, erratic, and unstable—will not give a creative impulse, and can even inflict harm. Lacking the correct coordination of attraction and repulsion, insignificant thoughts form, as it were, ugly conglomerates and pollute space. We call them spatial slime. Much energy is wasted in transmuting these stillborn monsters. One can imagine how greatly spatial production could be increased were it not for these progenies of men. In this matter let us not accuse only the primitive peoples. Their thinking is potentially not weak, but the average result of civilization is complete degeneration in quality of thought. Such degeneration produces the whole store of slimy products which threaten to turn the bliss of Agni into odium. Not rare are the instances of the harm of petty thoughts! So many of the best channels are clogged by chips only because humanity does not respect thought. Brainless superstition will undoubtedly rail against each reminder about the reality of thought; people will cite the contrast between nature and bliss, whereas the lower carnate strata are entirely incommensurable with the highest. Discipline of thought will inevitably lead up to the highest fiery spheres. Instead of becoming a source of infection man can become a purifier of space.

**550**. Petty thoughts not only clog space, they especially impede the transmission of thought to far-off distances. Every participant in thought-transmission knows how at times parts of the transmission are, as it were, corroded, as if a dark cloud obscures the precision of expression. In fact, these small, slimy, ugly creatures intercept the path of transmission. Singly, these little monsters are ineffectual because of their feebleness, but they form a slime sufficient to thicken space and thus intercept the currents. Therefore, to effect speedier thought-transmission humanity must be urged to desist from petty thoughts. Even a little carefulness in thinking will produce beneficial results. Moreover, the slime of petty thinking can be a source of epidemics.

**551.** In biographies it is highly instructive to trace the intervening circumstances which help to conclusively define a life task. It may be noted that many apparently accidental factors helped along in the predestined direction. As a matter of fact, not accident but many profound causes contributed to such achievement. In this can be seen the participation of the Subtle World. When the spirit chooses a definite task, it adapts itself to many assisting influences. Often there remain in the Subtle World allies and co-workers who control the contributory circumstances. Thus one can observe many scarcely perceptible impulses that lead to definite aims. One can only esteem such fireflies along with wayside guideposts!

**552.** When I advise continual striving toward Hierarchy, the full weight of such a Decree must be understood. Each one will readily accept it, but will forget it at the first occasion. He will remember the most minute details, but neglect the most important. The Guiding Image will be submerged in small fragments. But every Yogi knows the silver thread as the sole guiding star. When the heart forgets the most important, at least let the brain recall the words about the necessary salvation.

**553.** Throughout the entire world rises the sound of wailing. It is apparent that this cannot go on. The convulsions of the planet become more frequent. One should remember that these years are marked in all Teachings.

**554.** He who says that heroes are not needed expels himself from evolution. Observe that on the border of mediocrity, lack of faith, and egoism, lies self-annihilation. Decades may pass before the process of self-devouring becomes evident, but it grows from the very hour that Hierarchy is denied. It is impossible to imagine the affirmation of a progressive action without Hierarchy. One must repeat this most simple Teaching, because people are headed toward the abyss. The rays from the shoulders are causing pain not because of the convulsions of the planet but because of the raging of humanity. As waterspouts divide water into columns, so disunited humanity whirls about. It is a very significant year of the revolt of the human spirit. Fire can be held back only up to a certain point. Inevitably it will break through all manifested obstructions.

**555.** It is as easy to fall prey to obsession as it is difficult to effect cooperation with the Subtle World. In the first place, people as a rule give little thought to true cooperation; and in the second, they altogether refuse to admit the existence of the Subtle World. During obsession a most objectionable violation takes place, and rational cooperation is eliminated from the consciousness. Many dwellers in the Subtle World would like to offer their knowledge, but they are denied the opportunity because of various prejudices and fear. If you only knew what great turbulence now exists in the Subtle World when the new division of humanity rocks space! One should not assume that the present time is an ordinary one; it is unprecedented and can inaugurate a New Era. Nevertheless, create heroes—thus it is ordained.

**556.** One must have no small imagination to begin thinking of the Fiery World. One must be able to envision Hierarchy up to the Fiery World, and when the highest imagination has become exhausted, one will have to find all daring to turn to the great Fiery Images.

**557.** All killing is contrary to the fiery nature. Everyone who ponders about the Fiery World not only should not kill but is obligated to prevent the shedding of blood. He must understand that bloodshed not only creates confusion in certain strata of the Subtle World but is a violation of earthly nature. Among certain peoples sapping of trees in spring is prohibited for the same reasons. But if, since ancient times, people have understood the significance of the sap of trees, how can they fail to understand the significance of effused blood? The very passage into the Subtle World, if bloodless, saves one from the approach of those dark creatures which are immediately attracted to the emanations of blood. Besides these physical reasons, it is time to realize what it means to prematurely cut life short. The destruction of earthly enemies by murder means the creation of a powerful enemy in the Subtle World. More than once We have reminded about the meaning of karma, but if this word has no appeal to some, let us call it Divine Justice. Never burden the understanding of your companion with a persistent definition. The thought must be directed toward the essence of a concept, beyond its customary expression.

**558.** Premeditated murder is one thing, self-defense is another. When one is subjected to an attack by the dark forces, it is necessary to defend oneself. Thought about defense is not murder. Each one can defend himself first of all by the strength of his spirit.

Some strengthen their protective net, picturing it as a shield. But the fiery heart does not limit itself to a shield; it sends forth the spiral of Agni, which blunts the most malevolent arrows. Of course, courage and resourcefulness are needed for such action.

**559.** The resonance of nature is often sensed. The people of antiquity even divined the definite sound of peace or of confusion. But scientists can explain this manifestation by looking to fiery causes. Since the vortical waves of Fire resound, a sensitive ear can detect this great resonance even in complete silence. One may hear combinations of similar vibrations in the noises of Earth. It is said that Lao Tze often conversed with waterfalls. This is not a fairy tale, for he listened to the resonance of nature and sharpened the sensitiveness of his hearing to the point of discerning the qualities of the vibrations.

**560.** It must be remembered that Great Service brings one closer to cognition of the Great Goal. Comprehend it in its entire scope, to the best of your ability, in complete tension of the spirit. Beautiful is such tension when invisible co-workers gather around it. They strengthen the armor, protect from arrows, and illumine the path. Man can advance as if winged; he has gained numberless co-workers, and they are obedient to Hierarchy. Thus, above all physical considerations, let us at times lift our spirit toward the loftiest strongholds. This must be affirmed as the shield of the Great Service.

**561.** It is better to go to sleep with a prayer than with a curse. It is better to begin the day with a blessing than in bitterness. It is better to partake of food with a smile than with dread. It is better to enter upon a task with joy than with depression. Thus have spoken all the mothers of the world; thus have heard all the children of the world. Without Yoga, the simple heart knows what is needed for advance. It can be defined in any terms, but the significance of a joyous and solemn foundation is preserved throughout all time. The Yoga of Fire must strengthen the basis of ascent. The Agni Yogi is first of all not a hypochondriac; he summons all those who are strong and joyous of spirit. When joy keeps its glow even under the most difficult circumstances, the Agni Yogi is filled with impregnable strength. There, beyond the most difficult ascent, the Fiery World begins. The manifestation of the Fiery World is immutable. A Yogi knows that nothing can stop him from attaining the Fiery World. Thus, the first prayer of a mother and the very splendor of the fiery worlds are on the same thread of the heart.

**562.** When I permitted you to record Our Communions, I did not conceal from you that people would utter many evil words about the most lofty concepts. He who thinks about good must not be astonished when he is called a hypocrite, a necromancer, a murderer, and a liar. As if obsessed, people will apply the most unfitting epithets to him. Wherever there is no thought about good the evil tongue is always ready.

**563.** Today is a difficult day, therefore I shall narrate a tale. "A certain demon decided to tempt a pious woman. Dressing himself as a sadhu, the demon entered the hut of the woman, counting his beads. He asked for shelter, and the woman not only invited him in and set food before him but asked him to join her in prayer. The demon, the better to succeed, decided to accede to all her requests. They began to pray. Then the woman asked him to tell her about the lives of the saints, and the demon began to recite like the best of sadhus. The woman rose to such ecstasy that she sprinkled the entire hut with holy water, and naturally sprinkled some over the demon himself. Then she proposed to the demon that they perform the pranayama together, and gradually she developed such power that finally the demon was unable to leave the hut and remained to serve the pious woman and to learn the best prayers. A Rishi, passing by the hut, looked in, and seeing the demon in prayer joined him in praise to Brahma. Thus all three sat around the hearth, chanting the best prayers. Thus a simple woman, through her devotion, impelled a demon and a Rishi to sing in praise together. But in the Highest Dwelling Places this cooperation occasioned no horror, only smiles. Thus even a demon can be compelled to join in prayer."

564. Let us relate another tale about the heart. "Some people gathered together to boast of their prowess: some exhibited their muscular development; some boasted of taming wild beasts; one estimated strength by the hardness of his skull, another by his swiftness of foot—thus the various parts of the human body were extolled. But someone remembered the heart, which had remained unpraised. Then everyone began to think about how the strength of the heart could be estimated. Finally a newcomer said, 'You have discussed various types of competition, but you have forgotten one near to the human heart—a competition in magnanimity. Let your teeth, fists, and skull be at rest, and vie with each other in magnanimity. It will speed the path of the heart to the Fiery World.' It must be confessed that everyone became greatly concerned, for they did not know how to manifest magnanimity. And so the manifestation of love remained undiscussed, because even the gateway to it was not admitted to any place in the contest of prowess." Verily, if magnanimity is found, then love will kindle the fires of the heart.

565. Often the divisibility of the heart has spurred

the resourceful mind. Yet how can one divide that which is permeated with the one Fire? One can light many separate lamps from such Fire, but Fire itself cannot be divided. Thus, whole-hearted striving toward Hierarchy is undivided. I deem that many instabilities result from a lack of realization of the unity of Hierarchy. The time is coming when all the conditions of life will drive people to an understanding of the one Hierarchy. It has been wisely indicated that the greatest division will give the impetus for unity. Is not the present a time of the utmost disunity? Can humanity become still more divided? This is the dawn of the accomplishment of unity. The waning moon prepares for the coming of the new moon. Is not an infant upon it?

**566**. Let us pay especial attention to the battle in the Subtle World. Innumerable hordes are battling on all planes. A stout heart is needed to realize these forces. And even on Earth the shoulders can ache from these battles. One must warn people about the extent of their dependence upon the Subtle World. People often search for answers. Whence comes a seeming inner shock? Its cause may lie in some manifestation of the Subtle World.

**567**. Each incongruity and imbalance is a sign of chaos. When these signs are apparent in the lower forms of nature, one may hope that upon transition into a higher state they may be transformed. But what of the highest earthly creations—men, if they turn out to be filled with the most chaotic instability? Yet in the course of many ages, it is amazing to see the increase of imbalance among various achievements. No one and nothing impels people to ponder over the value of balance. The Teachings of all peoples speak of the Golden Path, yet men themselves actually think about this least of all. Through its imbalance, its chaotic state, mankind has brought on a coming uprising of fire. But even on the very brink of danger people reject each useful advice about self-preservation. As before, they will toss about from the very old to the very new, even if it be illusory. How can it be explained to them that Agni Yoga is neither old nor new? An element that is perpetual and omnipresent is not subject to the demarcations of time. Fire is at the very threshold! One must call to mind how it is to be encountered, and one must understand that only Agni, psychic energy, can be the interpreter at the approach of Fire.

568. One can carry on useful observations of the refinement of sensitivity to fiery manifestations. It is useful to note how our palm or our forehead senses human radiations at a distance. Such sensitivity varies, as does thermoradiation. Closing one's eyes and ears, by degrees one can sense the radiation of human heat at a considerable distance. Such observation is an affirmative demonstration of man as the focus of fiery energy.

569. Insomnia may be actually the result of non-admittance into the Subtle World when the tension of conflict is too powerful. Habitual ability to project the subtle body may bring it forth immediately upon falling asleep. But when tension is excessive one cannot risk this; one might even fail to return. Therefore, during the battle of Light and darkness one must not fall into a bottomless whirlpool.

570. Mental sendings ordinarily contain some unusual expressions, which you have frequently noticed with surprise. An unusual expression is sometimes used for the purpose of ensuring better remembrance. This is a very ancient method. It is difficult to retain the usual words, which may slip by instead of

penetrating the consciousness. The more unusual, the better assembled, the more definitive such a sending is, the better it is remembered. It is necessary to remind more than once of the far-off thought, which passes over the surface of the consciousness. One ought not reproach oneself for forgetfulness; on the contrary, these sliding thoughts projected from remote distances only prove that they come from outside and not from the inner consciousness. Also, in schools the receptivity to alien thoughts should be cultivated. People know so little how to listen or how to understand what they read that special hours should be assigned to the verification of what has been heard. How can one expect the fiery energy to be noticed if no attention is paid to even a loudly spoken word? More than once we have spoken of the development of the faculty of conscious non-hearing and non-seeing, this is quite different. In our normal state we must be highly receptive.

**571.** Here is another example of the influence of thought. True, in studying the scriptural records of all ages, one is struck by a seeming repetitious occurrence of identical thoughts. Not only do we find like expressions of the same thoughts but one may often find quite identical particular words. Yet it can be established that the writers not only did not know each other but could not possibly have read these writings. This manifestation can be observed in all domains of creativeness. Ignorance would suspect some form of concealed plagiarism, but anyone who has contacted true creative force knows that thought sent into space can impregnate the most varied receivers. Such manifestations should be studied. They can actually prove the possibility of the influence of psychic energy; besides, the same considerations may direct thought toward Hierarchy—in other words, to the shortest path.

572. One cannot fail to be amazed at the persistent refusal of people to envision the manifestation of the all-pervading fiery element. One can turn to the trite example of oxygen in its solid, liquid, gaseous and even etheric states. People will accept such action of substances quite calmly but never apply this striking example to the fiery element. Fire is lodged too strongly in people's minds in its coarsest form; but so utterly undeveloped is the human imagination that it cannot conceive the extension and refinement of the crude form into infinity. People will say, "Why don't we see the Fiery Beings?" Thus, they prefer to blame the Fiery World rather than ponder upon the state of their consciousness.

573. Pseudo-science impedes knowledge of the Universe. Thought cannot be limited by a mechanistic conception. Even the greatest mathematical minds have acknowledged something above mere formulas. But mediocrity has no flights of thought, and in its stupidity prefers to come up against a wall rather than look upward.

A certain teacher asked a pupil, "Where does stupidity dwell?" The boy answered, "When I do not know my lesson, you tap upon my forehead. Probably stupidity is there." One must understand why We now tap at the heart and not the forehead. The head has stored up many calculations, but the heart has been laggard in improving. Thus one must straighten out that which is backward.

574. Verily, the manifestation of the Great Sacrifice will sweep through all the world. It will be impressed upon the human hearts by striking evidences. Therefore, watch the signs keenly; they are numerous.

575. When people find themselves in the state of Preta-loka, they begin to regret that they did not

discard their outworn rags earlier. The Fire of Space must consume painfully that which should have been dissolved by the light of Agni. One can get rid of unnecessary burdens long before the transition. One's own vital Agni can purify one of harmful filth. The ability to turn in time to Agni is a goal-fitting action prompted by the experience of the heart. The manifestation of the oneness of life may elicit the inquiry, "If life were to be endlessly prolonged, how could the cognizance of its many sides be arrived at?" Indeed, if the body prevented penetration into the many strata of space, one would have to have recourse to the most artificial measures, which by their nature are contrary to free will. Only by direct fiery aspiration of the heart to Hierarchy, can one truly unite oneself with the higher spheres. One should not even divide Hierarchy according to personal criteria, but one should strive along the fiery thread to where the human word dissolves and is engulfed by radiance.

576. When I speak again of beauty, I wish to accustom you to the great beauty of the Fiery World. Everyone who loves the beautiful transforms thereby a portion of earthly life. Only by meticulous spiritual cognizance can one burn the unnecessary rags here in advance. Such burning does not take place in specially constructed bonfires in public squares, but in each day's smile of love. Only by degrees do we come to realize the beauty of the world of spirit. Our sojourns in the various strata are short, but on entering the Fiery World we can remain there. And when we come from there, we preserve the fiery solemnity wherever we are.

577. He who spends life pridefully is not of a fiery nature; he who spends it in self-disparagement is not of a fiery nature. Only simplicity is akin to Fire.

578. Even during earthly life people transform

their appearance through their passions. How greatly is this quality of justice magnified in the Subtle World! You have already seen how the dwellers of the Subtle World are transformed—some become luminous, some become darkened and even disfigured to the most horrible extent. With very few exceptions no one on Earth cares to see in this self-transformation the law of justice. People do not realize that they must take the necessary precautions in time, at least for the sake of their own appearance. Each thought honeyed by a hypocritical smile flowers according to its merit in the Subtle World. And if Agni has not been called into action, the ugly grimace of the true personality is almost ineradicable. Moreover, few of those disfigured by malice have enough sense to turn toward the Light in time. According to the law of progression, they keep rolling down into the dark abysses until a sudden reversal takes place, often bringing out even resistance from the wicked one himself.

Not through fear of any punishment, but in anticipation of their own destiny, should people turn to purification. What each one metes out for himself is not severity but justice. The thought of purification must lead to the realization of Fire. The Fiery Baptism is the wisest teaching, but how can it descend upon one if the heart is not softened and dwells in cruelty? The mask of cruelty is dreadful; it cannot be wiped away, just as Addison's disease cannot be washed off the face. Cruelty is a ferocious disease! Even a beast attacks a cruel being. Thus, I call to mind those with faces that cannot be cleansed, that have forgotten the heart, the Fiery World, and the Hierarchy of Light.

**579**. Do not speak ill of those who have crossed into the Subtle World. Even of a wicked man one should not speak badly. He has already assumed his true visage. And to speak badly of him means to invoke a harmful enemy. Often evil grows, and one may bring upon oneself a giant of evil with all his co-workers. It is better to send the evil one a wish that he be freed of his hideous mask—that will be wiser.

**580**. One must again recall that which should be familiar even to children. People often know and understand something, but later, when they arrive at the division of atoms, they are covered by the debris! They can only split, but no one can build a house in the wrath of destruction.

**581**. A mother told her son about a great saint, "Even the grain of sand beneath his foot becomes great." It came to pass that this saint passed through the village. The boy followed his footsteps, took up a pinch of dust therefrom, sewed it in a bag and wore it around his neck. And as he recited his lessons in school, he always held this relic in his hand. The boy was filled thereby with such inspiration that his answers were always remarkable. One day when leaving the school his teacher praised him and asked what he always held in his hand. The boy replied, "Earth from beneath the feet of the saint who passed through our village." The teacher commented, "This hallowed earth serves you better than gold." A neighboring shopkeeper, hearing this, said to himself, "What a stupid boy to take only a pinch of this golden earth! I will await the passing of the holy man and collect all the earth from where he trod. Thus I can obtain the most profitable merchandise." And the shopkeeper sat in his doorway and waited in vain for the coming of the saint. But he never came. Greed is not akin to the Fiery World.

**582**. Shamed be the land where teachers dwell in poverty and want. Shamed be those who know that their children are being taught by a man in want. Not to care for the teachers of its future generation is not only a disgrace to a nation but a mark of its ignorance. Can one entrust children to a depressed man? Can one ignore the emanation created by sorrow? Can one rest ignorant of the fact that a depressed spirit cannot inspire enthusiasm? Can one regard teaching as an insignificant profession? Can one expect an enlightened spirit in children if the school is a place of humiliation and affront? Can one perceive any construction during the gnashing of teeth? Can one expect the fires of the heart when the spirit is silent? Thus I say, thus I repeat that the nation that has forgotten its teachers has forgotten its future. Let us not lose an hour in directing thought toward the joy of the future. And let us make sure that the teacher be the most valued member of the country's institutions. The time is coming when the spirit must be enlightened and made joyous through true knowledge. Fire is at the threshold!

**583.** One must mellow the hearts of teachers, then they will abide in constant awareness. The child's heart recognizes what is aflame and what is extinguished. Not the given lesson, but the mutual aspiration of teacher and pupil reveals the world of wonders. To open the eyes of a pupil means to share with him the love of great creation. Who would dispute that one must have a firm foothold if one's goal is far distant? The archer will affirm this. Thus let us learn to cherish everything that affirms the future. Fire is at the threshold!

**584.** It is praiseworthy that you revere the days of the Great Sacrifice. Let every human heart draw strength for achievement from the Chalice of the Saviour. Let us not emulate savages, in hostility to one another. The time of crucifixion and killing must end. Hear ye! Apostles of Truth are needed, aspiring to the Baptism of Fire. Let malice cease, at least in the days of great suffering as happened when the Chalice was drained for the entire world! You should understand that the focus of All-Being is one. There cannot be two centers of rotation. Those are mad who deny the magnitude of Infinity! On this scale is the Ineffable Sacrifice measured. When an earthly body hastened to accept the Sacrifice for the regeneration of all the world, no human words could describe the reasons for this hallowed heroism. One may gather the most supreme expressions, but the heart alone, in the tremor of striving, understands this glorious beauty. Permit no slander or blasphemy, even from the ignorant. Each blasphemer plunges himself into the darkness of madness. Thus, teach the affirmation of the spirit's salvation, that there may be no touch of darkness in the days of the Fiery Chalice.

**585.** Not by accident do you receive in these Great Days news of treason and lies. What madness that the traitors are those who seem, as it were, the guardians of higher understanding! But the law of darkness is inexorable, and the devices of falsehood will not cease until the human heart becomes softened. If even the memory of the Great Sacrifice can instill only falsehood and treachery, then the Great Service is inaccessible. Let us turn away from darkness; even plants know enough to stretch out toward light.

**586.** To float against the current on a lotus was considered the symbol of Great Service in antiquity. The rapture of achievement admits no thought of the depth of the abyss or whether one will attain. The joy of spirit frees one from earthly fears. Only he who floats on a lotus knows this valor and joy. Thus, one need not think about sunken reefs when the spirit senses attainment.

**587.** During these Hallowed Days one should

remember all toilers. One must not dwell in cruelty even for an hour when even now the Crown of Thorns still bleeds. Let us abide in righteousness.

**588**. Each abuse of the Saviour, the Teacher, and the Heroes plunges the world into savagery and precipitates chaos. How can it be explained that chaos is very near, that there is no need to cross an ocean to find it? It is also difficult to explain that savagery begins with the very smallest. When the treasure of solemnity is lost and the pearls of the heart's knowledge are scattered, what remains? One can remember how people mocked the Great Sacrifice. Has not the entire world answered for this savagery? One can see how it is reflected in degeneration. This degeneration is the worst of all. I say, "Blessed be all energies; but let there be no sinking into the miasma of dissolution." Thus let us remember all Great Days!

**589**. He centered in Himself all Light. He was imbued with renunciation of self and of earthly possessions. He knew the Palace of Spirit and the Temple of Fire. One cannot take earthly objects into Fire, and the Palace of Spirit cannot be made a treasury of gold. Thus one should follow the Great Example. One can sometimes compare the objects of today, but how can one evaluate the objects of the future? So, also, the Fiery Images are incomparable and inaccessible to us at present. Therefore one should ponder deeply within one's heart, in order to glimpse the Fiery World through the help of the Great Examples. If but momentarily one could find oneself in the Lotus Boat, breasting the tide of all the waves of chaos! One can ask that in a really difficult hour one be permitted to experience the same rapture in the break up of chaos.

**590**. One may imagine the beauty of the conjoined service of multitudes of people when their hearts aspire in one ascent. We shall not say, "Impossible," or, "Denied." From Power one can borrow, and from Light one can become illumined. If one could only realize wherein lie Light and Power! Someone is already laughing boisterously at this, but he laughs in darkness. What can be more hideous than boisterous laughter in darkness! Yet Light will abide with him who seeks it.

**591.** Resurrection and immortality—do they not direct our thoughts toward the foundation of Being? But even these undeniable truths impel men toward disunity rather than cooperation. Many are the streams of Benefaction poured upon Earth. The manifestation of Benefaction occurs far more often than is generally supposed, yet the sacred gifts are accepted by men far more rarely than might be hoped. Thus is the law of free will peculiarly interpreted by Earth-dwellers. The dark forces try their utmost to prevent the manifestations of Benefaction. The self-will of people encourages various perversions. One should observe how at times benevolent thoughts flash out, to be extinguished as if by the pressure of a black hand. You were shown how even a powerful ray is subject to the schemes of the dark ones. Therefore I repeat about the unprecedented times. It is a fallacy for anyone to continue to regard the present time as normal. No self-hypnosis or reminiscing can help the ship in a storm; only the solid rock of the future can hold the anchor! So many raging voices are shrieking from out of space, intent on hindering the course of the ship! Therefore the black eagle struggles with such fierceness, but out of the Dawn comes the White One, and with him the streams of Benefaction!

**592.** Evil can be eradicated only by good. Such a truth is simple, and yet it remains not understood. The good in people is usually not operating and therefore remains inactive. They cannot imagine how good can expel evil, thus cutting short its existence. Good is the most active, vital, inexhaustible, invincible principle, but in its entire action it is devoid of cruelty. Therein, and also in its freedom from egoism and conceit, lies one of its most significant distinctions from evil. So if a religion and its emissaries display cruelty, it cannot be a religion that is a link with the Highest Good! How can one imagine a servant of religion as cruel? By his cruelty he would become the enemy of good. Moreover he would be indicating his ignorance with regard to the very Scripture of the religion. Good cannot sanction cruelty! But in affirming the sacred Teaching of active good one must ponder how to use one's entire time in the glorification of good. And such glorification will be not only a symbol, it will be the fire of the heart. If we want to advance we must apply active goodness. We must understand that we can replace a pit with a true temple. Step by step we must fill the abyss with strongholds of Light. We must put together the stones of good, over and above any personal moods. Let the small planet burn itself out, but our Father's house has many mansions. Each action for good is an eternal achievement. When the dross of evil shall have long since disintegrated, the sites of good will flourish.

**593.** Also, let us pray that our eyes be opened to good. Many eyes, dust-blinded, do not fully discern the good. Because of their affliction they discern only coarse forms. One must manifest extreme tension in order to avoid crushing the seedling of good. However, the heart that has expelled cruelty recognizes all seeds of good and ends up with magnanimity and love.

**594.** One should understand and encompass with good. Much that is done through forgetfulness is not evil, but absence of memory often makes criminals of men. True, egoism which is not overcome prompts one to forget others. But a fiery consciousness will not forget the goal of life when it serves the good of the world. People often do not know how to think about the good of the world, regarding themselves as insignificant. This is wrong, because the spirit, the fiery seed, emanates from the One Fire and strives toward the Light Eternal. It does not matter where burns the torch that points out the way to the lost traveler!

**595**. Even plants and trees influence each other. Every gardener knows this reciprocal action, knows where grow mutual friends and where enemies. Then how much more pronounced must be these interactions in the animal kingdom and certainly among men! During an ordinary conversation at dinner the experienced eye of a hostess detects such mutual attractions and repulsions. The fiery heart senses such mutual interactions far more clearly, but these manifestations should be noted. It is not enough to sense them; they must be transferred to the consciousness, to be utilized ultimately for good. The ability to transfer sensations to the consciousness is acquired through experience. For a discerning experiment one should premise a thought in this direction. Much is impressed upon the consciousness through simple thinking. Also, nature should be regarded as a great guide. Does not the purple of the swelling buds recall the purple of the protective net of the aura? Thus, one can find in color and sound great analogies to the foundations of Life.

**596**. Pay attention to the obvious fallacy of man when through prejudice he attempts to conceal that which he has long known in his heart. An eternal conflict ensues which can react on the physical body. One cannot deny with impunity that which our being knows from all past experiences. How many eyes full of suffering are encountered on the way! Great is the torment after condemning the consciousness to darkness. Great is the despondency when the energy Fire is directed against itself. And often we see those closest to us concealing the ancient knowledge under cover of dead husks of fear. One must pity those who are sick in spirit.

**597.** And so, the greatest misconception lies in the fact that people prepare themselves for death instead of educating themselves for life. They have heard often enough that the very concept of death is vanquished. They have heard often enough of the need for changing the seven sheaths. It has been sufficiently emphasized that these changes take place with the closest cooperation of Fire. This means that one should assist the fiery transmutations, since they are inevitable. Why spend ages and millenniums on that which can be accomplished far more quickly! We should prepare our consciousness for the fiery receptivity of our concentrated bodies. If something is subject to a fiery action, let this good be accomplished in the shortest possible time. Thinking about such transmutation in itself greatly helps our organism to assimilate this process into the consciousness. You already know that accepting something into the consciousness means a bodily assimilation also. In our general conceptions it is high time to become accustomed to the scope of the Fiery World. We are amazed at the difference between an idiot and a genius, but our imagination falls short in extending this divergence into infinity. Our imagination is equally uneducated in visualizing the closeness of the Fiery World, obscured solely by our body. Rarely do people see the highest spheres of the Subtle World, but those who are worthy to behold the splendor of the mountains and seas of the Subtle World, and the radiance of its flowers, can visualize the purity of the Fiery Kingdom! One can also imagine the omnipresence of the Fiery World, when even during physical existence one can project the subtle body to different places simultaneously. Thus let us become accustomed to the Fiery World as the only destiny of men.

**598.** The established facts of the simultaneous appearances of the subtle body in different places should do away with the ignorant prejudice that the Higher Beings cannot appear in various parts of the world at the same time. If even in the physical state one can know the divisibility of the spirit, then certainly in the fiery state, above all, there would be no limitation to one time, one place. When one succeeds, logically and intelligently, in visualizing the primary qualities of the Fiery World, one can immediately begin to assimilate its reality. What joy when Infinity ceases to be a void!

**599.** Insomnia was once again the reason for restraining the subtle body from excessive battle in the Subtle World. Drowsiness is often a sign of the projection of the subtle body, but the Guide must watch lest there be too great a subjection to excessive danger.

**600.** The Fiery World is reflected in the earthly consciousness as something contrary to all everyday concepts. Imagine a man who has slept through all sunrises; he knows only the sunset and the evening shadows. But if he is once awakened at dawn by an earthquake, he runs out of his house and stands astonished before the rising light, never hitherto seen. If a man cannot accept into his consciousness even so natural an occurrence, how can he assimilate the subtlest manifestations of Fire? People have acquainted themselves with only the most gross of the subtle and etheric energies, and the beautiful fiery signs are cast into the domain of superstition. It is terrible to observe that precisely ignorance comments upon superstition. It is difficult to imagine how repulsive is this obscuration of knowledge through dark stratagems! Chemistry and even elementary physics give an idea of the higher luminosity. But even such examples do not elevate thought. People want to dwell in evil, in other words, in ignorance. One should firmly remember that each allusion to the One Light will be the source of hostile attacks.

**601.** Furthermore, let us not forget that the fiery body not only does not fear blows but they even intensify the fundamental power. The statement that blows only strengthen energy does not belittle the Fiery World. By means of simple experiments in physics one is able to demonstrate this principle. Thus, let us learn to show reverence for the Fiery World, from the simplest to the Highest.

**602.** *Ahamkara* is the high state of the fiery seed when it can already affirm itself without egoism. Thus the Fiery Gates are opened when not only is egoism burned away but a worthy evaluation of self is achieved. Only then can the spirit verily bring its sole heritage to the altar of Light. But on this long journey what happens to the enemies who wrought such torment through their discordances? When darkness takes over its own possessions, the remaining ones who are able to ascend are divided according to rays. Thus discord disappears and the feeling of enmity dissolves by itself. The spirits gather and rise to the abode of containment like waves of harmonious light. Thus is settled the question, most incomprehensible to man, about the unity of the seeds of Light in ascent to the Higher World. Enmity, so insoluble in the physical world, disintegrates by itself in the etheric, purified rays. Not only in the higher but already in the middle spheres of the Subtle World, the feeling of enmity withers because of its uselessness. One must understand these laws of the distribution of the rays. The realization of these laws alone will mitigate the malice of enmity even here. Also let us not forget that enmity throws the organism out of balance, leaving it a prey to various sicknesses and obsessions. Therefore I advise you to consider enmity from the viewpoint of prophylaxis. Why should one be sick, infect others, and be a prey to fits of madness when a single effort of spirit preserves the invulnerability of the organism?

**603**. It is astonishing that even recently the transmission of pictures was considered unrealizable. But now images are already transmitted over great distances; the word thunders through many spheres, even further than people imagine. The fiery worlds likewise have no impediments in transmission and communication. One should not be astonished at such fiery potencies when even the material world has already mastered the crude forms of the same possibilities. And how many achievements are knocking upon the doors of the human heart!

**604**. Can human language express that which is beyond earthly expression? Notwithstanding, people must think about the Fiery World. They should picture it as the most vital and most guiding; otherwise, in confused dreams, they will be unable to approach it as has been ordained. Reverence for the One Light is as natural as the idea of the One Father. People are alike in their fiery seed, but physical atavism places them at varying distances from Truth. But the higher fires stand above all divisions. Read about the most diverse visions of Fiery Beings in all countries of the world, and you will find in them the same signs and results. Verily, all distinctions between peoples fall away before the Higher World. People sense equally the breath of the Higher World. They are set equally atremor in heart and body. They understand the Voice of the Envoy of Light. With difficulty they return to the common earthly state. Such manifestations, and the ecstasy of the spirit at contact with a Higher Being, are unforgettable to all alike. One should not forget that the most diverse peoples have beheld the Higher Beings in identical Images. Is this not a sign of the oneness of Light and of the Hierarchy of Good? Thus, one should accept the Fiery World with heart and mind. One must feel that all inspirations emanate therefrom. Honest creators and workers can bear witness that the best solutions come from without. Like a powerful dynamo, the Fiery World emits a shower of the best formulas. One should not only make use of them but also testify about them in the highest terms. Thus one can be united by the fires of the heart with the Supreme Light. This is not conceit, for Light knows no obstacles.

**605**. There is no salvation surer than that through devotion. One can forgive much where there is unswerving devotion. The man who is devoted in heart can be relied upon. It is cause for rejoicing when Hierarchy is upheld by devotion. At present it is especially needed. If yesterday's confusion seemed enormous, what can one say of tomorrow's? I have already prepared you for the growth of Armageddon, and you know that the black wings of darkness will not withstand the Fiery Sword. Be not astonished—the Battle increases!

**606**. Indeed, one must free oneself from egoism in order to transmute and affirm the radiant Ego. One may carry the transformed Ego to the altar of Light without fear of being burned. What, then, is subject to scorching if not egoism with all its appendages? Egoism, like a cancerous swelling is engendered by lack of Agni. Let us not forget that egoism attracts and fills itself with carnal lusts and begets evil. Around the bait of egoism flock the influences of family, clan, and nation. The very sediments of the physical and of the Subtle World seek to wind themselves about egoism; such a bristly ball is unsuitable for the Fiery World. But the tempered and conscious fiery Ego enters the Fiery World as a welcome guest. Thus, let us distinguish all that befits the Higher World. Let us not regard this attraction to the Higher World as an achievement. Let it be only a luminous duty. It is not fitting to consider the predestined assignment as a unique achievement. People should accustom themselves to the transmutation of the heart as a manifest path, known long ago.

**607.** Also, let us rejoice at such a path. Let the thought about transformation of the heart be a source of joy. Many sorrows and difficulties come from egoism. Many horrors arise from egoism. Many obstacles originate in egoism. One should cease to think about limitations. Since the fiery seed is bestowed, one should rejoice that we carry so great a pearl because of the trust of Hierarchy itself.

**608.** Do not falter at the sight of demons. Pity for them is sharper than a fiery sword. Through pity one can repel the most daring attack. A beast cannot withstand the look of compassion, whereas it attacks when it senses the trembling of fear. True, fear is evil, but an evil which intrinsically is insignificant because it is ignorance. You have had many occasions to convince yourself that the inventions of evil are begotten of ignorance. Thus, supply yourself with a coffer of compassion.

**609**. What crime is the most destructive to the monad of the criminal? Certainly treason. This crime abruptly alters the current already established, and a terrific counterblow results. A traitor cannot live long in the world of matter, and when he crosses into the Subtle World, being entirely without life-giving energy he is sucked into chaos and is doomed to disintegration. Treason is never impulsive. It is always premeditated, and thus its fate is aggravated. It must be understood that the return to chaos is, first of all, inexpressibly painful. In addition, the feeling of the primary seed remains, and facing the futility of hoping for a speedy transformation demands indescribable courage. But the traitor is devoid of courage. He is above all filled with conceit. Thus, people should be warned that even from a physical standpoint treason is intolerable. The traitor not only condemns himself but infects vast strata around him, generating storms of fire. One should not think that an unnatural human action will not react on the surroundings. It reacts first of all on children under seven, before the spirit has taken possession of the entire organism. During this early period the fiery tempests are especially dangerous; they impose a special nervousness upon the heart action of those who already carry the weight of heavy atavism. Thus the traitor not only betrays an individual, but at the same time outrages a whole generation and even affects the well-being of an entire country. Let each one who has pondered upon the Fiery World beware of treason even in thought. No treason is small—it is great in evil and is hostile to the Universe. Such evil is in itself a barrier to ascent.

**610**. It is instructive to observe from the scientific point of view the nature of the atmosphere surrounding the substance of the Subtle or Fiery World, when this atmosphere is condensed for a manifestation in the physical world. One may recall the draughts which precede manifestations; in one case one can sense a coolness as of mountains, even accompanied by fragrances, whereas in another case one can sense piercing cold and an unpleasant odor. In this way the strata of the worlds can be distinguished. But one might also discern various chemical compounds in the condensed atmosphere. Is this not a manifestation of the higher realities? Thus, spiritually and physically, it is possible to apprehend the magnitude of the Invisible Worlds. One must not only become accustomed to this beautiful reality, but must also adjust one's actions commensurately with the grandeur of Cosmos.

**611**. One may expect supernal manifestations in the life of the planet. Unprecedented is the time when events are poured cosmically into the Chalice of the Archangel!

**612**. If the Sublime Beings testify that they have not faced the supreme Origin of Origins, this should not be construed as a form of negation. On the contrary, this testimony of the sacred infinitude of the Supreme World only proves how unencompassable is the concept of Sublime Light. He is right who know the path toward Light, but only the ignorant, in conceit, will presume that the brain can evaluate the Sublime. One must learn to comprehend the oneness of the path of ascent. In the radiance of the microcosm one can envision the parallel with the Infinite. One must learn to value each drop of dew reflecting the myriads of worlds. By way of experiment, one may reject all negations. A manifestation of Hierarchy should be accepted exultantly. The directed consciousness can lead the spirit's eye to the string of pearls which loses itself in Infinity. One can understand the reverence for the concepts of concordance and co-measurement. One can raise the spirit toward Light and fly over masses of darkness. Does one not fly in dreams, and are not such flights inherent from childhood? The spirit remembers these qualities of other worlds. No earthly obstacles can deprive the human heart of the concept of flight, and the very same heart will teach reverence for the Origin of Origins.

**613**. Thought creates; the extent of thought in space is unencompassable. Thus, many experiments serve only partially to broaden the understanding of the power of thought. People are astonished at the inexplicable character of clairvoyance pertaining to the future, seldom realizing that the fire of thought kindles and constructs an image of the future. Thoughts of various times and content construct subtle worlds which are accessible to clairvoyance. Among many causes of evolution, thought-creativeness has a primary significance. Therefore I so often repeat about the quality of thought.

**614**. Earthly events are much spoken about in the Subtle World, yet there is much which cannot be understood there. One must have compassion for such lack of understanding, just as on Earth. Precisely, as on Earth, so also in Heaven, one should not aggravate a situation by irritation. One should follow the Hierarch in full trust, just as the Hierarch follows his own Hierarch. This path of devotion should be loved. One must cleave to it whole-heartedly, so that any other mode of thought becomes impossible. Verily, by such devotion are worlds built. One may read about most beautiful examples of devotion, and thus will be narrated a story about heroes. One should even learn to live like the heroes. One should love the Fiery Sphere.

**615**. Special complexities arise due to the varying

conditions of time in different worlds. True, one can see the very remote future, whereas an earthly date is deflected and appears quite different where no time exists. Moreover, our conventional days and nights assume differing aspects even upon other existing planets. But the Subtle World and the Fiery World even more are completely devoid of these conditions. This means that astrological signs may serve there, but even they are defined by different methods, because the chemism of the luminaries is refracted differently when Agni triumphs. But for us here it is difficult to imagine the conditions in higher worlds. The astral light is definitely affirmed according to the strata of the atmosphere; certain strata of the Subtle World dwell in twilight, because the light of their dwellers is faint. Few understand how the dwellers themselves can be like beacons of light. But precisely purified Agni serves as a beacon of light for all. Thus, thought about Materia Lucida serves as a beacon for achievement. Many ask themselves, "Will I shine?" Again, let us not forget that egoism is like a dark cobblestone upon the heart, but the pure Ego is like a radiant Adamant!

**616**. Thought-creativeness cannot be definitely discerned on the earthly plane; herein lies its difference from the Fiery World. The Higher Beings perceive the effect of their thoughts immediately, whereas here we can know only their direction, and the ultimate result is disclosed only after a certain lapse of time. Thus, one can gradually form an idea of the differences between manifestations in various worlds. Likewise, one can gradually approach fiery consciousness, eradicating the barriers between worlds. One can imagine the state when death will be no more, and the transition will be a usual attainment. It is impossible to understand how such separation between worlds came about, since it is not necessary for evolution, unless people have created a prideful concept of Earth. It can be discovered that in remote antiquity there was greater understanding of the spherical form of the planet than after the post-glacial period. True, many ancient traditions have been confused, and only now people begin correctly to extend their estimate of the continuity of the life of our Earth. It is amazing how apparently learned people discuss the greatness of God, yet at the same time seek to disparage his creations. If scientists two hundred years ago had dared to hint at the great antiquity of the planet, or to suggest other inhabited worlds, their contemporaries would probably have resorted to the well-tried remedy of the stake. And one may be equally sure that even now some moderate theory, though based on experiments, will be assailed as a fraud. Thus, people regard the destiny of this planet as the alpha and omega of the entire Universe. Much persuasion will be required to remind humanity that in all the promulgated Teachings the Era of Fire was foretold.

**617.** It is almost impossible to convey an idea of the imminence of the fiery invasion. There are numerous signs of it but people refuse to think of summer in winter. No one understands that the obduracy of nations cannot be settled by the methods of the past century. The Teaching about the most subtle physical processes presupposes everywhere something not susceptible to definition. One must accept this "something" also in the processes of national structures. The study of ethnography is greatly needed for the realization of the deplorable state of the planet. A concept of the world which embraces the Invisible World will change the psychology of the people. But this is as yet remote! Even in the circles devoted to psychic research the results of the experiments are not carried into life.

After their experiments the people remain as before. However, nothing should deter one from sharing his knowledge and encouraging the growth of consciousness. Therein lies love for one's fellow men.

**618.** Everywhere it is indicated that suffering is the best purifier and means of shortening the Path. This is undoubtedly true under the existing conditions on Earth. But could there have been Creation with an unalterable condition of suffering? No. Indeed, the Great Creativeness does not foresee a need for suffering. With terrific zeal people drive themselves into the circle of suffering. For millenniums people have tried to become mere bipeds. They try to weigh down the atmosphere of Earth with malice. Verily, every physician will bear witness that without evil there would be no suffering. Let us designate the ability to avoid suffering as a step toward Good. Truly, the passage of the Good through the furnace of Fire eliminates the sense of suffering. Thus, fiery transfiguration even on Earth lifts one beyond suffering. One should not evade suffering, for without suffering earthly achievement does not exist. But let each one ready for achievement kindle the fires of his heart. They will be the indicators of the Path, and a shield not fashioned by human hands. Someone has asked, "How does the Lord discern those who approach him?" The answer is, "By the fires of their hearts." If we are astonished by the power of Fire that even here envelops us and saturates our garments, then we can understand how supernal is the glow of the fires of the heart along the Chain of Hierarchy!

**619.** People erroneously believe that poison gases destroy only earthly life; there is a far greater danger in the death-inflicting gas fumes—they vitiate the strata of the atmosphere, in other words, disrupt the chemism of the luminaries. The gases not only endanger life but they can throw the planet out of equilibrium. Assuredly, if even the gas from dung fires is very harmful for the intellect, what of the exhausts from factories, and, above all, what of war gases? This last invention is the crown of human hatred. A healthy generation cannot be born if evil is set in the foundation of life.

**620**. Furthermore, it is the greatest infamy that humanity even now practices witchcraft, precisely the blackest sorcery bent upon evil. Such conscious collaboration with the dark forces is no less horrible than poison gases. It is incredible that men who consider themselves to be in the religion of Good perpetrate the most dreadful sorcery. I would not mention this black peril if it had not reached such terrific proportions at present. The most intolerable rituals have been reinstituted in order to harm people. In their ignorance the crowds have been inveigled into mass magic. It is impermissible to allow such disintegration of the planet! It is impermissible to allow the dark forces to succeed in annihilating all evolution. Sorcery is not permissible, being a pressure on space contrary to nature. Everywhere, stress the danger of sorcery.

**621**. It is a natural desire to want to know how the transitions into different spheres are accomplished. It is not difficult to understand that purified Agni is the decisive factor. If we gradually fill a balloon with combustible gas, it will begin to rise proportionately. If the balloon cannot retain the gas it will descend. This is a crude example of the principle governing transition into the various spheres of the Subtle World. The subtle entity can ascend by itself if its fiery seed is appropriately filled. Fire—the transmuter—helps to assimilate the new and higher conditions. Agni facilitates the understanding of the language of each sphere, because the intercourse of beings becomes more refined as the

257

ascent is made. Of course, the high Guidance does not forsake the striving ones, but for assimilation of Guidance devotion is needed. Thus, a being can ascend the ladder—there is no other symbol which can more accurately define the ascent of the spirit. If a being is detained on one step, the cause is apparent in the aura. So many travelers quite unexpectedly find themselves a few steps lower! The usual reason for such retrogression is some earthly remembrance which engenders cravings. The Guide considers a store of patience indispensable to protect those who stumble. But one should not draw too frequently upon this precious energy. The being who can discover the cause by himself will actually ascend more quickly. Truly, ascent is accompanied by the joy of new companions, and finally the earthly asp of envy falls away, and thought-creativeness is no longer impeded by the currents of malice. But one should prepare even now for mobility of consciousness. A torpid consciousness obstructs the striving of Agni. Thus, let us envision perfectly clearly the ladder of ascent.

**622**. One should in no way violate the free will of people. The Teaching of Light transforms life when the spirit voluntarily recognizes the necessity of ascent. Therefore, do not burden others with admonitions. People will improve and attain by themselves. In the history of mankind one can see how the spirit of people finds its way toward Light. By its light each spirit finds the path in its own way. Many are unwilling to accept everything proffered, seeking by themselves some secret approach to Truth. One must exercise the greatest care with such independent aspirants; not everyone likes the principle of a chorus. Observation will prompt the most appropriate measures. However, one must calmly accept human peculiarities. Even grains of sand differ from one another. But who should revere individuality if not the servants of Light! Thus, one should establish nothing by force. It is said, "Though today a man may not search for Light, tomorrow he may weep for it."

**623.** I commend your lack of surprise at learning that a shot did not affect the hypnotized woman. It is another evidence that psychic energy dominates physical laws. One should observe numerous examples in all of life. Besides cases where an outside command is involved, we often make use of our own psychic energy and with its help avert the most powerful hostile arrows. It should be remembered that the link with Hierarchy is stronger than armor. By what means did many warriors and leaders escape direct danger? Precisely through the link with the Highest Ones. The manifestation of such a bond demands the constant retention of the Image of the Lord in one's heart. One can traverse the most impassable abysses if the link with the Lord is strong. But if this link is temporary, the protection may be interrupted. Thus, one should observe the proofs in life. They provide many remarkable examples of the power of psychic energy and of the presence of the Forces of Light.

**624.** Even among contemporary forms numerous animal-like men can be found. Such monstrosities are usually ascribed to a fright or shock experienced by the mother. But, notwithstanding many explanations, the principal cause is usually lost sight of. It may be understood that in the Subtle World certain entities are subject to fits of carnal desire. During these obscurations they sink to the level of the animal kingdom. Moreover, Agni declines to such an extent that the animal principles take possession of the fallen ones. Of course, with time, they can again ascend, but the animal contact is so powerful that it may be transformed at reincarnation into animal form. Sometimes heredity contributes to such animal-like rebirths, for base spirits prefer corresponding forms for themselves. And sometimes it is neither atavism nor heredity, but a deplorable plunge into the animal world, which imprints the seal of madness. Again it is instructive to note how the decrease of Agni permits the manifestation of animal propensities.

Agni, the savior, leads to beautiful worlds, but one must cherish it and not forget its existence. Many spirits, while not lowering themselves to an animal state, disgracefully stamp about on one spot and even fear Agni. During their earthly journeyings these timid ones feared everything existing, and Fire was to them the most terrifying concept. They forgot the Light, which could draw them to the World of Beauty, and fear is a poor counselor.

**625.** A saturated solution forms crystals; various conditions pass before us similarly. So does the saturation of thought produce action. From thought is born a physical effect. So does the saturation of karma finally produce physical consequences. Many timid ones try to put off karmic consequences, but a fiery spirit wisely hastens it by all means. He understands that the ends of a torn fabric can but hinder the ascent. Ugly confusion should not disturb the hastening one. He recognizes within his heart that the inevitable must come to pass, and he only rejoices that everything can be passed through—the strength of Agni is in him.

**626.** Giving is a fundamental principle of the fiery divinity of the spirit. The analogy with fire is striking in all stages of development. From the crudest forms of life up to the highest, giving is manifest. One should not protest if a savage, not cognizant of the value of spiritual gifts, offers his deity his household treasures.

By such circuitous paths, humanity attains the highest giving. Beings of lofty degree understand giving as a joyful duty. One should strive for this degree of fieriness, for then we enter into balance with the Fiery Principle, and giving becomes receiving. Then, already devoid of selfhood, one's being accepts the highest gifts. And in such accelerated exchange an inflow of energy takes place. This constant regeneration renews the consciousness and spares one the breaks in consciousness during the transition into the Subtle World. Thus one can remember the exchange of substances in both the lowest and the highest. The unceasing interchange erases the boundaries between the lowest and highest, in other words, it raises the general level. Such work will benefit one's near ones, because it draws them into the orbit of striving of consciousness. Reveal understanding of the interchange of substances.

**627**. Sometimes you hear seeming wails and the din of voices. In fact, these are echoes from the strata of the Subtle World. These reach us either through our inner centers or as a result of tension of currents. With Us, perceptions of the Subtle World are transformed into voices, seemingly physical, but you know that the Subtle World has no physical sounds as we know them. Thus, energies are transmuted according to the different strata. The reverberation of vibrations around the Earth is heavy, but in their refined state they become just a certain aspect of electricity that is invisible to earthly eyes. So, also, a subtle vibration is inaudible in its highest tension. One can observe instructive changes in different worlds, but the principle of fiery manifestation remains inviolable throughout.

**628**. The loss of religion has shaken the movement forward. Without God there is no path. Call Him what one will, the highest Hierarchic Principle must be observed, otherwise there is nothing to adhere to. Thus, one must understand how the upward aspiration of people's wills surrounds the planet like a protective net.

**629.** In primitive beliefs the worship of the Deity was based on fear. But fear evokes terror and inevitable indignation. Human nature inherently preserves the consciousness that the great Origin of Origins has nothing in common with terror. He who feels love for God can utter his Name in his own language. Only with such an all-pervading concept can one express worthy veneration. Nothing on Earth can so kindle the fire of the heart as does love. No existing glory is comparable to love. People are not ashamed to reveal anger and irritation in their basest forms, but the sacred concept of love is accompanied by confusion and even derision. A man who dares to display loving devotion is already regarded as somewhat dubious; from this confusion of fundamental concepts issues the world chaos. The human heart cannot flourish without striving toward the Origin of Origins—inexpressible in words, but cognized through the fire of the heart. Thus, amidst violated world foundations, let us kindle the fires of the heart and of love for the Supreme. Let us realize that even science, by its relativity, keeps open the path to Infinity. Amidst the grandeur of the worlds, can one dwell in malice, in murder, in treason? Only darkness can harbor all insidious crimes! No law justifies ill will. Ill will is terrible, for it leads into darkness. But by what earthly means alone can one prevail against darkness? Verily, the fire of love.

**630.** They will ask, "How can we best serve on Earth to effect the utmost benefit at present?" One must restore the health of Earth. By innumerable ways, one must carry out the world task of regeneration. One must bear in mind that people have destroyed the resources of Earth without mercy. They are ready to poison the earth and the air. They have laid waste the forests, these storehouses of prana. They have decimated animal life, forgetting that animal energy nourishes the earth. They believe that untried chemical compounds can take the place of prana and earthly emanations. They plunder the natural resources, unmindful that the balance must be maintained. They do not ponder over the cause of the catastrophe of Atlantis. They do not consider the fact that chemical ingredients must be tested over the course of a century, for a single generation cannot determine the symptoms of evolution or involution. People like to calculate races and subraces, but the very simple idea of calculating the plundering of the planet never occurs to them. They think that by some act of mercy the weather will clear, and people will become prosperous! But the problem of restoring health does not enter their thoughts. Hence, let us love all creation!

**631**. The decline of the earthly garden is dangerous. No one thinks about the importance of the health of the planet. One thought about it—a single thought—would in itself produce a spatial impulse. One can grow to love the Origin of Origins and all the creations of the grandeur of thought.

**632**. In the acquisition of qualities one cannot keep to one system or one order of sequence. Whoever feels at heart the need of acquiring patience, let him set himself this task. Whoever strives to develop courage, let him gather this experience. One cannot forbid him who wishes to think of compassion or express himself in cooperation. Still worse are conventional coercive methods which force the disciple to strive for the quality farthest from him, which cannot yet be assimilated.

With all the discipline of the Greek schools of philosophy, imposition on a pupil's free will was forbidden. For example, all abusive words were forbidden by mutual agreement, without coercion, otherwise a man could send mentally still worse abuse. One should definitely indicate to the beginners the need for improving their qualities, but in the sequence of predilection. The fires of the heart kindle the centers according to the individuality. Thus, one should appreciate these fiery guideposts. It must be understood why We so insist upon a natural transformation of life. It is because otherwise the effects of deviation from the very nature of striving will result in a violation of all foundations.

**633.** Ancient alliances were sealed by leaping through fire. In oaths the hand was held over fire. As a consecration one walked through fire. Such testimonies to fire have occurred through all ages. This must be taken as a recognition of the fiery element of purification. Even in thinking, one should form the habit of straining thought, so to speak, through the fire of the heart. This advice must be applied in action. One can feel in this action a moment of bliss, as it were, evoking the warmth of the heart. The feeling in the heart of warmth or heaviness or tremor will confirm the participation of the heart's energy. One should not consider these indications as merely preliminary to the Fiery World. Intensity of many of the aforementioned qualities will be needed for the Fiery World itself.

**634.** Self-control is a very complex quality. It comprises courage, patience, and compassion. But courage must not become anger, compassion should not border on hysteria, and patience must not be hypocrisy. Thus, self-control is complicated, but it is imperatively needed upon entering the higher worlds. One should develop this synthesized quality with the utmost care.

In schools the students should be confronted with the most unexpected circumstances. The teacher should observe the degree to which impressions are consciously assimilated. This is not the austere Spartan schooling of physical endurance and resourcefulness, it is drawing upon the heart energy in order to apprehend things with dignity. Not many persons remember self-control. As soon as they pass beyond the borders of the usual they begin to display a series of strange movements, to utter needless words, and, in general, to assume an affected pose of spirit and body. It can be imagined how such people lose their composure when crossing the great boundaries! It must be remembered that in approaching Light one must carry one's own lamp unspilled. Such guiding perfection must be acquired in the physical state. Therefore experienced people ask for tests; otherwise upon what can they affirm their strength? Let each earthly action lead to the higher path. Let each thought be such that it may be repeated before the Fiery World.

**635**. One more difficult achievement—it is not easy to gain respect for earthly creativeness, yet liberate oneself from the sense of possession. He who feels the grandeur of Infinity will certainly understand the entire incommensurability of illusory possession on so transitory a place as Earth. He who understands the magnitude of the creativeness of thought will value the Sublime in all earthly creativeness. Hence, let us perceive the one great Path and give over the fruit of our labor to those who come after us. Thus we will preserve the value of labor, not for ourselves, but for those who follow and continue this bond of perfectment. Also, this point of view regarding possession must be affirmed in one's heart here upon Earth, otherwise we shall carry into the Subtle World a most burdensome feeling of earthly possessions. Let people combine the concept of inner perfectibility with the acceptance of beauty in earthly things. Beauty for many, is this not a salutary fire for the wayfarers? Thus the refining of one's self for others will be a worthy decision.

**636.** The times are very complex. Hate among men has reached extraordinary proportions. One can no longer speak of the erstwhile rivalry of ancient clans. This was child's play compared to present day hatreds. Therefore, let us manifest the self-control of which I spoke.

**637.** He who dares the stream chooses firm stones. He understands to whom and when he may entrust the Teaching. The Bird of Life, the radiant Swan, also reveals straight-knowledge as to where lies the boundary of usefulness. The determination of this boundary cannot be expressed in human language. It can be unalterably sensed, but cannot be calculated by physical measurements. Thus a great test for each treason is created. Another great test lies in the acceptance of homelessness. There may be much mockery over the great sense of homelessness. To the earthly mind the concept of a home is an absolute necessity. If anyone dared to speak about the House of Light he would be taken for a lunatic. Therefore a change of earthly dwelling places is a useful expansion of the concept. Another great test is that of hearing every thought. The pitiable concept of earthly secrecy leads people into many errors. The feeling of pride and egoism rebels against the absence of secrecy, but co-workers of the Hierarchy of Light already understand this degree of cooperation. "I am ready," he says, and hastens to open his heart. The successful mastery of all trials lies within our hearts and consists in our love for the Lord. If we are filled with love, can obstacles exist? Earthly love itself creates miracles. Does not the fiery love for Hierarchy multiply our forces? These forces will help to transform homelessness into a beautiful Home, vast and unlimited! One cannot think of beautiful expanses in the midst of a fog of contentment. It is said that hunger obstructs the path to God, but we will also add that contentment is like murky waters. He who understands the difference between hunger and contentment will enter the current. But he who touches the Light will be transformed into a Bird of Life. So long as the Bird of Life remains a poetic abstraction, that spirit is still unready.

**638.** It is said, "Do not enter Fire in inflammable garments, but bring a fiery joy." In this indication lies the entire prerequisite for communion with the Fiery World. Verily, even the garments of the Subtle World are not always suitable for the Fiery World. So, too, the joy of ascent must transcend any earthly joy. It must shine, and by its Light be a beacon to the many. Who, then, can deride joy and Light? The mole does not know the attraction of light; and only an evil spirit does not understand what joy is! When you rejoice at flowers, when you seek in thought to penetrate into their wondrous structure, into the creation of a small seed, when you value the fresh fragrance, you already have contacted the Subtle World. Even in the flowers of Earth, in the plumage of birds, and in the wonders of the heavens, one can find that very joy which prepares one for the gates of the Fiery World. Chiefly, one must not be dead to beauty. Where can one find a better setting than beauty for devotion, for aspiration, for indefatigability? Amidst earthly conditions one must learn to find that which is applicable to all worlds. There will be no time for deliberation at the moment of crossing into the Subtle World; the illumination by joy can and must be instantaneous. Thus, consciousness is actually preserved by joy. But one must not lose even an hour here on Earth in learning to rejoice at each flower.

**639.** Let the days of great heroic deeds live in your memory. Like spring flowers they can regenerate your consciousness. The labor of achievements was hard because of their exclusion from the consciousness of the masses. It usually happens that a Great Spiritual Toiler does not know his true co-workers; only rarely can he send them his greetings from afar. Therefore you do well in your writings to point out about sending greetings over far distances. Thus is expressed friendliness and the kinship of souls.

**640.** One may wonder at times why and how people can meet again after many incarnations. There are many reasons for this, but the principal one is the Cosmic Magnet. One may notice that people are attracted precisely through a sense of karma; nothing can hold back the debtor. But earthly concepts make it difficult to coordinate Infinity with the manifestation of karma. How great must be the attraction in order to hold such divergent energies in conformity! Moreover, one side will always try to escape, but the law will lead it to the immutable realization of inevitability. In this one can observe a psychic attraction that only proves the oneness of the basic law. People also find it difficult to accept the fact that incarnations vary according to psychic principles and not according to earthly distinctions. Not many will understand that a king may find himself a laborer, and a shoemaker may become a senator. But the concept of Agni solves the riddle of change. The change of existence is assigned according to Agni. The fiery energy conveys to us the superterrestrial actions. We do not value earthly revolts in the form of murders—enlightenment alone is the real victory of Agni.

**641.** Economy of forces distinguishes him who has entered the current. No senseless dissipation is possible where the value of energy is appreciated. If we have a precious remedy that cannot be replenished, should we destroy it senselessly? One must accept Agni as verily the most precious substance. One must realize the difficulty of developing this energy, and that it is impossible to compensate for the excessive expenditure of it. One must simply guard this Divine Fire with especial care. He who can admit dark whisperers does not safeguard Agni. Even in moments of especial consternation one must preserve self-control, of which We have already spoken. Much has been said, but one should apply it in action. No one desires that time should be spent in idleness, but sleep and the waking state are both parts of the same activity. Thus, in this connection also, one should not judge by earthly measures alone. Let people become accustomed without delay to thought about the two worlds. Thought—one and ever-existing—must not be confined to the earthly plane alone.

**642.** The seed of the spirit is in need, as it were, of strengthening blows. Deathlike contentment and senseless dissipation of life are actions contrary to nature. People cannot comprehend the salutary character of blows that push one forward like explosions of a motor. The explosions of energy move humanity. One must cognize the degree to which Agni begins to act precisely during the manifestation of energy. One can observe many examples in nature, but people prefer to exempt themselves from the law of unity. It is true that without an understanding of the future the blows, as motive forces, are incomprehensible. They can give rise to complaints and despondency. Therefore it is so necessary to adopt the fundamentals of self-perfection for the great future. Striving toward the future will already be an evidence of Agni. Do not think it superfluous that Agni and the future are again spoken about. The infant must be reconciled to its first pain. Expressions of complaint mean lack of understanding of the problems of life. During the propelling blows it is especially difficult to understand their true significance. But the inception of heroic achievement in itself denotes the acceptance of the propelling blows. Let us not forget the formula of propelling blows.

**643**. Verily, one must have discrimination to ascertain true significances. Many are the illusions and phantoms that obscure an evaluation of the real advance of the spirit. Many appearances of the dark forces attempt to seduce or terrorize one. Such attacks are especially preponderant in the vicinity of obsessed or mentally diseased persons, who are like open gates, not only attracting entities to themselves but creating a kind of channel for all surrounding people. The border lines of psychic illnesses are quite imperceptible, therefore I advise great caution. I consider it useless to expend one's strength in experiments with obsession when one's own ill health disturbs the equilibrium. Whisperers can attach themselves to the ear that is ailing. And only a firm consciousness can shake off these asps without delay. You already know that no sickness should be neglected. One must immediately inoculate oneself with vigor and not forget about Agni.

**644**. Bliss, Nirvana, Divine Nearness and all analogous terms for the higher state are usually understood in an earthly sense. Thus, Bliss is always understood as an ecstatic oblivion and the rapture of some kind of indolent rest; but oblivion may be understood only as the erasure of all earthly means and examples. Truly, why such limited earthly ways, when one can already act through the higher energies? Is it possible to identify Divine Nearness with indolence and immersion in oblivion? Such a correlation is contrary to the very meaning of approach to the Highest Principle. This conjoining with the Highest, this transformation through the higher energies, primarily impels one to an increased tension of all forces. Even in extreme tension a man must not lose hold of himself. But amidst the contacts with fiery radiances, the seed of the spirit will be kindled the more, and its striving toward thought-creativeness, unrestrainable. One may wonder why people try to limit and disparage the significance of the Fiery World. They wish to clothe it in earthly limitations and also stipulate that the inhabitants of other worlds must exist in earthly bodies and dwell in earthly conditions. Only an undeveloped imagination can limit the Universe to such a degree. Therefore I so greatly emphasize the development of imagination as the basis of striving toward the higher worlds.

**645**. How can man create mentally when he is even unable to imagine a desirable environment for himself? How can he think of the refinement of forms when he never pictures them in thought, thus trying to make his surroundings worthy of the Higher Beings? The essence is not in luxury but in conformity. Only the evidence of conformity can uplift the spiritual consciousness. The ancients turned to the law of proportion, seeking the solution in numbers, but the fiery consciousness is beyond numbers and creates through immutability. Nothing is disparaged in this immutability, which in itself reflects the fiery law on the earthly paths. Thus can one gradually perceive the Higher Law.

**646.** Churning is a symbol of cosmogony. He who has accepted so simple a process as the symbol of a great action, has verily understood the correlation between microcosm and Macrocosm. On the physical plane spiral rotation is the basis of the accumulation of substance, and thought also acts in an identical way. From the Summits down to chaos, Space is intensified by the spirals of consciousness. Thought spirally transforms itself into substance, permeating all Cosmos. One must understand and accept the transformation of thought into substance. This welding preserves the supply of substance, for thought is inexhaustible. On Earth much benefit may be reaped from the realization of the substantiality of thought. People are especially fearful of overtiring the brain, but this is absurd because thought cannot cause excessive fatigue. Mental disease is caused by numerous other excesses. Smoking, drinking, sexual overindulgence, lack of sleep, overeating, irritation, a wearying depression, envy, treason, and many horrors of darkness cause the overstrain which is ascribed to mental labors. As a prophylactic force, thought not only does not occasion fatigue but contributes to the interchange of higher substances. To blame thought for overfatigue is equivalent to expulsion of Agni from the heart. Both conductors connect humanity with the higher worlds; one must value these threads without which one can sink into chaos. In the West, religion signifies the link with God, with the Highest Principle; this means that every tie must be cherished, and the most important intercourse will be through the fiery thought process. Therefore, one must free oneself from the fear that thought can cause fatigue. But if you notice fatigue during the process of thinking, seek other causes; usually they are nearby. Perhaps the cause is not in you.

Perhaps poisoned air has entered through the window or the firewood is not pure. Petty causes often produce grave consequences, and it is especially deplorable that a light-bearing thought should be regarded as the source of fatigue. Thought is health, renewal, interchange of substance—thus let us understand the salutary quality of thought.

**647**. When I say, "Burden Me more," I do not deviate from the aforementioned economy of forces. It should be known that burdening develops the resistance of the seed of the spirit. One cannot reject the law of gravity. Thus should one understand the value of burdening. Any seaman can tell you about the need of ballast for a ship. No sailor would even consider putting to sea on a ship without cargo. Equally useful is a load amidst earthly tempests. Do not fear burdening, it will only reveal the fire of the heart. Thus should one think upon each action. And thus should one end each advice.

**648**. The "fiery embrace" signifies the formation of a planet when a complex of chemical aggregates sends forth its cooperation toward the embrace of Fire. Should not man, as a microcosm, strive toward the "fiery embrace?" Through a fiery embrace man is drawn toward the highest concepts. He begins to seek fiery substance in all his surroundings. Thus he surrounds himself with fiery consonances, recognizing in the most varied objects a principle close to him. To observe the objects surrounding a man with opened centers is to perceive fiery harmony. One must pay attention to the habits of fiery people; with all their broad outlook, they are sensitive to their surroundings. They sense to the point of pain much that remains unnoticed by others. Not without reason is it said that it is difficult for fire during a whirlwind. It is precisely the earthly vortex which strains the centers. But this essentially does no harm; on the contrary, it creates a useful tension. A fiery man feels deeply the evanescence of earthly existence, and with all his being knows about the higher path. Nothing can divert the fiery man from his goal. Neither by day nor by night does he forget his predestined path. He is indifferent as to where his ascent will be accomplished. The condition of his body has lost importance for the striving spirit. Let us not understand this as referring specifically to the lives of saints, but let us regard the fact of such achievement as possible in life. Many signs are bestowed on humanity, only let us not forget them. Each of you remembers these landmarks which are scattered throughout different years of life. When the Tablets are revealed, one must just read them and courageously walk on toward the Light.

**649**. You already understand why it is better to tell too little than too much. You have many examples of how the unprepared consciousness can distort instruction. It can be shown how the simplest indication is deflected when it is given to an unprepared consciousness. So many earthly considerations are brought in, in order to apply non-earthly measures to Earth! Not only perfect strangers but even those already familiar with the Teaching can be warped by lack of understanding, therefore I am so concerned that instruction be given according to place and to consciousness. Sometimes, too, one must read between the lines, especially when some who are obviously friends still do not comprehend what is pointed out. People accept with great difficulty instruction outside their usual standard. There are many examples of people limiting themselves. For instance—a woman has lost husband and children; they are nearby, but she will mourn her loss, and will not bestir herself to search for them. Thus it happens not only on Earth but also in the Subtle World. One must develop cooperation and persistence here and also there.

650. In all Teachings the dark forces are represented as shooting their fiery arrows at the Illumined One. This battle is depicted in beautiful symbols. No less beautifully is it indicated that the malevolent arrows do not reach their target but form a protective net. Let us not regard this heedlessly; this symbol is entirely realistic, even from the viewpoint of modern science. The malevolent flame encounters the great fire of the heart and becomes subservient, only augmenting the Agni of the Great Spirit. Thus, the heart which manifests all its power is invincible. In case of retreat, search nearby. Has the heart maintained all its force? Has not some transitory earthly circumstance interfered? Has not self-pity arisen? Did not a quiver of fear overcast the heart? And did not doubt allow clouds to set in? Verily, where the Agni of the heart is not overcast, there can be no defeat. Often it seems to a man that he has reached his limit, but he is deceived by faulty vision, and a large expanse still lies before him, precisely where victory may come. Prematurity leads to misfortune.

651. How many unalterable truths have been rejected! They say eternal life does not exist. Yet it exists. They say the Subtle World does not exist. Yet it exists. They say no intercourse between the worlds exists. Yet it exists. They say no Higher Guidance exists. Yet it exists. Thus dark deniers would screen the light from the heart. But no lock exists which can debar the heart from achievement. One should not only discuss and read, one should also sense the warmth of the heart. This warmth of the heart can be measured; this means

275

it is accessible to simple apparatuses. Agni will point the way to that land where the victory of the heart is preordained. The Fiery World summons to victory.

652. Self-perfectment is the most difficult achievement. People inject into this process so many inconsistencies that the manifestation of true self-perfectment is obscured. Self-perfectment is simplified primarily when Hierarchy is accepted. Everyone should realize that the perfecting of the consciousness in itself contains all other aspects of improvement, but one cannot accept the mechanical betterment of the details of daily life as perfectment. One may be able to forge the most deadly blade or discover the most fatal poison, but it is impossible to consider such intellectual craftiness as worthy improvement. Nevertheless, to understand the ideas of the higher worlds, it is necessary to determine what self-perfectment is. We can come to a decision as to what beautiful achievements are when we ourselves realize for what they must be accomplished. There will be not even a thought about achievement if we have no conception of the desirability of improvement of life. Affirmation of the physical world alone cannot advance the true development of consciousness. Take the history of humanity. Observe how brief were the periods of materialism; they invariably ended in bloody convulsions. Indeed, the trend of thought became rebellious, and the correct path having been lost, crimes multiplied. Self-perfectment is possible only through refinement of consciousness by its seeking to surround itself with worthy manifestations. Thus can consciousness protect us from small and shameful thoughts. Consciousness leads to the Fiery World.

653. Indignation is indeed justified when people wish to crown their city with a monstrous tower and

build a tavern on top of it. Not accidentally have we already referred to this symbol. Ask anyone with what he would like to adorn himself, and you will discover his level of consciousness. It is not only illiterate persons but often the most sensible who are not averse to adorning themselves with primitive and crude objects. At times one marvels at a flash of sensitiveness in so-called savages, and one may stand aghast at the absurd displays of so-called civilized leaders. Consider where there is more of the fire of the heart, and where it is easier to awaken the consciousness.

654. Let us recall an ancient Chinese tale about the Elusive Decrees. A man passed by the dwelling of eight Blessed Ones and noticed that they were strangely occupied. One of them was rushing about attempting to jump upward. When the passer-by asked the reason for such exercise, he answered, "I am catching the Elusive Decrees." Another Blessed One held his hands over the fire and referred to the same Elusive Decrees. A third stood in an icy stream and spoke of the same Elusive Decrees. Thus eight Blessed Ones strained their forces in striving to the higher Decrees. The passer-by thought to himself, "If even those who have already attained beatitude must strive so vigorously to cognize and catch the Decrees, then how much greater tension must I exert lest the Higher Will escape me!" In this story one can perceive several useful concepts. First, the state of greatest tension can indeed assist transcendental receptivity. Second, having already attained initiation does not necessarily relieve one from the danger of failing to fulfill the higher Ordainments. Third, one must welcome all forms of tension, in order to enter into accord with the Higher World. How often the Elusive Decrees flash through space and return again to the treasury of the

unapprehended! It is surprising how great a breach of convention it is even to speak about Elusive Decrees. Some smirk in ignorance, some reprove in pride, some take offense in cruelty. Thus each one in his own way ignores the Decrees—subtle decrees, vanishing into the ether. Thus, an old Chinese tale can remind us of the attention due the Elusive Decrees.

**655**. The Fiery Decrees must not only attain their destination, they must not remain aquiver like the wings of a frightened bird. One may ask how a Decree can be compared with quivering wings when the Decree is a fiery arrow? Truly, the Decree can be likened to an arrow, and it will reach its destination, but such a destined heart must be constantly aflame!

In other cases the Decree may be compared with the wings of a frightened bird. Moreover, one must always take into consideration the physical state of both men and nature. During a thunderstorm the fiery arrow may increase the tension to a perilous degree. True, electrophorous manifestations are mutually reinforced, but during these manifestations one should not transgress the safety line of tension in earthly actions. It is wise to observe the physical state of your companion. Unfortunately, a speaker too often listens only to himself and pays no attention to his listeners. Only a fiery consciousness focuses its entire attention to meet the characteristics of the listeners. Such attention in itself partakes of magnanimity.

**656**. When I speak of tension it must not be interpreted as fanaticism. On the contrary, the tension that links one with Hierarchy may be precisely a spiritual departure from customary conditions. Though formerly people fell into bodily fanaticism, this does not mean that in a more spiritually advanced time the same primitive methods need be used. If formerly it was necessary to threaten people with the torments of hell in order to curtail their partaking of bloody food, nowadays the vegetable diet enters life quite naturally. So, also, when it is realized that the heart is the focus of the spirit, then the physical manifestations of fanatics will be replaced by the revelation of the life of the heart. Thus, gradually, even in the most difficult epoch, the spiritualization of life is entered upon. There are many grave examples before you of entire nations losing their image. But when the Fiery World is realized, the highest earthly state appears small and transitory.

**657**. You are quite right in saying that the existence of an Invisible Government perplexes many, but if there exists an unseen dark government, then why should there not be a Government of Light? Is it possible that the human mind is so utterly obscured that it will acknowledge anything dark rather than think about Light? People actually understand and have heard more than once about the dark forces, which are universally united, but the Government of Good and Light is especially suspect. People are unaccustomed to being united for Good. They look upon Good as a prime pretext for disunity. One can regard the entire illness of our planet as the result of the complete discord among those who could have united their forces for Good. It is most deplorable that even in a temple the hearts of men are not transformed for cooperation. Thus, let us ponder upon each act of friendliness, which is already a spark of cooperation.

**658**. Our Communions are not merely for information, but are to be accepted with the heart. Soon you will finish the first part of the writings about the Fiery World. They should not be given only to the curious, for this may give birth to blasphemy. The meaning of blasphemy must be understood and full attention paid to it. Blasphemy not only repels Light, it inherently carries an actual infection. The blasphemer is not quite the same after his utterances, for he has rent a part of his protective net. One may then expect various sicknesses, for the protective net is not only a spiritual protection but also a physical one. Therefore blasphemous utterances should be forbidden, even in childhood. It is deplorable that people have lost the sense of responsibility to the extent of forgetting the significance of words. At the Fiery Gates blasphemous words will not come to one's mind, but if we consciously let them take root, they will burn the heart like red-hot knives. Losing the word *harmony* degrades men. How was Pythagoras able to understand the significance of the glory of the body of Light? Moreover, the appearance of numerous mechanical inventions has destroyed to a considerable degree the evidence of culture. Indeed, the forces of disintegration are very active; they strike all that is beautiful with putrescence, infection, and insensateness. There is a wealth of data on the activity of the dark forces; not superstition, but documents corroborate their intentions. It is possible to guard against them by use of all the fiery energies, but to do this one must recognize Agni itself. Hence, let those who wish to receive a continuation of the records about the Fiery World prove that it is really important to them.

**659**. Samadhi is only a partial fiery state. It is difficult on Earth to understand the potentiality of the fiery existence, when even Samadhi does not correspond to it entirely. If Samadhi even endangers life, then what tension of energy must be required for the assimilation of Fire! But the transmutation of consciousness creates such an intensely ecstatic state that the action of fiery tension merely corresponds to the power of the new being. Somnambulism sets up this fiery resistance even on Earth. In a certain state the somnambulist acquires a phosphorescence that completely safeguards him from burning, even in a strong fire; such cases are well known both in the East and in the West. But of course somnambulism is a transmutation of consciousness, which kindles, as it were, the entire nerve substance, and thus the fire is absorbed by the fire of the aura. Hence it gives some idea of the transformation of the fiery body. One can recall instances from the most ordinary lives when mothers saved their children and in so doing have withstood the most furious assaults of the elements. A certain substance transformed their strength. Not without reason is it said that metaphysics does not exist—only physics. Also, physics teaches that success is created in joy. But what can establish the undaunted joy of the spirit if not the realization of the Fiery World? One must cultivate this realization like a precious flower. The Silvery Lotus glows as a sign of the opening of the gates of the future.

**660.** Discrimination is one of the most pronounced fiery qualities. It is not straight-knowledge, but a glimmer, as it were, of the language of the Fiery World. Truly, the man with open centers does not judge by words; he understands all the inner meaning of speech. If all judges were at such a level of fiery discrimination, many offenses would appear in a different light. But such discrimination needs cultivation. It exists in the seed of the spirit, but one must evoke it from the storehouse of the Unmanifest. Therefore a sharpening of the consciousness must be urged. Let each approaching one manifest himself as an exemplary judge. Let one begin to judge according to the eyes; another by the intonation of voice; a third according to the bodily movements. It is immaterial where one begins, because the inner fire is reflected on all the nerve centers. And it is instructive to observe how words often fail to reflect the inner condition. With patience one can attain great results and disclose signs of fiery understanding. Certainly, this will be only a glimpse of the Fiery World, but each spark of such cognizance is already an achievement. Upon entering the Subtle World one should firmly bear in mind the resolution to go toward Light, to hasten to self-perfection, and for this each advice is extremely important. If here upon Earth we already approach discrimination, then upon crossing into the Subtle World this achievement will be a benefaction. The principal difficulty is that despair and perplexity hinder the assimilation of the new conditions. But if we remember firmly whither and wherefore we go, we will instantly find many helpers. Yet people are especially disconcerted by the absence of secrecy when the Ineffable Light penetrates all that exists. Blessed are those who do not have to be ashamed of their heart's accumulations. Love everything that can uplift the heart.

**661**. Fanaticism is inadmissible. It contains neither devotion, nor love, nor magnanimity, but is only a reversion to the animal state. Fanaticism begets treason, hostility, and cruelty. The fanatic does not reach the Fiery World, because love is the key to it. Fanaticism is like a neglected ailment, if not immediately attended to it becomes incurable. Such a consciousness must encounter great shocks in order to understand true devotion. By repulsion alone one cannot acquire the quality of the magnet. Therefore, I am so concerned that you should not lose a single opportunity for manifesting friendliness. The best fuel should be preserved for the fire of the heart. The store of friendliness generates true compassion, which is directly opposed to the cruelty of fanaticism. Fanaticism knows only the egoism which presumptuously says, "All or nothing." And since *all* is impossible, there remains nothing. Therefore, take notice of even the slightest signs of fanaticism. Cure them with the greatest patience as you would a contagious disease. It is precisely fanaticism which has shaken the most beautiful Teachings and corroded the seeds of love. One should carefully prepare everything that can facilitate the access of Agni to one's heart.

**662.** The growth of consciousness is usually considered a slow process. Yet it can be perceived how, even in the midst of earthly conditions, consciousness grows before one's very eyes. Certainly, for such growth there is needed, on one side, tension and, on the other, rapport with the magnet of an already fiery consciousness. One may rejoice when at each progress of consciousness the ancient acquisitions of the spirit come to life. One may rejoice when the essence of life is regenerated through the proximity of a kindled heart; however, one must discern the difference between broadening and illumining consciousness and a low psychism. We are not at all pleased to see that intercourse with the lower spheres of the Subtle World is increasing. One must not forget that the lower entities, even aside from permanent obsession, can benumb, as it were, the consciousness. From the lowest comes only the lowest.

Thus, once again let us understand why the heart's striving to the Highest is so necessary. Simple maxims must not be arrogantly scorned; in them the most essential is attested simply. When a warrior is ready for battle, his leader examines him. Thus, especial caution is needed when I speak of that subtlest element, fire. One should not understand fire as a chemical formula. One should fittingly understand its utter indefinableness. Already in antiquity we can find all kinds of descriptions of the characteristics of Fire; how it permeates all objects; how all heavenly bodies, without exception, are permeated with fire. Thus, we cannot escape this most luminiferous element; and it is wise to prepare oneself to meet it and to know that the cognizance of higher Fire is useful in overcoming the lower fires.

**663**. How can one attain success? Remember, through joy—not through despair, but joy. Do not for an instant believe that We ponder the probability or improbability of success. The thought is, Does your joy suffice to quicken the ascent? We always counsel joy. It is necessary to realize and remember that you have succeeded when you rejoiced. Certainly this is not the frisking of a calf on the meadow, but the creative joy which transforms all difficulties. The play of the Mother of the World is in joy. She enfolds the enlightened ones in Her veil of joy. Rejoice amidst flowers; and in the midst of snow—equally redolent—also rejoice!

**664**. If we look on our planet from above, we will observe, besides the evident volcanoes, particular vortices of light and darkness. The human spirit can create powerful manifestations of energy. One may state that the vortices of Light are saviors of the equilibrium of the planet. Nor is it far from the truth to state that the vortices of darkness contain a destructive gas, which is not only deadly to the crust of the planet but can alter the climate and even significantly effect a shifting of the poles. Thus powerful is the significance of the human spirit. Hence We treasure the Ashrams where purified Agni is gathered. Many teachings have pointed out the importance of pure places where psychic energy can be affirmed. References to the importance of pure places are found in the Sacred Writings, in the Bible, and in the Rig-Veda; the Tao likewise contains knowledge of these treasure-places of Earth. We rejoice when We notice the rise of new Ashrams, for people so seldom think of the power of their spirits!

**665**. The Fiery Wall, the Fiery Mist, the Fiery Baptism affirm the fiery reality. For example, people do not wish to understand that the quality of the fire borne by them depends upon themselves. They do not imagine that they themselves can kindle both the salutary and the destructive fires. Perseverance in various directions inevitably imparts to the fire its power and color; therefore it is so difficult to extinguish the consuming fire, which is kindled by the nature of habits. But the Yogi understands the great need of kindling the fire connected with Good. The thought of Good is the measure of consciousness. He who attains begins the ascent in self-abnegation and measures his steps by the criterion of Good. He knows that no mask of Good can disguise him, for deceit is only the illusion of an instant. Therefore, do not forget how the saint revered by you sent greetings to his friend from a great distance. He knew that his friend had set out for an achievement, and their hearts became one in revelation. Nothing can impede the revelation of the heart. Thus, a mutual confession of faith is in itself a foretaste of the language of the Fiery World, where the hidden becomes revealed. It is not surprising that the word of Truth is constantly repeated through the course of the ages. How can Truth be forgotten, though times may vary! One can rejoice at every mention of Truth, for that which we love we speak about, in words and in the heart.

**666**. True human cognizance will always be in harmony with the One Truth. All human developments should be compared with the Teaching of Light, and one can rejoice when world understanding continues to follow the one possible Truth. But for this purpose one must constantly compare the Fundamentals with human actions. Of course, true science cannot be contradictory to immutable laws. Consequently, in new researches the Tablets of the Fundamentals must be kept constantly in mind and in heart. They will give an invincible enthusiasm to the scholar who, freed of egoism, with honesty continues his researches for the benefit of humanity. He will sense the waves of Light and detect new energies amongst the vibrations. Fire, the Great Agni, is the manifest Gatekeeper of the Ineffable. Light has the power of attraction, and he who enters it will not turn back. What traveler would willingly descend into darkness?

Let the Sacred Image, guarded in the heart, serve as a guidepost. Thus, let friends realize the might and beauty of the Fiery World. Let them not be merely curious, but let them find within themselves a steadfast bond with the World of Beauty.

When you are asked about the second part of *Fiery World,* answer, "It will be given immediately, provided you keep in mind the affirmed valediction on the long journey and preserve joy and the resolution to hasten in spirit." Meanwhile collect the new findings that science is offering and observe how they are utilized. Do not forget that Agni is nourished by joy and courage and endurance.

Thus, let us follow the path of the fiery consciousness.

## AGNI YOGA SERIES

Agni Yoga Society
www.agniyoga.org